International Bar Association Series

# Liability of lawyers and indemnity insurance

*Albert Rogers*

*John Trotter*

*Willem G. van Hassel*

*James R. Walsh*

*Ralph P. Kröner*



*Co-edited by: Karin C.J. Frikkee*

KLUWER LAW INTERNATIONAL
LONDON – THE HAGUE – BOSTON
*and*
International Bar Association

Published by Kluwer Law International
Sterling House
66 Wilton Road
London SW1V 1DE
United Kingdom

Kluwer Law International incorporates
the publishing programmes of
Graham & Trotman Ltd,
Kluwer Law & Taxation Publishers
and Martinus Nijhoff Publishers.

Sold and distributed in the USA and Canada
by Kluwer Law International
675 Massachusetts Avenue
Cambridge MA 02139
USA

In all other countries, sold and distributed
by Kluwer Law International
P.O. Box 85889
2508 CN The Hague
The Netherlands


First published in 1995

ISBN 90 411 0876 9

**British Library Cataloguing in Publication Data and Library of Congress Cataloging-in-Publication Data is available**



Printed and bound in Great Britain by Hartnolls Ltd., Bodmin, Cornwall.

# Table of Contents

# Preface

When I came into office as Chairman of Committee H on Insurance, of the Section on Business Law of the International Bar Association at the end of the Cannes Conference in 1992, I felt the first stirring of the idea to devote an entire conference of Committee H to the subject of the liability of lawyers and indemnity insurance for the legal profession. When some time thereafter the President of the Section on Business Law suggested to each committee to try and make a special effort at the occasion of the 25th Anniversary of the Section on Business Law, it became clear to me that this would be the opportune moment to deal with this subject.

The Committee therefore has had the benefit of a longer than usual preparation time. And indeed I was able to present the first outlines of a programme for the 25th Anniversary Conference to be held in Paris in September 1995 at the Melbourne Conference in September 1994.

On this occasion, I was also able to have a word with Lukas Claerhout of Kluwer Law International Publishers, who was susceptible to the idea of publishing a book on the liability of lawyers and indemnity insurance for the legal profession, and in fact became quite enthusiastic when I showed him the first preliminary programme and explained the scope of the project to him.

Committee H had set itself the following aims:

1. To prepare a preliminary text analysing on what basis the law relating to the civil liability of legal advisers might be harmonized in the principal jurisdictions of the world.
2. To produce draft guidelines for recommended minimum standards and financial levels of professional insurance cover appropriate to those jurisdictions.

The objective of this book would be that the implementation of the recommendations of Committee H would:

1. Enhance the status and reputation of the profession,
2. Produce a better service for clients,
3. Provide security for clients.

Two Working Groups were established, consisting of members of Committee H on Insurance. The Working Group A, which had the task of structuring the programme for the Paris Conference, consists of:

- Ralph Kröner of Trenité Van Doorne Rotterdam (chairman of Committee H)
- Peter Rogan of Ince & Co., London (vice-chairman of Committee H)
- Louis van Zyl of Findlay & Tait, Cape Town
- Christian Bouckaert of Cabinet Jeantet, Paris.

The members of Working Group B had the task of preparing the questionnaires, analysing the answers, summarizing the individual country reports and each writing a chapter on the various aspects of this subject in close coordination with each other and finally drafting the recommendations. Working Group B consists of:

- Albert Rogers of Ince & Co., London
- John Trotter of Lovell White Durrant, London
- James Walsh of Walsh Donovan Lindh & Keech, San Francisco
- Willem van Hassel of Trenité Van Doorne, Rotterdam.

Further, some eighty lawyers were invited to act as national rapporteur for their country. The choice of the country rapporteurs was made primarily from the existing list of members of Committee H, as it was felt that this should be very much a Committee H project. For various reasons, Committee H members could not be found as national rapporteur in every country.

Working Group A and B sat together to establish the questionnaire, which consisted of twenty-four carefully drafted questions, for which it must be said that Albert Rogers gave the main input. The questionnaires were then sent to about eighty countries and we were very pleased with the overwhelming response, which enables us to present a book at this occasion, reflecting the situation on the liability of lawyers and indemnity insurance of the legal profession in some sixty countries all over the world.

This is the first comprehensive overview ever made. Of course the subject has been touched upon at earlier IBA Conferences - especially during the period that Dennis Nelson was Chairman of the sub-committee on Professional Liability - and also in other international bodies like the *Union Internationale des Avocats* (UIA) and *Association Internationale des Jeunes Avocats* (AIJA). It is also a subject of continuous interest and discussion within the various national Bar Associations and the Council of the Bars and Law Societies of the European Community (CCBE). The construction of this book, together with its table of contents and index, should ensure easy access to the material and to the main elements of liability and insurance of each country.

It is always a benefit to mankind that work in distant perspective seems less than it actually proves to be. It is doubtful whether we would have undertaken the enormous task of producing this book if we had realised what this would entail. The enthusiastic support of the members of the Working Groups, the national rapporteurs and especially the pro-active help and execution by my legal assistant Karin Frikkee, ensured that each of us actually felt that working on this project was not only worthwhile but in the final analysis pure pleasure.

Although this book is obviously a coordinated effort, chapter two on the professional liability of lawyers, and chapter three dealing with trends in relation to professional indemnity claims were written by Albert Rogers and John Trotter. Chapter four on indemnity insurance for the legal profession and chapter five with an overview of survey results were written by Willem van Hassel. Chapter six on lawyers' liability indemnity insurance policies was written by James Walsh. The introductory chapter was written by Ralph P. Kröner.

The country reports, as summarised, have been compiled on the basis of the answers to the questionnaires by the national rapporteurs and have been approved by them and therefore should be regarded as the opinion of the particular rapporteur on the liability and insurance situation in that country. The descriptive chapters in this book are of course based on those reports and are not the result of a separate investigation into each country. It goes without saying, that the scope of this book reflects information and comments received from the countries surveyed, together with the knowledge and experience of the authors.

Where in this book a word is used which could be read as expressing the masculine gender only, the feminine gender should be regarded as meant to be used equally. This also applies vice versa, and for neutral genders as well.

As this book spends some time on the efforts of lawyers to restrict their liability by contract and because of the very wide scope of this project, I should make it clear that this book is no substitute for a specific investigation in detail into the prevailing situation in any given country and the liability of the authors and editors of this book is limited to the price of it. The reader is deemed to have accepted this term by opening the book.

Ensuring that a book of this nature is up to date at the time of publication as far as every technical detail of the law is concerned in every jurisdiction covered, is almost impossible. We are reasonably confident that we have represented the position correctly as of June 1995. The Committee trusts that the reader will benefit from reading this work.

Ralph P. Kröner
Chairman, Committee H on Insurance
of the International Bar Association's
Section on Business Law

Partner, Trenité Van Doorne,
"Plaza", Weena 666, Rotterdam

July 1995

# National Rapporteurs

**Argentina**
*Alfredo M. O'Farrell*
Marval, O'Farrell & Mairal
Carlos Pellegrini 885
1338 Buenos Aires
Tel. +54 1 348 0600
Fax. +54 1 322 4122

**Australia**
*Norman Lyall*
Ebsworth & Ebsworth
135 King Street
Sydney NSW 2000
Tel. +61 2 234 2366
Fax. +61 2 235 3606

**Austria**
*Hellwig Torggler*
Schönherr Barfuss Torggler & Partner
Tuchlauben 13
1014 Wien, P.O.B. 41
Tel. +43 1 534 370
Fax. +43 1 533 25 21

**Belgium**
*Claude Verbraeken*
Liedekerke Wolters Waelbroeck & Kirkpatrick
341 Avenue Louise Boite 8
1050 Brussel
Tel. +32 2 627 1411
Fax. +32 2 627 1500

**Bermuda**
*Dianna Kempe*
Appleby Spurling & Kempe
Cedar House, 41 Cedar Avenue
Hamilton HM 12
Tel. +1 809 295 2244
Fax +1 809 292 8666

**Bolivia**
*Fernando Rojas*
C.R. & F. Rojas - Abogados
Frederico Zuazo 1598
Edif. Park Inn, 11°piso
La Paz
Tel. +591 2 36 0655/0651/0866
Fax. +591 2 37 6380

**Brazil**
*J.M. Pinheiro Neto KBE*
Pinheiro Neto - Advogados
Rua Boa Vista, 254, 9° Andar
01014-907 Sao Paulo
Tel. +55 11 232 5022
Fax. +55 11 232 9161

**Canada**
*V.R.P. (Sas) Bersenas*
Paterson MacDougall
Box 100 Suite 2100
1 Queen Street East
Toronto Ontario M5C 2W5
Tel. +1 416 366 9607
Fax +1 416 366 3743

**Channel Islands**
*David Moore*
Ozanne Van Leuven Perrot &
Evans Advocates
P.O. Box 186,
1, Le Marchant Street
St. Peter Port
Guernsey, GY1 4HP
Tel. +44 481 723 466
Fax. +44 481 714 653

**Chile**
*José María Eyzaguirre Garcia de la Huerta*
Claro Y Cia
Gertrudis Echenique 30, Piso 13
Casilla 1867, Las Condes
Santiago
Tel. +56 2 206 1230
Fax. +56 2 206 0658

**China**
*Ambrose Chua*
Lovell White Durrant
Office 5D CITIC Building
19 Jinguomenwai Dajie
Beijing, 10004
Tel. +86 1 506 3588
Fax. +86 1 500 1972

**Colombia**
*Alvaro de Brigard*
Brigard & Urrutia
Calle 70 N° 4-60
Apartado Aéreo 3692
Bogotá
Tel. +57 1 2103955/3462011
Fax. +57 1 310 0609 / 0586

**Cyprus**
*Kypros Chrysostomides*
Dr K. Chrysostomides & Co
29 Stasikrates Street 1st Floor
PO Box 2119
Nicosia
Tel. +357 2 448278
Fax +357 2 451391

**Denmark**
*Flemming Andersen*
Kromann & Münter
14, Rådhuspladsen
DK - 1550 Copenhagen V
Tel. +45 33 11 1110
Fax +45 33 11 8028

**Ecuador**
*Christina Pérez*
Pérez, Bustamente & Pérez
Av. Patria 640
P.O. Box 17-01-3188
Quito
Tel. +593 2 5617 98
Fax +593 2 5617 10

**Egypt**
*Ali Shalakany*
Shalakany Law Office
12, Marashly Street
Zamalek 11211
Cairo
Tel. +202 340 3331
Fax +202 342 0661

**England and Wales**
*Albert Rogers*
Ince & Co.
Knollys House, 11 Byward Street
London EC3RN 5EN
Tel. +44 171 623 2011
Fax +44 171 623 3225

*John Trotter*
Lovell White Durrant
65 Holborn Viaduct
London EC1A 2DU
Tel. +44 171 236 0066
Fax +44 171 236 0084

**Finland**
*Tomas Lindholm*
Roschier-Holmberg & Waselius
Keskuskatu 7 A
00100 Helsinki
Tel. +358 0 228 551
Fax +358 0 664 303

**France**
*Christian Bouckaert*
Jeantet & Associés
87 Avenue Kleber
75784 Paris Cedex 16
Tel. +33 1 4505 8008
Fax +33 1 4704 2041

**Germany**
*Klaus Grossmann*
Wessing Berenberg-Gossler
Zimmermann Lange
Konigsallee 92 A
40212 Düsseldorf
Tel. +49 211 8387 0
Fax +49 211 323616

**Greece**
*C. Lascaratos*
Theologidis & Lascaratos
25, Bouboulinas Street
185 35 Piraeus
Tel. +30 1 412 2230 / 411 8747
Fax +30 1 411 4497

**Guatemala**
*S. Guillermo Bonilla S.*
Bonilla, Montano & Toriello
Avenida de la Reforma 15-54
Zona 9
Guatemala CA 01009
Tel. +502 2 32 6062
Fax. +502 2 32 2361

**India**
*Ashwani Kumar*
Ashwani Kumar & Associates
C-9 Friends Colony
New Delhi-110065
Tel. +91 11 684 2758
Fax +91 11 683 1146

**Ireland**
*Anthony Collins*
Eugene F. Collins Solicitors
61 Fitzwilliam Square
Dublin 2
Tel. +353 1 6785 766
Fax +353 1 6618 906

**Israel**
*Peter Gad Naschitz*
Naschitz, Brandes & Co.
136, Rothschild Blvd
Tel Aviv 65 272
Tel. +972 3 685 7766
Fax +972 3 685 7535

**Italy**
*Mario Riccomagno*
Studio Legale Riccomagno
4/8 Via Assarotti
16122 Genoa
Tel. +39 10 839 1095/2385
Fax. +39 10 87 31 46

**Jamaica**
*H. Martin Payne*
Myers, Fletcher & Gordon
21 East Street, P.O. Box 162
Kingston
Tel. +1 809 922 5860 8 / 9
Fax +1 809 922 4811

**Japan**
*Takashi Ejiri*
Asahi Law Offices
New ATT Building
11-7, Akasaka 2-chome
Minato-ku, Tokyo 107
Tel. 81 - 3 - 3505 0003
Fax. 81 - 3 - 3505 1333

**Kenya**
*K. Hamish W. Keith*
Kaplan & Stratton
PO Box 40111
Nairobi
Tel. +254 2 335333
Fax +254 2 340827

**Korea (South)**
*Yong Suk Yoon*
Lee & Ko
C.P.O Box 8735
Seoul
Tel. +82 2 753 2151
Fax +82 2 753 0373

**Latvia**
*Janis Volksons*
Volksons & Petersons
Tirgonu Street 9
Riga 1050
Tel. +371 2 220 630
Fax +371 2 210 471

**Liechtenstein**
*Markus Wanger*
Advokaturbüro
Landstrasse 36
FL-9490 Vaduz
Tel. +41 75 232 0062
Fax +41 75 232 0064

**Luxembourg**
*René Faltz*
Faltz & Associés
P.O. Box 1147
L-1011 Luxembourg
Tel. +352 485 050
Fax +352 481 385

**Malawi**
*Babazelenge Jacob Mwafulirwa*
Lawson & Co
Press Bakeries Building
Churchill Road
Limbe
P.O. Box 2074
Blantyre
Tel. +265 644 943 / 641 687
Fax +265 641 504

**Malta**
*Richard Camilleri*
*Emily M. Camilleri*
Tonna Camilleri Vassallo & Co.
52 Old Theatre Street
Valletta VLT 8
Tel. +356 232 271 / 223 316
Fax +356 244 291

**Mexico**
*Daniel del Rio*
Basham, Ringe Y Correa, S.C.
Liverpool 123, 1° Piso
Apartado 24, 521 or 65 Bis
Col. Juárez, 06600 México D.F.
Tel. +52 5 227 0400
Fax. +52 5 227 04 96/97/98/99

**Netherlands**
*Hugoline de Groot*
Houthoff
P.O. Box 1507
3000 BM Rotterdam
Tel. +31 10 2244666
Fax +31 10 2244668

*Willem van Hassel*
Trenité Van Doorne
P.O. Box 190
3000 AD Rotterdam
Tel. +31 10 4042111
Fax +31 10 4042333

**New Zealand**
*Christopher P. Browne*
Russell McVeagh McKenzie
Bartleet & Co
PO Box 8
Auckland 1
Tel. +64 9 309 8839
Fax +64 9 377 1849

**Nigeria**
*Gbenga Oyebode*
Aluko & Oyebode
35 Moloney Street
P.O. Box 2293
Marina, Lagos
Tel. +234 1 260 0080
Fax +234 1 263 02249/264 7505

**Norway**
*Ole A. Bachke, Jr.*
Wiersholm • Mellbye & Bech
Postboks 400 sentrum
0103 OSLO
Tel. +47 22 400 600
Fax. +47 22 410 600

**Panama**
*Carlos Raúl Moreno*
Patton Moreno & Asvat
P.O. Box 6-4298
El Dorado
Panama City
Tel. +507 64 8044
Fax +507 2 637 887 / 2 637 038

**Papua New Guinea**
*Timothy John Glenn*
Blake Dawson Waldron
PO Box 850
Port Moresby
Tel. +675 211 977
Fax +675 212 630

**Paraguay**
*Guillermo F. Peroni*
Peroni, Sosa & Altamirano
Casilla de Correo 114
Avenida España 2012
Asunción
Tel. +595 21 208 791
Fax. +595 21 222 42

**Peru**
*Jorge del Busto V.*
Estudio Oleachea
Bernardo Monteagudo 201
Lima 27
Tel. +511 4 62 1090
Fax. +511 4 61 8931 / 62 2406

**Philippines**
*Roberto C.O. Lim*
Philippine Airlines Inc
PAL Building II
Legazpi St Legazpi Village
Makati Metro Manila
Tel. +63 2 817 9119
Fax +63 2 818 8661

**Portugal**
*Manuel P. Barrocas*
M.P. Barrocas & Associados
Av Fontes Pereira de Melo 15-7.°
1000 Lisbon
Tel. +351 1 52 21 56
Fax +351 1 57 62 02

**Puerto Rico**
*Antonio J. Rodríguez*
McConnell Valdés
P.O. Box 364 225
San Juan
Puerto Rico 00936-4225
Tel. 1 809 759 9292
Fax. 1 809 759 8282 / 9225

**Russia**
*Theodore P. Matheny*
Salans Hertzfeld & Heilbronn
9 Rue Boissy D'Anglas
75008 Paris
Tel. +33 1 4268 48 00
Fax +33 1 4268 15 45 / 46 / 47

**Scotland**
*Michael Walker*
Maclay Murray & Spens
151 St Vincent Street
Glasgow G2 5NJ
Tel. +44 141 258 5011
Fax. +44 141 248 5819

**Singapore**
*Victor A.P. Wong*
Wong & Lim
143 Cecil Street
# 09-02/03 GB Building
Singapore 0106
Tel. +65 2236166
Fax +65 2247465 / 3235653

**South Africa**
*Louis van Zyl*
Findlay & Tait
PO Box 248
Cape Town 8000
Tel. +27 21 247 015
Fax +27 21 241 688

**Spain**
*Jorge Angell*
L.C. Rodrigo Abogados
Velazquez 75, 1st floor
28006 Madrid
Tel. +34 1 435 5412
Fax +34 1 576 6716

**Sri Lanka**
*Badharani Yasoja Devasurendra*
21 Roberts Road
Dehiwala
Tel. +94 1 71 6706
Fax +94 1 44 0840

**Sweden**
*Elisabet Fura-Sandström*
Advokatfirman Vinge
Smålandsgatan 20
P.O. Box 1703
111 87 Stockholm
Tel. +46 8 614 3000
Fax +46 8 614 3190

**Switzerland**
*Donald Reichenbach*
Reichenbach & Partner
Talacker 50
8001 Zurich
Tel. +41 1 212 4477
Fax +41 1 221 2656

**Taiwan**
*Vincent W. Liu*
Ko Lin & Wei Law Offices
4th Floor 11 Chingtao West Road
Taipei 100
Tel. +886 2 331 7585
Fax +886 2 314 1485

**Thailand**
*Pakdee Paknara*
Tilleke & Gibbins R.O.P.
64/1 Soi Tonson
Ploenchit Road
Bangkok 10330
Tel. +662 254 2640/58
Fax +662 254 4304 (Local)
+668 621 0172/73 (Int'l)

**Turks & Caicos Islands**
*Owen B. Foley*
Dempsey & Company
PO Box 97 Caribbean Place
Providenciales
Tel. +1 809 94 643 44
Fax +1 809 94 645 64

**United States**
*James R. Walsh*
Walsh Donovan Lindh & Keech
595 Market Street, Suite 2000
San Francisco 94105-2831
Tel. +1 415 9578700
Fax +1 415 5439388

**Uruguay**
*Mariana Silveira &*
*Nicolás Herrera*
Guyer & Regules
Plaza Indepencia 811,
11.100 Montevideo
Tel. +598 2 92 1515
Fax. +598 2 92 5454

## *The International Bar Association Series*

*Other Titles in this Series:*

*Acquisition of Shares in a Foreign Country*, (M. Gruson, S. Hutter)
ISBN: 1 85333 755 2
*Agency and Distribution Agreements - An International Survey*, (Editor, A. Jausàs)
ISBN: 1 85966 100 9
*Arab Comparative and Commercial Law - The International Approach*, Volumes 1 and 2
Volume 1 ISBN: 0 86010 977 1
Volume 2 ISBN: 0 86010 978 X
*Capital Markets Forum Yearbook Vol 1/1993*, (Editor, S. M. Revell)
ISBN: 1 85966 066 5
*Civil Appeal Procedures Worldwide*, (Editor, C. Platto)
ISBN: 1 85333 725 0
*Current Issues in Cross -Border Insolvency and Reorganisations*, (Editors, E. B. Leonard, C. W. Besant)
ISBN: 1 85333 958 X
*The Developing Global Securities Market*, (Editor, F. W. Neate)
ISBN: 0 86010 979 8
*Due Diligence, Disclosures and Warranties in the Corporate Acquisitions Practice*, (2nd ed.) (Editors, D. Baker, R. Jillson)
ISBN: 1 85333 633 5
*Energy Law '88*, (Section on Energy and Natural Resources Law)
ISBN: 1 85333 097 3
*Energy Law '90*, (Section on Energy and Natural Resources Law)
ISBN: 1 85333 477 4
*Energy Law '92*, (Section on Energy and Natural Resources Law)
ISBN: 1 85333 759 5
*Enforcement of Foreign Judgements Worldwide*, (2nd ed.) (Editors, C. Platto, W. G. Horton)
ISBN: 1 85333 757 9
*Environmental Liability*, (Editor, P. Thomas)
ISBN: 1 85333 561 4
*Global Offerings of Securities: Access to World Equity Capital Markets,* (Editors, M. Brown, A. Paley)
ISBN: 1 85966 045 2
*Insider Trading in Western Europe*, (Editors, G. Wegen, H-D. Assmann)
ISBN: 1 85966 079 7
*Joint Ventures in East Asia*, (Editor, J. Buhart)
ISBN: 1 85333 739 0
*Law Without Frontiers*, (Editor, E. Godfrey)
ISBN: 90 411 0851 3
*Legal Opinions in International Transactions - Foreign Lawyer's Response to US Legal Opinion Requests*, (2nd ed.) (M. Gruson, S. Hutter, M. Kutschera)
ISBN: 1 85333 192 9
*Life After Big Bang*, (Editor, S. macLachlan)
ISBN: 0 86010 982 8

*Mechanics of Global Equity Offerings,* (Editor, M. Brown)
ISBN: 90 411 0855 6
*Nuclear Energy Law After Chernobyl,* (Editors, P. Cameron, L. Hancher, W. Kühn)
ISBN: 1 85333 110 4
*Obtaining Evidence in Another Jurisdiction in Business Disputes,* (2nd ed.)(Editors, C. Platto, M.Lee)
ISBN: 1 85333 082 5
*Pre-Trial and Pre-Hearing Procedures Worldwide,* (Editor, C. Platto)
ISBN: 1 85333 758 7
*Transnational Environmental Liability and Insurance,* (Editor, R. P. Kröner)
ISBN: 1 85333 778 1
*The Impact of the Freeze of Kuwaiti and Iraqi Assets,* (Editors, B. Campbell, D. Newcomb)
ISBN: 1 85333 558 4
*Trial and Court Procedures Worldwide,* (Editor, C. Platto)
ISBN: 1 85333 608 4
*Using Set-Off as Security - A Comparative Survey for Practitioners,* (Editor, F. W. Neate)
ISBN: 1 85333 363 8
*Warranties in Cross-Border Acquisitions,* (Editor, M. Rubino-Sammartano)
ISBN: 1 85333 946 6
*Water Pollution - Law and Liability,* (Editor, P. Thomas)
ISBN: 1 85333 874 5

Chapter 1

# Introduction

In a world where individual prosperity and well-being seem to take precedence with the exclusion of the benefit of collectivity, it seems to have become unacceptable that damage should be borne by the individual. If something has gone wrong, somebody must reimburse you. If the outcome of legal proceedings is not completely satisfactory, somebody must have done something wrong. Justice is only justice if you have been put in the right.

Against this background, it is understandable that lawyers start to worry. In the next chapter of this book we will see a consideration of the various notions on the subject of liability of lawyers and the acceptability of limitation of this liability and on insuring against the financial risk of being held liable. When we started to do the survey, we knew of course that these questions are very closely linked to notions of ethics and morality, which obviously differ hugely in the world. The historical backgrounds for the disparity of notions on morality would fill volumes and indeed the public libraries have rows of books, which touch on this matter. Even religious concepts have bearings on these existentialist questions.

There are countries where the legal profession argues that if a plumber is allowed to limit his liability, there is no reason why the lawyer should not also be allowed to do so. There are also countries where the position of the lawyer is so elevated, that the mere thought of limitation of liability is blasphemous. However, in major jurisdictions, claims against lawyers are the order of the day. We do not believe that the reason for this is that the lawyers in these jurisdictions make so many more mistakes than the lawyers in other jurisdictions.

As in realms of, for instance, environmental law and liability, there are jurisdictions where a mistake and ensuing liability for the lawyer are more easily assumed than in other jurisdictions. These lawyers therefore run a higher risk. We are quite confident that the situation of no-fault liability or strict liability will not easily be reached in the field of lawyers' liability. Nevertheless, in some instances elements thereof are present. During a conference in Marrakech in 1994, a German lawyer friend offered the example of a lawyer not adhering to a time limit set by court and thereby losing the case. Irrespective of whether this particular lawyer had exoneration grounds, the German court held that the lawyer has strict liability in these cases.

In that part of the world, where the risk for the lawyer is enhanced by the developments in society, one sees also that insurers tend to leave the market place and insurability for lawyers' liability risks tends to become a problem. Could this trend be halted by compulsory insurance up to a certain amount, with limitation of liability for lawyers up to that same amount?

This book addresses these questions. The Conference of Committee H at the occasion of the 25th Anniversary of the Section on Business Law in Paris from September 18 to 22, 1995, will go into detail. The Committee has set itself perhaps over-ambitious goals when trying to offer guidelines on the subject of liability and insurance for lawyers. The thinking appears to be so diverse that it is difficult to envisage consensus on the direction of such guidelines. In the letter to the national rapporteurs, we wrote — perhaps naively:

> Harmonisation of jurisprudence on the subject of the liability of lawyers and indemnity insurance for the legal profession within Europe could be within our grasp. The reflex-effect on the other large jurisdictions of the world could be of major importance.

It is of some comfort that in a part of the world like Europe, where civil law countries become more and more united with common law countries, a tendency towards harmonisation, also on the subject of liability of its lawyers and the possibility of limitation thereof, can be discerned.

The Commission of the European Communities issued a draft proposal for a directive relating to the liability of suppliers of services on December 20, 1990.[1] The latest official position on the proposed directive is that the Commission withdrew the proposal. As the proposed directive covered only damage to the health or physical integrity of persons or the physical integrity of private property, it is clear that the legal profession was not materially affected by the directive or its withdrawal.[2] However, Mrs Scrivener stated on behalf of the European Commission on April 25, 1994[3] that the Commission is once again dealing with the directive on the liability of services as proposed on December 20, 1990.

---

1 Doc Com (90) 482 Final Syn 308.

2 See answer of the European Commission dated September 16, 1991, Official Journal of the European Communities, No C 241/23: "*The Commission considers that services provided by lawyers and tax consultants are not as such covered by the proposal since they cannot result in direct damage through injury to the physical integrity of persons or property.*"

3 Official Journal of the European Community, January 23, 1995, No C17/37.

On June 23, 1994, the European Commission issued a communication on "New Directions on the Liability of Suppliers of Services" where it is stated:

> All the above considerations — the negative reaction of the Economic and Social Committee and the responsible Committee at the European Parliament, severe criticisms from various professional circles in the services sector, and the need to examine the problem of the liability of suppliers of services in a wider context — have led the Commission to adopt new directions in this important domain. This means that the proposal of 20 December 1990 has to be withdrawn. In doing so we are not abandoning our concern for the safety of services. On the contrary, it is necessary to reconsider the best way of achieving this goal on the basis of appropriate consultations.[4]

We will all be looking forward to what Professor Dr Mario Monti, European Commissioner for the Internal Market, Financial Services and Financial Integration, Customs and Taxation, will present us with at the occasion of the Paris Conference.

Being Dutch lawyers and therefore living in a country adjacent to Germany, we have always looked with particular interest to legal developments in Germany, where we have seen in June 1994 the adoption of a law whereby lawyers are compelled to insure their liability for a minimum level of cover, at the same time allowing contractual limitation of liability, both in individual contract and general conditions, however with varying ceilings. We appear sometimes also to cross-fertilise.

In the Netherlands — where indemnity insurance has been compulsory for the members of the Bar Association since 1986 and contractual limitation has been possible since January 1, 1992 (moves towards limitation by general conditions are on the verge of being implemented) — an advisory committee (Kamphuisen and Arisz) has suggested the introduction of limitation of liability by royal decree. The possibility thereto was introduced in the new civil code (6:110 BW).

Meanwhile, one of the larger law firms in the Netherlands has (June 1995) printed a limitation of its liability on its stationery as follows:

> Any liability shall be limited to the amount which is paid out under the firm's professional liability policy in the matter concerned.

There are people who argue that this sort of general limitation of liability may not be upheld in court. We fail to see, however, why different tests should be applied as to the acceptability of such clauses, other than those which are applied for the determination of the legitimacy of general conditions in other areas.

It would seem that the European Commission feels the need within a short time to issue directives on the subject in order to achieve harmonisation within Europe, as it is clear the differences of liability levels may distort competition. A level playing field should be established soon.

---

4 Com(94) 260 final, Brussels 23.06.1994

The Netherlands is incidentally also one of the countries where — almost unperceived by the profession — liability for some lawyers has come closer. On September 1, 1993, Book number 7 of the new Civil Code entered into force. In this Book of Statutes, the concept of mandate is dealt with (articles 7:400 a.f.). This provision is of specific importance for lawyers who profess to be or are known to be specialists in a certain field. If a particular lawyer is instructed by a client and is held liable for negligence, his firm can also be held liable, which enhances the risk for his partners considerably. The law allows lawyers to contract out this special liability, but of course no lawyer in his right mind will do so.

This diminishes the possibilities of limitation of liability often mentioned, like the incorporation of the practice of the lawyer. In other words, the lawyer does not issue his advice in person but a legal entity is established which employs the lawyer and either the legal entity acts as lawyer or the lawyer as employee only practises law. It is argued that thereby the liability of the lawyer could be limited to the equity of the legal entity. Many objections are voiced against this argument and indeed some national Bar Associations have allowed incorporation only if the lawyer cannot hide behind the corporate veil. More about this in the next chapter.

Let me conclude with an extract from the judgement of Lord Griffith in Smith v Eric S. Bush [1989] 2 All England Law Reports:

> I would not ... wish it to be thought that I would consider it unreasonable for professional men in all circumstances to seek to exclude or limit their liability for negligence. Sometimes breathtaking sums of money may turn on professional advice against which it would be impossible for the adviser to obtain adequate insurance cover and which would ruin him if he were to be held personally liable. In these circumstances, it may indeed be reasonable to give the advice on a basis of no liability or possibly of liability limited to the extent of the adviser's insurance cover.[5]

We are sure that any reader wishing to know more about the matter in a particular country, would gladly be advised by one of those who have acted as authors or national rapporteurs in this book.

There are a number of valuable nuggets of wisdom for practitioners to be found scattered all over the chapters of this book. We particularly have in mind the topic of insurance policies and their wording, dealt with in detail in the last chapter.

---

5 Also quoted by Professor Mr B. Wessels in Nederlands Juristenblad, February 1995.

# Chapter 2

# The Professional Liability of Lawyers

> Woe unto you, lawyers! for ye have taken away the key of knowledge.

The Bible, St. Luke's Testament.

> The first thing we do, let's kill all the lawyers.

Shakespeare, Henry VI Part II.

> Why do priests and doctors swimming in shark-infested waters get eaten, but lawyers survive? Professional courtesy.

Recent comment, probably of American origin.

As those practising the law have for so long had such a bad reputation it is surely safe to assume that the rules of the profession have been organised entirely for the lawyers' own convenience and to protect their interests. Those reading the results of this detailed survey should be reassured that the clients' interests are fairly balanced against those of their legal advisers and generally the means are available to resolve claims against lawyers. There is a surprising degree of unanimity in the approach adopted in the sixty or so jurisdictions considered.

## THE PRINCIPLES OF LIABILITY

In a lawyer's office or a courtroom almost anywhere in the world any consideration of the liability of legal advisers is likely to follow similar lines. The conduct of the professional relationship between the lawyer and his or her client is determined principally by reference to the law of contract. This is supplemented to a greater or lesser extent in most jurisdictions by the law of tort or delict, which may have some impact on the lawyer's retainer as well as any liabilities owed to other parties.

It is recognised throughout the world that lawyers, in common with other professional advisers, are not usually under a strict liability to guarantee the results sought by their clients. Rather, they are obliged to use the degree of skill and care to be expected from a competent member of the profession. It is also a prerequisite of liability that the client should have suffered damage, and that there should be a causal link between the negligence and the loss.

Whilst many lawyers embark enthusiastically on the preparation or analysis of the lengthy standard conditions which appear in contracts of others, their own contract of retainer is usually a purely oral arrangement and if anything is in writing it is likely to be no more than a confirmation of the task which the lawyer is being asked to carry out. If more is committed to paper it is probable these days that it will deal with the question of legal fees. Other questions equally important to the client, such as what quality of service and what results can be expected from his legal adviser, as far as the client is concerned are left to the imagination. Perhaps the client does not ask because he assumes his attorney will be able to do everything he requests; perhaps he does not want to pay the additional fees which might be involved in getting a detailed answer; in more sophisticated countries he may have read the law firm's glossy brochure which has convinced him of all the virtues of the practice, with pictures to prove it.

The simple answer to the question: "what am I entitled to expect from my lawyer?" is that there is an implied term of the contract of retainer that the lawyer will carry out his or her services with the skill and care of a reasonably competent member of the profession.

The lawyers, and probably most clients, would not be surprised to know that there are more complicated answers to the question as well. The level of expertise to be expected from the legal adviser is explained by reference to various analogies, which generally reflect the trust and confidence there should be between lawyer and client. One obvious comparison is with the prudent man of business. Elsewhere a more homely comparison is applied and the lawyer is seen as the "good father of his family". Such distinctions are probably not of great significance in practice. The duty can be over-ridden by the lawyer's duty to the court where he is an officer of the court, but again that is thought unlikely to be a factor of everyday concern. China is apparently unique, as a communist country, in imposing a duty on its lawyers above all to protect the interests of the state. Of practical importance is that in various countries distinctions are made between lawyers with different qualifications or functions, or between specialists and those in general practice.

One major distinction, which exists in England and Wales together with most British Commonwealth jurisdictions, is between those who have rights of advocacy in the higher courts and those who do not, effectively creating "a divided profession". The limited immunity from claims enjoyed by advocates in those jurisdictions is considered later, suffice to say here that it does appear to be against the general trend. However, in Germany a similar division exists, between those who are admitted to practise as attorneys in court and those who are not. The former are subject to special standards of liability, the latter are judged by the general principles of professional liability. In Norway the term "lawyer" strictly applies only to those with a law degree who are admitted to the Norwegian Bar, although others with a law degree may give legal assistance. Until recently perhaps the most "divided" profession was in France, with a variety of two types of *Avocats,* two types of *Avoués*, *Agréés*, *Notaires*, and *Conseils Juridiques*, but legislation is working towards a more united profession. For example, the *Avocats* and *Conseils Juridiques* have been unified since the beginning of 1991 into the profession of *Avocat*.

Whilst in most countries the legal profession is unified in theory, very real differences are developing in the everyday practice of the law between specialists and generalists, with an increase in specialisation, particularly in commercial areas. The extent to which this is recognised in considering the standard of care to be expected from the practitioner varies. Perhaps the usual position is typified in Sweden, where if a lawyer claims to possess "expert competence" within a particular field then a higher degree of skill will be expected and that factor would be taken into account in judging the issue of liability. In the United States the point can be put to a jury on the basis that a lawyer has a duty to use the care and skill ordinarily expected in like cases from reputable members of the profession practising in the same locality under similar circumstances. That itself is a distillation of the principles adopted in some fifty different state jurisdictions in the U.S.A. The South African approach is that each case is decided strictly according to its particular circumstances.

It is probably dangerous to make any generalisations which try to establish principles applicable to all or even most jurisdictions beyond the basic implied term of reasonable skill and care. For example, in Germany the courts have extended the duty of care as far as an obligation to advise a client on the risk that an earlier decision supporting his case might be overruled, whereas across the border in Austria "any possible changing developments in the relevant law need not be anticipated". On closer investigation these statements might not be so contradictory; rather, this is an area in which the law is developing in jurisdictions where professional indemnity claims are becoming more frequent, and different aspects are brought to the fore and developed in each country in its own time, as legislation is passed and individual cases decided.

Further, differences can be apparent in analysis of the relevant law which may not be so real in practice. In some systems a distinction is made between contractual obligations which give rise to no more than a duty to use reasonable skill and care, and obligations which impose a stricter liability. In Belgium the former are called *obligations de moyens*, being obligations to use one's best efforts without guaranteeing results. The latter are *obligations de resultat*, which do create a duty to achieve a specific result. The same distinction is made in Luxembourg, and no doubt elsewhere. Even if the distinction does not feature in the theory of the law, in practice it appears effectively to distinguish between those cases where the onus of proof rests with the claimant and those where it rests with the lawyer. To use the Belgian terminology, if the lawyer is alleged to have given inadequate advice and to have acted in breach of his *obligations de moyens*, it is for the client to prove that reasonable skill was not used in the preparation of the advice. On the other hand, if the lawyer misses a time limit and has thereby acted in breach of his *obligations de resultat* the onus of proof is on the lawyer to provide an excuse if he is to avoid liability, and almost always there is no answer to such claims.

Statutes have had some impact where consumer legislation has been applied to the professional services provided by lawyers. Perhaps against the trend, in Brazil the Consumer Protection Code which imposes strict liability on "service renderers" excludes the legal and other professions from its provisions. In contrast, Indian lawyers have been brought within the country's Consumer Protection Act, in company with those who provide "entertainment, amusement or the purveying of news or other information". This legislation has imposed a liability on lawyers for any "deficiency" in their services, defined as "any fault, imperfection or shortcoming or inadequacy in the quality, nature and manner of performance". As the pressure on governments increases in various countries to pass legislation to improve the rights of consumers this might well have a considerable impact on the profession, as considered later.

Reference has already been made to one anomaly which is found in England and Wales and other British Commonwealth jurisdictions, that of the advocate's immunity from suit. There is another at the other end of the spectrum, that of strict liability for undertakings given to other lawyers or third parties in the course of professional practice. Such undertakings may not have contractual force, if they are given without any consideration from the recipient, but they are nonetheless enforced either by the courts or by the lawyers' professional body. They are most frequently given either to guarantee a payment of money or in the context of property transactions as a method of facilitating completion of a sale before the documents of title are available. If in the latter situation the deeds can never be produced the court will generally make an award of damages to reflect the purchaser's loss. In any event, the lawyer is strictly bound to comply with the terms of the undertaking provided its terms are clear.

## THE SOURCE OF THE PRINCIPLES

In about half of the jurisdictions reviewed the principles of lawyers' liability are defined by statute, either in the country's Civil Code or, more rarely, a statute limited to the legal profession, such as the Code of Ethics and Professional Liabilities of Lawyers of Panama. Civil Codes do not always directly consider the liability of professional advisers. Often the principles are to be extracted from provisions which deal with the law of contract and delict generally. Several jurisdictions, as diverse as Austria, South Africa and Taiwan, look to their contract of mandate. Elsewhere emphasis is placed on the retainer being a contract for services, hence the impact of consumer legislation.

In many countries the framework set out in codes and statutes is developed by decisions of the courts. Elsewhere reliance is placed entirely on court decisions, again often by the application of authorities which deal with broad issues of contractual and tortious liability. Such is the case in China, although there the principles are established by court decision and government directives. More typically, in such jurisdictions as England and Wales and throughout the British Commonwealth, South Africa, Japan and Denmark the standard of care to be expected of lawyers has evolved over the years, generally in the context of the law of contract.

Decisions and statements of individual Bar Associations may also be taken into account by the courts, as happens in Denmark, as can the decisions of disciplinary tribunals, for example in Greece and several Scandinavian countries. Within the European Community a further factor intervenes, in that a Code of Conduct has been established by The Consultative Committee of the Bars and Law Societies of the European Community (CCBE). It is being incorporated into the disciplinary rules of member countries by adoption through Bar Associations. For example, this Code provides that lawyers who conduct "cross-border" services between parties in member states should have adequate professional indemnity insurance.

## THE APPLICATION OF THE PRINCIPLES

Claims against lawyers are dealt with by the civil courts within each jurisdiction, although in many countries the parties may by choice submit to arbitration. In virtually all the countries considered a very clear distinction emerged between the jurisdiction of the civil courts and the role of local Bar Associations or Law Societies in investigating professional misconduct and other disciplinary matters. There are exceptions. In Israel the disciplinary tribunal of the Bar has the power to order compensation to a person aggrieved by a disciplinary offence up to a sum equivalent to approximately USD9,000, as well as repayment of fees. In some South American jurisdictions, for example Bolivia, Honor Tribunals of the local Bar Associations are competent to decide claims, subject to the case being taken up in an ordinary court once a decision has been given. In Korea local Bar Associations may act as mediator in disputes between lawyer and client, but their findings are only recommendations and they cannot be enforced. Such a system might not be acceptable elsewhere as sufficiently independent. In a few jurisdictions, such as Puerto Rico, China and the Philippines, the courts do become involved in disciplinary matters. In China, because compensation awarded is often relatively low, the courts either substitute punitive sanctions like disbarment or take disciplinary steps as well.

It should be mentioned in passing that membership of a Bar Association or Law Society is not a practice requirement in several countries, which can restrict the ability of such organisations to impose sanctions on the profession.

Usually the relief granted is restricted to compensation and it reflects the financial losses suffered by the client. In addition, in some jurisdictions awards are made in respect of "moral" damages (Colombia) or punitive damages (New Zealand). There is a further trend, in New Zealand and other common law jurisdictions such as England and Wales, to make modest awards of general damages, extending the principles applicable to compensation for physical injury to the mental anguish, worry and vexation which a client may suffer at the hands of a negligent lawyer.

The position of the defendant lawyer is generally not of concern to the court. However, in Denmark rather exceptionally the courts have a discretion either to waive or limit compensation after taking into account such factors as the degree of negligence, the size of the award and the insurance position. The Dutch courts may also take into account the lawyer's financial resources, as a general principle of law. In the overwhelming majority of jurisdictions there is no limit on the financial compensation which can be awarded against the defaulting lawyer, subject to the assessment of a realistic sum in each case.

Often there can in theory be further relief available by way of mandatory orders which might be imposed on lawyers as part of the remedies for breach of contract and breach of duty generally. Such orders are made rarely, if at all, in many jurisdictions. In the United States disciplinary steps can include mandatory orders against attorneys, for example for restitution of monies taken by the attorney, with the threat of further disciplinary action if the order is not obeyed. They do feature in the English courts, as solicitors are officers of the court and judges therefore can and do require them to perform undertakings given to other solicitors and third parties.

## RESTRICTIONS ON LIABILITY

The most obvious bar against bringing a claim is the imposition of a time limit for instituting proceedings. Here there is considerable diversity. One suspects the more complicated the procedural provisions and the shorter the limitation period then the more claims result against the lawyers themselves for failure to take action in time. There is one small jurisdiction where this is not of concern to the lawyers: in Cyprus all time limits for making civil claims are currently suspended!

The differences between countries are apparent from the start, that is when time begins to run. That may be when the lawyer's error is committed, when the client suffers damage, or when the client either realises or should realise that he can make a claim. There may then be anything between one year and twenty years in which to institute proceedings. The most usual periods are three, five, six or ten years, all of which have their adherents.

It is common ground throughout the world that lawyers cannot restrict any liability arising out of their own fraudulent or reckless conduct. In a few countries lawyers have no opportunity to make agreements with their clients to limit their potential liability for the consequences of their negligence. India, Switzerland and Puerto Rico all have legislation to that effect. In Kenya the Advocates Act makes void any agreement which would otherwise have the effect of relieving an advocate for liability for professional negligence, although the ambit of the prohibition is still to be clarified by the courts. Elsewhere it is the view that such a limitation would be void on grounds of public policy.

In theory, lawyers in many countries may by agreement with their client restrict their potential liability for negligent acts or omissions, but not for gross negligence or fraud. Such agreements can be either general by way of standard conditions or for a particular matter. However, whilst such agreements might be allowed as a general principle of contract law they are only very rarely set up in practice. It is easy to imagine the difficulties which could be involved in negotiating any agreement with the client before the lawyer sets to work on the client's behalf, let alone the loss of confidence in the attorney which might well result from such a matter being raised at all.

In New Zealand the Rules of Practice contain a clause making void any agreement which would limit the lawyer's liability, but with the interesting proviso that the practitioner may limit his liability to the minimum compulsory insurance cover for the profession, equivalent to about USD1,345,000, if the client is fully advised of the position and the limitation is reasonable in all the circumstances. Apparently such agreements would only be applied where the lawyer's retainer presents a substantial or unusual risk but, as ever, they are a rarity. Recent legislation in Germany has introduced a similar provision, the minimum compulsory insurance cover being the equivalent of just over USD350,000. There the restrictions may be excluded for certain kinds of work.

Typical of current trends perhaps is the approach in Sweden. In principle restrictive agreements can be made, but they would be deemed unreasonable if the client, as a consumer, was seen to be in the weaker position. A limitation of liability could also raise ethical issues and lawyers appreciate the disadvantages they could face from a marketing and competition point of view. In England and Wales such restrictions would be subject to the terms of the Unfair Contract Terms Act. This characteristic piece of consumer legislation requires clauses restricting or excluding liability to be tested according to their "reasonableness". The factors to be taken into account by the court include the respective bargaining powers of the parties and the availability of insurance. Finnish lawyers are subject to very similar legislation.

One rather anomalous restriction on liability is the immunity from being sued which is enjoyed by those undertaking advocacy in England and Wales and in other British Commonwealth countries and South Africa. It has arisen historically as a consequence of the divided profession which exists in England and Wales, where clients generally only have direct access to solicitors and all advocacy in the higher courts is carried out by barristers, who generally are instructed only through solicitors. There are various explanations for the immunity enjoyed by barristers. They cannot sue for their fees, they owe a duty to the court as well as to the lay client, and as a matter of public policy the courts are unwilling to relitigate actions for a second time by a further action brought against the barrister who is alleged to have been negligent in his conduct of the original proceedings. Also, it reflects the principle that is common to the countries surveyed that a legal adviser should not be held liable to his client for a mere error of judgment that falls short of a breach of his duty of care. The advocate on his feet in court must make many decisions on the spur of the moment. The question is where the dividing line comes between negligence and a matter of judgment that in retrospect looks wrong.

There are few reported decisions on the extent of this restriction, but it is reasonably clear that the immunity now only extends to a barrister's work in court and to work intimately connected with or preliminary to the conduct of the case before a judge. The principle may well be further eroded if and when more cases are decided by the courts, particularly as professional indemnity insurance becomes the norm for the entire profession and the distinctions between solicitors and barristers become less significant.

## LIABILITY TO NON-CLIENTS

The point should be made that lawyers as men of business must face the same risks of claims and litigation as everyone else in the community. Several rapporteurs mentioned that attorneys can be at the receiving end of defamation proceedings, and not necessarily from their own clients. Subject to that, in some jurisdictions the question of liability to any third party does not arise at all, simply because lawyers can only be liable to their clients, by operation of the law of contract. They are in a minority.

More often than not it is accepted that lawyers may be the subject of claims for negligence by non-clients under the general principles of the law of delict or tort. The occasions on which such claims can arise may be rare, but there will be a remedy where the lawyer owes a duty of care to a third party and that person suffers loss as a result of the lawyer's default. Various countries provide different examples: the lawyer may be deemed to owe a duty of care to both husband and wife, to both parties in a property transaction, or to lender and borrower, even though he has been instructed by only one of the parties.

In England the principle has quite recently received approval from the highest appeal court, the House of Lords, although only by a narrow majority of three judges in favour and two against. The court allowed a claim by a beneficiary who lost his entitlement to a legacy through the negligence of the solicitor instructed by the testator. The lawyer unfortunately delayed for an unreasonably long time and the testator died before the intended will was executed. It is interesting that one of the judges took the opportunity to review the experience of other countries, particularly decisions in the Commonwealth and the United States, as well as referring to the position in Germany. There the courts accommodate claims from disappointed beneficiaries by doctrines which extend contractual causes of action for the benefit of third parties, especially the doctrine which translates into English as "contract with protective effect for third parties". In England the same result has been achieved by extending principles of liability in tort, although two of the judges could not bring themselves to be sufficiently "flexible" to decide for the plaintiff despite what appeared to be the merits and justice of the case. Certainly worldwide the most quoted example of third-party liability is of the beneficiary who loses entitlement to all or part of a deceased's estate as a result of someone else's lawyer acting negligently.

It is arguable that in the growing practice of writing Legal Opinions in commercial transactions, a higher degree of skill may be expected. Generally, it is thought, however, that from a lawyer issuing an opinion, the same level of expertise may be expected as in any other case, provided that the lawyer realises that the opinion may have to be issued to a foreign recipient (perhaps unfamiliar with the law of that jurisdiction), may have to cover grey areas of the law and may be relied on by third parties. In the case of a bond issue, an example of a third party would be a foreign purchaser. Thus the language of the opinion should be especially clear, unambiguous and understandable for any foreigner.

One of the concerns expressed about the development of liability to non-clients in the law is that it will lead to an excessive number of additional claims against lawyers: the "opening of the floodgates" argument. In the United States the claims from non-clients have increased dramatically over the past two decades and now about thirteen per cent of all malpractice claims against lawyers are brought by non-clients. Despite that particular experience, the general reaction of those who answered this survey was that in practice such claims do not arise very frequently.

# Chapter 3

# Trends in Relation to Professional Indemnity Claims

Two clear themes have emerged from the recent survey. First, in many jurisdictions those who consider they have suffered loss as a result of negligence by a lawyer are increasingly willing to use the law to obtain compensation. Second, as lawyers become aware of this factor in their professional life they are considering how to limit its impact by obtaining insurance cover or by taking steps to restrict their potential liability.

## INCREASING CLAIMS AGAINST THE PROFESSION

There is little doubt about the growing inclination to make claims on the part of those who are dissatisfied with the performance of their lawyers. That is borne out by insurance statistics in countries where they are available. In England and Wales claims notified by solicitors on the fund which provides compulsory insurance have increased on average by nearly twenty per cent each year since 1988, although the number of notifications has recently decreased. In the United States the increases have been equally dramatic; currently lawyers are sued each year nineteen per cent more often than in the previous year. Until the 1970s lawsuits against lawyers were almost unknown. During the last ten years more lawsuits have been filed against lawyers than in all United States' judicial history. Rapporteurs have confirmed a change has taken place by comments such as "a more aggressive climate for claiming compensation from lawyers", which has developed in Denmark. In India there is now a change in attitude by the "litigating public" hitherto disinclined to sue a member of the legal profession. Elsewhere, particularly in some South American and Southern European jurisdictions, claims against lawyers are comparatively rare, but it may well be just a question of time before that is no longer the case. An increased willingness on the part of lawyers to take on claims against other members of the profession and improved chances of success might well contribute to this trend. The survey has shown that generally rights of redress are available as a matter of law and, for example, it is suggested that in Uruguay the trend which already exists in pursuing claims against doctors might well be reflected in due course in the legal profession.

How has this come about? Consumer legislation has made a considerable impact, in part directly by increasing the rights of potential claimants, and in part indirectly by creating an atmosphere in which the position of professional advisers has become less sacrosanct. The very fact that legal advisers can be brought within the ambit of such legislation is perhaps an indication of the changing status of lawyers. Providing legal services becomes little different from mending the plumbing or selling a car. Unquestioning reverence for the lawyer's words of wisdom is replaced by a critical and sceptical attitude, which is encouraged by the pressures exerted by consumer groups and on occasions by the media as well.

In this atmosphere clients are becoming less reluctant to raise such issues as fees and to negotiate terms with their lawyers as they do elsewhere in the market place. In the United States and Europe clients now want to know hourly rates and the likely level of fees before they instruct a lawyer. Increasingly they want to know about the lawyer's indemnity insurance arrangements. This more business-like approach should have its advantages for the profession, in that legal advisers may feel less inhibited to raise such issues as the limiting of their liability. However, one definite consequence of these changes is that clients who are dissatisfied with their lawyers no longer have any reservations about pursuing a claim against them.

In circumstances where the lawyer is still "the father figure" advising private clients as a close friend of the family there may remain the inhibitions which have traditionally provided legal advisers with an effective immunity against any criticism from their clients. There are good reasons why this is no longer the case for those lawyers who act for commercial clients. It must be tempting for those who have suffered as a result of a stock market crash, times of economic recession generally, or even their own lack of business acumen, to look to their advisers for compensation if there is any chance that their losses might be recouped, especially if the advisers have the benefit of an insurance policy. In a parallel trend directors are becoming increasingly aware of their duties to protect their shareholders' interests, so much so that the directors themselves more frequently consider it necessary to obtain their own insurance cover. They will look critically at the conduct of their lawyers should the occasion arise.

The economic problems of recent years have also made an impact within the profession, in that where there is more competition between lawyers there is another source of pressure in providing a service. Certainly in England the boom of the 1980s created a substantial increase in the number of lawyers in practice, who are now chasing a decreasing amount of work in the more restrained 1990s. Added to that, improvements in communications and information technology have led clients to expect a faster response, whilst their problems are generally becoming more complicated. No doubt each lawyer has his or her own catalogue of the pressures which affect their own particular practice and hence their ability to perform consistently to a high standard.

If the dice are becoming loaded against the lawyers in the risks they face of a claim being made, the odds are probably worsening against their successfully defending a claim when one is brought. Whether the law is developed by statute or decided cases there are indications that the standards imposed on the profession are becoming increasingly severe. The South African rapporteur commented that traditionally a professional person enjoyed a privileged position as he did not guarantee his product, unlike a supplier of goods. However, developments in the law of contract and delict have caused that privileged position to be eroded. Decided cases in the Netherlands show that ever more strict requirements are being imposed on the quality of work carried out by all professional people, including lawyers. The survey has shown that in several areas the law has developed over recent years to present new or wider bases for claims against the profession. Examples are in relation to conflicts of interest and liability to non-clients, such as liability to an intended beneficiary under a will who does not benefit because the will is prepared wrongly or too late.

It is difficult to assess whether this is a trend which is still gathering momentum or whether the law develops in cycles, at one stage favouring the client and at another stage swinging in favour of the lawyer. In some common law-based jurisdictions there has in fact been a general move to hold back the expansion of negligence claims against some professionals, by narrowing the definition of those to whom, for example, accountants owe a duty of care. However, no rapporteur has suggested that the pendulum is currently swinging in favour of the legal profession. As an example of the trend against the profession, reference has been made in the previous chapter to the immunity from suit which benefits advocates in England and Wales and other Commonwealth jurisdictions. The general principle predates the Commonwealth and the British Empire as well, originally extending to all work undertaken by barristers. These days it is limited to advocacy and work closely connected with the conduct of litigation in court. Further inroads are likely to be made if and when appropriate cases come before the higher courts, and this restriction on liability seems rather anomalous when compared with the position in other jurisdictions which have not been influenced by the English legal system in the course of their history. Certainly the defence of immunity from suit looks somewhat vulnerable to those who defend barristers or insure them.

If a case comes before the court two factors often seem to work against the lawyer. The judge inevitably has the benefit of hindsight, which is difficult to exclude from anyone's thought processes. Also, when a professional negligence claim comes to trial usually the outcome of one transaction or a single set of proceedings is being considered in isolation and subjected to a detailed analysis which ignores the everyday working pressures on the lawyer who is alleged to have made an error. That leads judges to impose a high duty of care on their own profession.

An extreme example of this tendency has occurred in cases where the court has concluded that lawyers have been negligent notwithstanding that they have followed an accepted practice. The Supreme Court in the Republic of Ireland held in 1986 that a solicitor had been negligent following the "universal practice" of the profession as to the timing of a search against a company on the grounds that the practice had "inherent defects". Solicitors in Hong Kong were also held liable in the aftermath of a conveyancing transaction they had conducted in 1976, in which they had followed the customary local practice on completion. Unfortunately that created a risk that the vendor's solicitor would abscond with the purchase monies and leave the buyer without title to the property. The judge at first instance held that the risk of embezzlement by the other solicitor was foreseeable and liability was established. The Court of Appeal of Hong Kong came to the opposite conclusion and the case was only finally decided in 1983 by the final appellate court for Hong Kong, the Privy Council sitting in London. The solicitors were held liable, despite the fact that they had carried out the transaction in accordance with the standard practice for "Hong Kong style" completions.

If the outcome of such cases is of concern, an even more disturbing development has appeared in several jurisdictions, although as yet it has made no direct impact. It is the proposal that the burden of proof should not be on the claimant to establish negligence by the legal advisers, but that the lawyers should have to prove they have no liability. That has been put forward in recent years in Argentina, in an act unifying the Civil Code and the Commercial Code, but vetoed by the President. In Greece consumer laws which became effective in 1994 placed the onus on "service providers" to prove lack of fault. It is assumed the statute applies to the legal profession. A rather wider threat was presented by a draft proposal of a European Community Directive which sought to reverse the onus of proof for claims against professional advisers generally. The scheme has been withdrawn by the Commission in the face of the opposition it aroused, but it is understood the idea may not have been abandoned.

## THE PROFESSION'S REACTION TO INCREASING CLAIMS

In a society with a well-developed infrastructure one of the usual reactions to a substantial financial risk is to insure against it by some means or other. As far as claims against the legal profession are concerned this is the option probably best understood by lay clients, although the arguments put forward by consumer pressure groups sometimes appear to ignore the fact that insurance premiums borne by the profession are an expense which is paid for at the end of the day by the clients in higher fees. From the profession's point of view there is everything to be said for avoiding the risk of a large award of damages against the practice which would have to be found from the personal financial resources of the members of the practice, failing which they would be made bankrupt. That is an acceptable solution provided the cost is not prohibitively high, but a least insurance premiums are largely predictable and can be allowed for in the management of the business. However, in jurisdictions where the number of claims has been increasing and the level of awards is perceived to be spiralling upwards the questions are being asked whether there is enough insurance capacity available on the market and whether insurance on its own is enough.

The real risk is the large claim where the amount of damages substantially exceeds the insurance cover obtained by the practice. Any member of the profession may become involved in a situation which is akin to a game of Russian roulette with whatever wealth those in the practice have acquired for themselves and their families from their years in practice. What is more, the fatal shot may be fired before they realise they are playing. It is easy to imagine how the worst might happen. In the course of a hectic period of work new clients are found whose need for legal assistance promises a substantial fee income for the rest of the financial year and well beyond. In the course of sorting out their problems the lawyer enthusiastically becomes involved in what is likely to be the largest and most complicated piece of litigation in his career. Then a time limit is missed. Only at that stage is it realised that the clients' claim against the firm is likely to be well in excess of that year's indemnity cover. By then, of course, it is too late to consider any "one-off" policy to insure against the additional risk. This kind of situation is all the more a lottery because the smallest claim can arise from a long period of total incompetence by someone who should not be allowed to practise at all, and the largest claim can be precipitated by a moment's inadvertence on the part of a very experienced and conscientious practitioner.

The law firm which appreciates such risks exist, but believes it has a reasonable level of indemnity cover, may consider two further options. The first is limiting its liability, either by agreement with the clients or by pressing for appropriate regulation. The second is incorporation, following the common practice of much of the business community generally and, in some countries, other professions. The lawyers are to some extent following the accountants down the same road. In some countries the very large awards and settlements paid by accountants for their liability as auditors, often of failing companies, have meant that insurance cover is either prohibitively expensive or is available only with very large deductibles. It is hardly surprising that the issues of a financial ceiling and incorporation are being carefully explored by them.

## METHODS OF RESTRICTING LIABILITY

Restricting liability is controversial. The idea that there should be some fixed monetary limit to lawyers' liability for their own mistakes provoked a very mixed reaction from the profession in the countries surveyed. There is agreement everywhere that such a principle can have no application where the legal adviser's liability results from dishonest or reckless conduct. Some rapporteurs have gone further, to express the view that any attempt to limit liability for lawyers' negligence would be unprofessional. In a few countries legislation has been passed to that effect. Several rapporteurs pointed out that it is hardly an auspicious start to working on a major new set of instructions, or with a new client, to enter into a discussion about the extent of the lawyer's liability should matters be mishandled.

Elsewhere the reaction is more favourable. In numerous jurisdictions arrangements for limiting liability are not thought to be in conflict with the dignity of the profession, although individual agreements between lawyers and their clients might well be subject to the strictures of consumer legislation. However, one-off negotiated arrangements with clients are either non-existent or a rarity in virtually every jurisdiction. It is another matter to put forward a system which would be appropriate for general application. In the forefront is Australasia. Mention has already been made of the practice rule adopted in New Zealand which in limited circumstances allows legal advisers to limit their liability to the amount of their minimum compulsory insurance cover. The Parliament of New South Wales in Australia has recently passed a statute which will enable lawyers to put in place a scheme to put a limit on damages, although as yet no detailed arrangements have been implemented.

As far as Europe is concerned, in Germany a recent statute which alters the regulations for the practice of attorneys at law has created three options. First, by specific agreement with the client the attorney can limit liability to the mandatory minimum for indemnity insurance, which is just over the equivalent of USD350,000. Whilst this provision allows liability to be limited for "gross" as well as "ordinary" negligence there is some doubt as to the areas of practice it covers. Second, liability for "ordinary" negligence can be limited by general conditions, although such a clause is only valid if the attorney has indemnity cover of at least four times the compulsory minimum. Third, liability may be restricted to the individual attorney who conducted the matter. How this last alternative might work in practice is particularly unclear, if only because the giving of legal advice is so often a team effort within a firm. Other uncertainties arise, especially as to how the courts will react to general conditions: one effective way to limit their application would be to condemn the mistakes complained of as "gross" rather than "ordinary" negligence. In Holland, lawyers may limit their liability to the amount of their compulsory indemnity cover, as in Germany. Discussions on the same topic are taking place in Austria and no doubt elsewhere.

Within the European Union, individual agreements to restrict liability to the client will be subject to the national legislation implementing the Unfair Terms in Consumer Contracts Directive, where the client is a consumer rather than a business. A clause avoiding or limiting liability on the part of the lawyer will be ineffective unless it satisfies the tests as to fairness and good faith set out in the Directive. In some jurisdictions there are similar obstacles for any contractual limitation of liability, even to business clients. For example, in England and Wales, under the Unfair Contract Terms Act such a clause must pass the test of reasonableness. The criteria for making that assessment include the relative bargaining position of the parties and, importantly, the availability of insurance to both parties.

Experience with the operation of these arrangements is very limited. They certainly have attractions for the legal profession but it is safe to assume that the vast majority of clients need to be convinced they are reasonable. It is one thing to suggest to a client that a particular transaction warrants additional indemnity cover in view of the amount involved, and even to invite the client to pay the insurance premium. That has some benefit for the client as well as for the lawyer. Only the lawyer benefits from the prospect of reducing his own liability. However, if some law firms try to restrict their liability and others in the same market do not, it would be a very confident commercial client who instructs the former rather than the latter on a substantial matter if the firms were all of the same calibre.

To suggest to a client that there should be a limit on liability might well be justified if the legal advisers are unable to obtain adequate insurance cover on reasonable terms. It is likely to be the case that such situations arise where the client is a corporation or other institution of considerable substance and better able to carry the potential losses which might be involved than their legal advisers, even taking into account their indemnity cover. It is the reverse of the uneven bargaining position which has led to legislation to satisfy consumer interests. Instead of the private individual seeking legal assistance from what he sees as a large and wealthy law firm, the multi-national corporation is relying on the expertise of an individual adviser or a team of lawyers whose judgement will influence executive decisions involving millions of dollars. In the former case the argument for restricting liability is not at all persuasive; in the latter case the balance of interests is far less clear-cut. If any limitation of liability is to be generally accepted it must be on the assumption that the lawyers do have in place reasonable indemnity insurance arrangements with a level of cover commensurate with their type of practice. Further, if the argument in favour of restriction is convincing it must follow that in the interests of all concerned it should be a matter for general regulation rather than individual agreement between lawyers and clients. One purpose of any legal system is to introduce an element of certainty in the relations between members of the business community. To introduce the principle of limitation on the maximum financial liability of lawyers, but to be negotiated on a piecemeal basis, is taking two steps forward and one step back.

Once the principle is accepted two main questions need to be addressed. First, when does the "balance" between client and lawyer, as consumer and service-provider respectively, tip in favour of the lawyer? To put it another way, what factor or factors should be decisive in defining when lawyers are justified in limiting their liability? Second, how should the limit of liability be fixed? Apart from the very few jurisdictions where schemes have actually been introduced, these are issues which have received little consideration. In South Africa its Law Commission investigated the possible need to introduce legislation but came to the conclusion that no system of statutory restriction was required. More positive results might be achieved if there was at least consensus within the legal profession as to where the lines should be drawn.

## INCORPORATION OF PRACTICES

In some quarters the prospect of lawyers being able to incorporate their practices provokes similar objections to those that are made to the limiting of liability. For members of the legal profession to "hide behind the corporate veil" and to use such a device as a means of avoiding personal responsibility is dismissed as unprofessional. Although there may be opposition from within, much of the outside world, which the legal profession services, has been organised along corporate lines for many years and to commercial clients the idea is probably not so hard to accept. Indeed, over the last two decades or so that part of the profession which handles corporate work, particularly with an international aspect, has become more businesslike in every sense, more aware of their clients' business and eager to impress on clients that lawyers are aware of the commercial realities of life. If this outlook is acceptable to the clients it is difficult to imagine that they would find incorporation by the lawyers themselves to be unprofessional in principle.

The results of this survey suggest that incorporation should not lead to a decline in professional standards. In the vast majority of jurisdictions questions of misconduct and other disciplinary matters are the responsibility of local Bar Associations or Law Societies, functioning entirely separately from the courts. It should therefore be within the power of the governing bodies of the profession to keep its distinct character and maintain proper standards. A client is unlikely to believe that the quality of service that he is to receive would be any lower after incorporation. He is also unlikely to have thought that unlimited liability was a prerequisite for his lawyer in the sense of taking comfort that he could if necessary enforce a judgment against the lawyer's personal assets. This is because, in many jurisdictions, he will know that professional indemnity insurance is in place to protect both himself and his lawyer.

If incorporation of law firms, with limited liability, were to become the norm the clients would become all the more interested in the level of indemnity insurance carried by the firm. Indeed, it would become standard for clients to insist on being given that information as a matter of course.

It should be borne in mind as well that incorporation does not invariably lead to lawyers acquiring the advantage that their liability is limited to the assets of the corporate vehicle they use for the conduct of the practice. In Sweden current regulations allow lawyers to carry on their business within the scope of a limited partnership or company but their personal liability to clients nonetheless remains unrestricted. Elsewhere incorporation is still something of a novelty. Since April 1992 lawyers in Finland have been permitted to establish limited liability companies and partners have become shareholders. In 1994 in Germany the Superior Court for Bavaria decided that law firms may in restricted circumstances establish themselves as limited companies. This ruling was made in the face of various arguments against allowing incorporation within the legal profession. It was said that limitation of liability conflicted with the very personal responsibility of the attorney, that an attorney could not maintain his independence as an employee subject to management directives, and that incorporation would result in the commercialisation of the profession. In the event all those points were rejected by the court. However, it did rule that only attorneys working for the company could be "investors" and that there should be substantial minimum requirements for indemnity insurance. In neighbouring Austria incorporation is still at the discussion stage.

In all probability the issue of incorporation, if considered at all, is discussed in the context of various factors, limitation of liability being only one of them. Taxation consequences are likely to be an aspect in the forefront of any consideration, and this option apparently may produce tax disadvantages in Germany. Incorporation is on the decline in the United States as a reaction to changes in tax and retirement laws, which have removed benefits on pensions. The image the firm wishes to present to its clients will no doubt be another element to be taken into account, as will experience elsewhere, for example in accountancy, where incorporation is already a feature of professional life in some countries.

## RISK REDUCTION METHODS

In countries where there is now a history of increasing claims against the profession and rising insurance premiums, further strategies have on occasions been adopted based on the principle "prevention is better than cure".

The initiative may come either from within the profession or from the insurers. Bar Councils and Law Societies can publicise both general trends and specific cases which highlight the major areas of risk faced by lawyers in the course of their practice, and how those risks can be averted or at least reduced. The provision of continuing education after qualification is also becoming a feature of professional life, in some countries on a compulsory basis. The fact that completing so many hours of continuing education is being introduced as a condition for continuing in practice at all, for example in England and Wales, is either a reflection of the importance attached to the scheme or a comment on the probable attitude towards the scheme by the weaker members of the profession. There is perhaps a greater incentive to react favourably towards the quality control procedures which can now be adopted by law firms. If the firm is eventually certified under the International Standards Organisation ISO 1900 process that is an accolade which can be advertised and placed on the firm's notepaper. Another process, considered in South Africa, is for the certification of lawyers as specialists in particular fields of practice. On the one hand this may well be seen as a very worthy method of improving standards, but on the other hand it will almost inevitably lead to an even higher duty of care being imposed on specialist practitioners, thus increasing their vulnerability.

Concern about preventing the escalation of claims comes to the fore from the insurers' side when the profession introduces a compulsory single "master policy" or a mutual fund. These schemes, which are considered further elsewhere, have to justify themselves to their insured lawyers as the most effective and cheapest way to provide indemnity cover. One crucial advantage which these schemes both have over insurance in the open market is that in time very full statistical information can be accumulated in relation to claims. That information is of course essential for the purposes of fixing premiums or contributions. It also enables a constructive and organised approach to be adopted towards any risk management programme. The Speedman Report, commissioned to review the Law Cover Scheme of compulsory insurance for members of the Law Society of New South Wales, commented:

> Insuring through one scheme or through one insurer is the only effective method of ensuring that proper and complete statistics are collected and maintained and used effectively in the implementation of risk management and loss control programmes.

Also:

> If the frequency and cost of claims is to be reduced with a consequent reduction in the cost of indemnity which in turn should lead to a reduction in the cost of legal services, there must be a greatly increased profession-wide awareness of risk management and loss prevention.

After almost two decades of compulsory insurance for solicitors in England and Wales a recent development makes possible a more direct impact being made in certain cases. Hitherto there has been concern that detailed information about claims against specific firms should not be disclosed by those responsible for the mutual scheme, the Solicitors Indemnity Fund, to the Law Society, which is responsible for disciplining the profession. It was thought that the possibility of a firm's defaults being disclosed to the Law Society might result in some solicitors being less than frank with the Solicitors Indemnity Fund. Now the managers of the Fund have the power to reveal to the Law Society the name of any firm which they consider has such a bad claims record that it would benefit from investigation by the Society. This could be an indication of one way forward for improving standards in the profession and therefore the service given to clients.

# Chapter 4

# Indemnity Insurance for the Legal Profession

## INTRODUCTION

Professional liability is still a relatively new subject, that is to say as a subject of legal publications and case law. For as long as professionals have been practising, they have no doubt made errors from time to time, but this has only been receiving more serious — legal — attention since the sixties, with a noticeable growth in the eighties. The number of claims against professionals since then shows a distinct increase.

The increase in the number of claims would seem to be related to, *inter alia*, the following factors:

- injured parties are more readily inclined to sue (people have become more assertive, have less regard for old power patterns, have access to state-funded legal aid, take out legal expenses insurance etc.);
- the professional-client relationship (notably in larger law firms) has become more businesslike, much less of a personal relationship;
- the growing complexity of rules and regulations (due to which there is a greater risk of errors);
- people's awareness that the risk of professional liability may be covered by insurance (the loss will ultimately be borne by an insurance company);
- the economic situation (economic recession increases the number of claims).

The developments in case law pertaining to malpractice suits in the various jurisdictions all over the globe appear to be kaleidoscopical. In certain jurisdictions, malpractice suits against lawyers used to be relatively minor compared to the claims against other professionals like medical doctors and accountants. This was probably due to the larger social role of the latter professionals in those countries. This trend does not exist everywhere, and indeed in countries like the United States lawyers seem to be as vulnerable as medical doctors and accountants. It can therefore be observed that throughout the world the legal profession finds itself in different stages of awareness that using great prudence and diligence is of paramount importance. This does not only apply to specialized and internationally-operating lawyers, but equally to lawyers with a general, domestic practice. Elsewhere in this publication the trends with respect to professional indemnity claims are analyzed more comprehensively. This section will deal with insurance against the risks emerging from legal practice, insurance being one of the usual reactions to financial risks in societies with a well-developed infrastructure.

## INDEMNITY PRINCIPLE

In many jurisdictions, the doctrine of indemnity was traditionally based on the principle that "fundamentally everyone has to bear the damages he has incurred". Social developments in this century, closely followed by the developments in the various legal systems anywhere, have moved in another direction. Particularly in those countries which shaped into an — increasingly — affluent society from the fifties onward, the aforementioned principle has become an exception. Nowadays, the average citizen believes that either the community, by means of a collective scheme, or the person who has caused the damages should compensate losses and damages: responsibilities are being transferred and risks are being hedged, both as much as possible. Here we enter the market of indemnity insurance.

## THE PROFESSIONAL INDEMNITY INSURANCE MARKET

Professional indemnity insurance is a species of general indemnity insurance, which in general only covers damages to goods or injuries to persons (apart from punitive damages). Professional indemnity insurance distinguishes itself from general indemnity insurance in that it covers damages which solely consist of financial losses.

It should be postulated that the worldwide potential of professional indemnity insurance is much smaller than the possibilities for covering fire risks, transport risks and the like. Many insurance companies refrain from giving professional indemnity insurance because they lack the expertise and insight to weigh the risks involved. The circumstances under which professionals carry out their practice vary from country to country and the risks involved are widely divergent. Hence the rather reserved attitude of the insurance world in this field, with the London-based market as a clear exception.

Hardly any insurance company for professional indemnity insurance seems to be prepared or capable to bear fully the risks involved for its own account only. In nearly all cases there are co-insurers or reinsurers that have an important say in the policy conditions of the direct (or primary) insurer. One of the consequences of the reinsurance mechanism is that developments in other countries do influence local circumstances, which means that this subject does not lend itself to just a domestic approach.

Globally, the insurance market was quite profitable until the eighties. Profits were made not only because the premium earnings were higher than the claims for insured damages but also because the interests accrued on reinvested reserves were considerable. The latter was indeed an important factor in the period that the interest rates in countries like the United Kingdom and the United States went up to about twenty per cent. After 1980, interest rates fell at a high speed, whilst at the same time, especially in the United States of America, the number and the extent of claims granted by the courts increased enormously. The indemnity insurance market became less and less attractive. Insurance companies shrunk from covering risks which they felt were difficult to cover. In the light of the foregoing, it should be no surprise that the market for professional indemnity insurance was heavily affected by these developments: the number of insurances available fell and premiums increased considerably.

## THE ALARM BELL

On April 14, 1986, the International Bar Association devoted a conference to (the problems with) professional indemnity insurance in London, where it was felt that the situation "is now verging on the impossible". Taking a closer look at the situation at that moment, the picture becomes quite distorted. In some countries, such as the United Kingdom and Hong Kong, with collective schemes, the situation was indeed alarming. In Hong Kong, for instance, the so-called loss ratio at that time amounted to two hundred per cent over the past five years. On the other hand, the situation in a country such as Sweden seemed to be rather stable, with only a slight increase in claims.

As a result of these negative trends, collective schemes with commercial insurers ran out of favour. As per September 1, 1987, the Law Society of England and Wales introduced a new system whereby the Master Policy taken out by the Law Society ceased to provide cover in respect of the future and was replaced by the Solicitors Indemnity Fund, providing for an indemnity limit of now USD1.5 million for each and every claim.

It should be noted that the situation in 1995 does not significantly differ from the situation at the time of the IBA conference in 1986, when, at the closing of the conference, the Chairman felt that legislation was the only way out for the problems in various countries. So far, however, we are not aware of any legislation in this field in any country. At the same time, however, quite a number of Bar Associations and Law Societies are studying and discussing the subject of limitation of liability, explained in chapter 3, on trends in relation to professional indemnity claims.

Returning to the situation on the insurance market for professional indemnity insurance, it seems that the crisis felt by the mid eighties has quietly been solved in a number of countries. For instance, the United States has recently shown a slight decrease of premiums. Other countries, however, report a continuous annual increase in the cost of professional indemnity insurance. The fear that the tide of claims and the enormous rise in the amounts claimed might result in a situation in which professional indemnity insurance with acceptable premiums and adequate coverage would no longer be available has appeared unfounded. But perhaps one can also conclude that the legal profession has learned to live with the permanent cost factor of professional indemnity insurance.

In connection with the cyclical character of the insurance market, it is now felt that the mid nineties will again demonstrate a development towards both higher premiums and lower coverage. This is being attributed not only to claims records but also to problems on the London market and the fact that insurers are being forced to make provisions in connection with the threat of future claims on old policies (asbestos claims!). The latter has a price-inflating effect on other forms of indemnity insurance.

## THE NEED FOR PROFESSIONAL INDEMNITY INSURANCE

Going through the responses to the questionnaire, it does not require much imagination to establish a connection between the socio-economic situation in a country and the way in which the legal profession in that particular country deals with professional indemnity insurance. Practising law in developing countries is still a traditional profession — and in a number of non-democratic societies even a vocation — whilst it has become more businesslike in the highly-developed post-industrial economies. Elsewhere in this publication attention is paid to the lawyer as "the father figure", advising private clients as a close friend of the family. There are indeed a number of countries where at the end of the twentieth century the title of advocate still has its classical meaning of "friend", which dates back to the classical Roman era. In those countries, the need for adequate professional indemnity insurance is hardly felt, or rather non-existent. The problems are felt there where practising law has become more and more a commercial activity, and this could perhaps also justify a commercial approach when it comes to the question of which risks and responsibilities should be borne and insured and which should not.

Following this line of reasoning, one could argue that there should always be an obligation for a lawyer to take out an adequate insurance coverage when his client is heavily dependent on his lawyer for his personal well-being and way of life, and does not engage a lawyer for business or commercial purposes. Such dependence exists in any case in those areas of the law where assistance or representation in court proceedings by a lawyer is mandatory. This approach could also give an answer to the ethical dilemma of whether or not a limitation of liability by the lawyer can be deemed acceptable.

## COMPULSORY INDEMNITY INSURANCE

It follows from the questionnaire that quite a number of Bars and Law Societies in countries which at present do not require the lawyer to take out professional indemnity insurance are considering a compulsory scheme. Consumer expectation appears to be the driving force behind this development. Throughout the world, more and more countries are entering the age of the "empowered consumer", with his ever higher demands on suppliers of goods and services, the latter including professional advisers like lawyers. It should be noted that without compulsory insurance not only would some clients be left unprotected against faults of their lawyer but the legal profession itself would suffer from the bad image this would entail. These and other arguments can be found in various studies, of which the Speedman report[1] is mentioned here because it holds an extensive and independent review of this subject. Mr Speedman reports:

> Everyone I spoke to on this subject was in favour of compulsory insurance.

and indeed there is not much to add to this statement but two other arguments in favour derived from the same report:

- compulsory indemnity insurance creates a much larger premium pool for coverage;
- it also averts the situation that the client has to make an informed choice about the risks of retaining the services of a lawyer.

## THE SHIELD OF INDEMNITY/DEDUCTIBLES

Professional liability was discussed during the 1995 spring meeting of the Council of the European Bars (CCBE), which is the representative body of the independent Bar Associations and Law Societies in the European Union and Norway and Iceland. As early as 1985, the CCBE made a recommendation on the need for all lawyers in the European Community to be insured against professional risks. This recommendation was reflected in article 3.9.1 of the CCBE's Code of Conduct of 1988, which stipulates that the lawyer shall be insured

> against claims based on professional negligence to an extent which is reasonable having regard to the nature and extent of the risks which lawyers incur in practice.

In his preliminary memorandum on behalf of the aforesaid CCBE meeting, Mr Dag Wersen, Head of the Swedish Delegation to the CCBE, raises the question of what level of insurance protection should be deemed "reasonable". It would seem natural to limit the lawyer's responsibility to amounts corresponding to the possible or actual insurance protection for the lawyer, which would mean that the lawyer carries no risk whatsoever after having paid the insurance premium. As Mr Dag Wersen has put it, this is hardly satisfactory from a client's point of view, because insurance is usually limited to a certain amount and to a restricted number of claims against the insured lawyer. Moreover, the lawyer who is aware of a personal risk for reimbursement of damages

1 J.A. Speedman "Review of the Solicitors Mutual Indemnity Fund", published by the Law Foundation of New South Wales, November 1994.

to a certain extent will presumably remain more careful than the lawyer who knows that negligence will not cause personal loss to him.

This dilemma can be solved in various ways. In this respect deductibles seem to be the most efficient because they are not only a penalty for a bad claims record but also an instrument to keep the premium down. Here the results of the questionnaire again show a great variety in "deductible systems", and it might be that in the near future risk assessment regarding the type of practice of the lawyer or a partnership will influence both the premium level and the extent of the deductibles. Anyhow, there are quite a number of arguments in favour of — perhaps even compulsory — deductibles, such as:

- they are an incentive to practice with care, as lawyers without claims save on premium costs;
- they may cut out minor claims, which also saves premium costs.

Especially in those jurisdictions where the Bar or the Law Society has instituted its own mutual indemnity fund or an independent mutual fund, one finds the most advanced deductible schemes because there the administrators of the fund have an overall picture of both the nature of the claims that are filed and the type of practice causing the claims. In this connection Mr David Cox, a corporate counsel to an international chemical concern, suggested during the aforementioned CCBE meeting that insurance should be arranged according to the area(s) of practice. To quote Mr Cox:

> Different areas of practice would have different levels of cover (monetary ceilings) and different premiums. Levels of cover could also be related to annual levels of fee income. In these circumstances, for example, the sole practitioner who practises in the areas of family law and small real property matters in a rural community would be able to obtain a relatively low level of cover at a modest cost. Whereas, the large law firms practising in the areas of cross-border mergers and acquisitions and corporate finance would require a much higher level of cover at considerably higher cost.

Bearing in mind Mr Cox's suggestion, it seems at present to be generally accepted in countries with a compulsory insurance scheme that the lawyer should have a coverage of at least USD500,000 ("the exceptions confirm the rule"). Although the questionnaire does not provide a better insight in the nature of the practice for which this level of coverage is required, we feel we are on safe grounds stating that this coverage deals with the ordinary general practice and aims at protecting the interests of the individual rather than the risks involved in business transactions with sometimes a high risk profile.

## RISK PREVENTION

Although this chapter concerns indemnity insurance, we cannot avoid paying some attention to risk prevention, as, for instance, has also been done in the report from South Africa. Only recently did the legal profession become aware of the fact that the quality concept does not only reflect the substance, i.e. legal skills and knowledge of the law and of the courts' jurisprudence. The quality of the practice is also determined by procedural aspects aiming at avoiding risks as well as improving the service to the clients. Nowadays a lawyer, apart from reading weekly/monthly/regularly(?) the law gazette and the most recent publications and court cases in his area of the law, should also develop certain managerial skills related to his practice. To quote Mr Dag Wersen, who proposes in this field:

a. Introduction of routines for those parts of the practice normally exposed to damage risks, such as observation of dead lines which should be noted in registers etc.
b. Control systems for legal opinions and/or important documents, for example, through cross-checks by a lawyer not involved in the matter.
c. Including in the education and training of lawyers awareness of and techniques aimed at the prevention of risks.
d. Appointment of risk manager(s) in the law firms and preparation of guidelines for risk managers based on what experienced lawyers would suggest from what they have been through, and what they know that colleagues have been through.

Much more could be added in respect of this interesting subject. Take, for instance, the law offices in the United Kingdom, and recently also in the Netherlands, which have obtained the ISO quality certificate. There can be no doubt that this is only the very beginning of a development which in the near future will be adopted by the legal profession on a large scale.

## MUTUAL FUNDS

One of the problems in the area of professional indemnity insurance is that reliable statistics on claims are lacking in most countries. As commercial insurers are inclined, not to say obliged, to calculate their own risks in a prudent and thus conservative manner in order to remain profitable, they will always try to be on the safe side when fixing the premium level. In this respect, the worst case scenario seems to be the guiding principle.

In a number of (mostly Anglo-Saxon) countries the legal profession has therefore developed its own or an independent mutual fund, which offers the advantage of self control. Research carried out by the Law Society of England and Wales and recently by Mr Speedman in New South Wales demonstrates that insuring through a single scheme is the only effective method to collect proper and complete statistics. Only in this way effective risk management and loss-control programmes can be implemented. But there is another very substantial argument in favour of not only one insurer but also of one compulsory mutual fund, which is the amount available for indemnification.

This is illustrated by a calculation in the Speedman Report, which shows that only USD76.50 is available to meet claims from every USD100 paid to a commercial insurer, whilst the amount available to meet claims in case the same USD100 is paid to the Solicitors Indemnity Fund, is USD109.25. This difference is caused by the absence of insurance brokerage fees, lower operating expenses and higher investment earnings of the mutual fund.

Of course, it should be recognized that a mutual fund can only be organized in countries where the legal profession is highly organized and has a very professional organization with sufficient staff at its disposal also to develop and administer a mutual fund. This entails that the members have to pay significant annual contributions to keep up the organization. It may furthermore be argued that as a consequence of a mutual fund, lawyers with a good claims record are subsidizing their colleagues with a poor record. Perhaps there are also other disadvantages involved in a mutual fund, but studies like the Speedman report make it worthwhile to explore the pros and cons of such a scheme, especially in those countries where the legal profession is at present considering the implementation of a compulsory system.

# Chapter 5

# Overview of Survey Results

## INTRODUCTION

For the sake of easy reference, this chapter consists of the following three sections:

- countries (eight) where indemnity insurance is not available;
- countries (thirty-three) where a lawyer's indemnity insurance is taken out on a voluntary basis;
- countries (nineteen) where it is compulsory to take out a lawyer's indemnity insurance.

## COUNTRIES WHERE INDEMNITY INSURANCE IS NOT AVAILABLE

These are the following eight countries: Bolivia, China, Guatemala, Korea, Panama, Paraguay, Thailand and Uruguay.

A number of the responses show that the insurance business has not yet developed professional indemnity insurance because in these countries a lawyer's liability toward his clients is of little or no relevance. The observation from Guatemala is interesting, i.e. that professional indemnity insurance is expected to be introduced within three to five years as a result of the internationalization of trade and economy and the implications for the legal practice.

## COUNTRIES WHERE PROFESSIONAL INDEMNITY INSURANCE IS VOLUNTARY

These are the following thirty-three countries: Argentina, Bermuda, Brazil, the Channel Islands, Chile, Colombia, Cyprus, Ecuador, Egypt, Greece, India, Israel, Italy, Jamaica, Japan, Kenya, Latvia, Malawi, Malta, Mexico, New Zealand,

Nigeria, Peru, the Philippines, Portugal, Puerto Rico, Russia, Spain, Sri Lanka, Switzerland, Taiwan, the Turks and Caicos Islands and the United States (with the exception of the state of Oregon).

In twenty-one of the thirty-three countries mentioned above, a negligible percentage of lawyers (less than ten per cent) is insured against professional liability. In these countries claims against lawyers are rare.

In seven of the thirty-three countries where professional indemnity insurance is voluntary, only part of the members of the Bar take out this insurance; for example Portugal (twenty-five per cent), the Turks and Caicos Islands (thirty-five per cent), the United States — California (sixty-six per cent) and Malawi (seventy-five per cent).

In the remaining five countries — the Channel Islands, Israel, Italy, New Zealand and Switzerland — practically every lawyer is insured against professional liability.

This tripartition will be maintained in the following review of the various aspects.

## Countries where less than ten per cent of the lawyers take out professional indemnity insurance

These countries are: Argentina, Bermuda, Brazil, Chile, Columbia, Cyprus, Ecuador, Egypt, India, Japan, Kenya, Latvia, Malta, Mexico, Nigeria, Peru, the Philippines, Puerto Rico, Russia, Sri Lanka and Taiwan.

### *Insurance facilities*

In most of these countries it is possible to take out insurance with a commercial insurer in one's own country. In some countries, such as Egypt and Ecuador, it is also possible to take out insurance abroad, subject to the approval of a supervisory authority.

In Malta insurance is taken out through a local agent with foreign insurers (the London market).

### *Level of cover*

With respect to the level of cover generally obtained by the legal profession, most respondents could not give an indication because there were no statistics available. A number of countries have indicated that insurers offer a limited cover. In some countries the level of cover rises high above that of other countries (Japan: USD2.3 million[1] per claim and USD6.9 million for the total number of claims in a period of 2 years; Kenya: USD5 million; Puerto Rico: for the larger law firms USD15 million for the total number of claims during the term of a policy).

Most rapporteurs found it impossible to estimate what proportion of the annual expenses of a practice is represented by professional indemnity insurance premium.

1 All amounts mentioned in this book are in US Dollars and are based on exchange rates as per June 1995.

Of the rapporteurs that answered the question, Kenya's answer was the most remarkable: for a firm with a level of cover of USD5 million — although most practices would carry a significantly lower level of cover —, the professional indemnity insurance premium can represent approximately 8 per cent of the annual expenses of the practice.

*Deductibles*
Taking into consideration what was said above under *Level of Cover*, little can be said about deductibles either. Of the rapporteurs that answered this question, Kenya and Nigeria report that the range of deductibles payable by the insured lawyers themselves is negotiable.

*Recent developments*
In a number of countries (Latvia, India and Malta) it is expected that there will be an increase in interest in professional indemnity insurance and that this kind of insurance will be developed further.

The Law Society of Kenya is at an advanced stage in the development of a compulsory system for professional indemnity insurance as well as a compensation fund. They hope that these will be realized by the end of 1995. Both the system of professional indemnity insurance and the fund are drawn up after the English example.

The Philippines rapporteur informed us that the Integrated Bar of the Philippines has examined if, and to which extent, compulsory professional indemnity insurance is desirable. The legal profession is not in favour. It is expected that compulsory insurance will lead to additional costs. Furthermore, it is felt that making insurance compulsory may lead to a flood of claims against lawyers. From the consumer's point of view it is believed that the available legal remedies and sanctions provide adequate protection.

**Countries where ten to ninety per cent of the lawyers take out professional indemnity insurance**

These countries are: Greece, Jamaica, Malawi, Portugal, Spain, the Turks & Caicos Islands and the United States.

*Insurance facilities*
In Malawi professional indemnity insurance is taken out with local commercial insurers.

In Portugal there are the following options:

- an indirect voluntary collective scheme introduced by the Social Security for Lawyers Institution (associated to the Portuguese Bar Association);
- a direct voluntary scheme between individual lawyers and a commercial insurance company;

- a combination of the above.

In Spain, lawyers are offered voluntary collective schemes through the Law Societies. Insurance policies offered by commercial insurers are also available as well as commercial insurance policies approved by the professional body.

On the Turks and Caicos Islands, professional indemnity insurance is taken out with foreign commercial insurers.

In the United States there are a large number of possibilities:

- insurance taken out with commercial insurers;
- most State Bars have a list of approved insurers, including one company that the Bar sponsors. The State Bar recommends this insurer and in return the recommended insurer will pay the State Bar a fee — the Californian State Bar receives approximately USD1 million per year from its sponsee);
- some State Bars have a collective scheme whereby the Bar acts as a separate corporate entity offering insurance;
- the large law firms self-insure themselves by joining a mutual insurance company. The deductibles are very high, usually from USD100,000 to USD500,000;
- client security funds in nearly all of the states.

*Level of cover*

In Malawi, the level of cover depends on the number and the sort of cases as well as the size of the law firm. The cover is an aggregate of all the claims in a policy year.

In Portugal, the maximum level of cover for the indirect voluntary collective scheme is USD200,000 per claim per year for each individual lawyer. The average level of cover for law firms is USD500,000 per claim per year. The maximum level of cover is USD1 million. The insurance premium for the indirect voluntary collective scheme and the direct voluntary scheme is respectively USD3,000 and USD4,200 per year.

In Spain, the minimum level of cover differs per Law Society. The Madrid Bar provides a cover of USD19,230, while the Vizcaya Bar requires its members to take out a minimum cover of USD192,300. This cover is a maximum per claim, with a total maximum of claims per policy period of USD769,230. The insurance premium is estimated between 0.1 and 0.5 per cent of the annual expenses of a practice.

On the Turks and Caicos Islands, the level of cover is USD500,000, up to a maximum of USD1 million for every claim, with a total of USD2.5 to 5 million for every year. The cost of the professional indemnity insurance is estimated to be approximately three per cent of the annual expenses of a practice.

In the United States, the level of cover ranges between USD100,000 and USD5 million per claim for all claims in a policy period. In Oregon, the limit is USD300,000 per claim for every claim made against a firm.

*Deductibles*
In Malawi these can be negotiated. Usually the deductibles will range between one and ten per cent of the claim.

In Portugal the deductibles are ten per cent.

In Spain, the range of deductibles is between USD769 and USD7,692 with an average of USD3,846.

On the Turks and Caicos Islands the deductibles vary between USD5,000 and USD25,000.

In the United States the lowest deductible is approximately USD2,500. The maximum is usually between USD100,000 and USD250,000, but some large firms will pay up to USD500,000.

*Recent developments*
In Malawi, it is deemed necessary to make the professional indemnity insurance compulsory. The Malawi Law Society has requested the Association of Law Societies of the Republic of South Africa to supply background information to facilitate the establishment of professional indemnity insurance to be taken out by the Law Society on behalf of all its members.

Spain expects that the Council of State Bars will make a professional indemnity insurance compulsory in the near future.

**Countries where ninety to one hundred per cent of the lawyers take out professional indemnity insurance**

These countries are: the Channel Islands, Israel, Italy, New Zealand and Switzerland.

*Insurance facilities*
On the Channel Islands, law firms either negotiate individual policies with commercial insurers or take out insurance direct with underwriters. The insurance is generally obtained locally, or in England, or is negotiated directly with Lloyd's.

In Israel, insurance is taken out with domestic commercial insurers. The Bar pursues collective insurances on behalf of its members and annually concludes an agreement with an insurance company on the basic premiums.

In Italy, insurance is generally taken out with domestic insurers as well.

In New Zealand, large law firms often take out insurance abroad, while the smaller firms and sole practitioners engage domestic insurers. Barristers are usually insured with C E Heath Insurance which offers a special policy to barristers.

In Switzerland, insurance is generally obtained from commercial insurers within the country. The Swiss Bar Association is exploring the possibility of a voluntary collective insurance scheme, but so far has not found a cheaper form of insurance.

*Level of cover*

On the Channel Islands, the major law firms often have a cover of USD7 to USD15 million for all claims in a policy period. The insurance premium is estimated to be approximately two to three per cent of the annual expenses of a practice.

In Israel, a basic insurance cover negotiated between the Bar and an insurance company provides a cover of USD75,000 per claim and USD150,000 for the total of claims during a specific policy period.

In Italy, the level of cover is determined by the size of the law firm and the nature of their legal activities. The insurance can be concluded with a cover for a total of claims in a policy period, but also with a cover with a maximum for each claim. Risks usually excluded are

> the loss, destruction and damage to money, precious metals, bearer bonds, the auditing of the balance sheets of joint stock companies listed at the stock exchange, the offices of director or of auditor in companies or institutions (which nevertheless can be insured otherwise).

In New Zealand, the average level of cover is approximately USD3 million per claim. The insurer usually imposes a maximum for each claim and can limit the aggregate total liability for the policy period. Approximately three to five per cent of the annual expenses of a practice are represented by the insurance premium.

In Switzerland, the level of cover generally ranges between USD770,000 and USD3.8 million. The average level of cover is estimated to be USD1.5 million and usually provides a maximum for each claim. The cost of insurance represents approximately two to five per cent of the annual expenses of a practice.

*Deductibles*

On the Channel Islands, the likely range of deductibles is between USD15,000 and USD90,000.

In Israel, deductibles range from USD3,500 to USD6,500 for non-land matters and from USD5,500 to USD9,000 for matters related to land.

In Italy, deductibles are normally in the range of ten per cent.

In New Zealand, depending on the size of the law firm, deductibles vary between USD31,000 and USD150,000.

In Switzerland, normally, the deductible is ten per cent of the total claim, with a maximum of USD38,500 per claim.

*Recent developments*

New Zealand is looking into compulsory professional indemnity insurance. Policies are considered which have been approved by the New Zealand Law Society. The New Zealand Law Society has proposed a minimum basic cover of USD150,000.

## COUNTRIES WHERE PROFESSIONAL INDEMNITY INSURANCE IS COMPULSORY

In nineteen out of the sixty countries it is compulsory to take out professional indemnity insurance. They are the following countries: Australia, Austria, Belgium, Canada, Denmark, England and Wales, Finland, France, Germany, Ireland, Liechtenstein, Luxemburg, the Netherlands, Norway, Papua New Guinea, Scotland, Singapore, South Africa and Sweden.

Ireland distinguishes between barristers and solicitors. Only the former were required to take out professional indemnity insurance, but as of January 1, 1996 the Irish Law Society will introduce an obligatory scheme for solicitors too.

In the majority of the countries, professional indemnity insurance is required by law or government regulation. In a number of countries, including Belgium, Finland, Luxemburg, the Netherlands and New Zealand, this requirement follows from the regulations of the professional organization (e.g. the Bar or the Law Society), which in turn has the statutory power to impose binding regulations on its members. Combined with the fact that the law in these countries prescribes compulsory membership of these professional organizations for all "advocates", it may be concluded that the requirement to take out insurance as directed by the professional organizations is indirectly also a statutory requirement.

In South Africa, every lawyer needs a Fidelity Fund Certificate to practise. This certificate automatically carries with it professional indemnity insurance according to the Attorneys Fidelity Fund Professional Indemnity Insurance Scheme, which was established by arrangement with the Association of Law Societies. This scheme provides for cover from USD280,000 to USD560,000 per year, depending on the number of lawyers in a firm. The cover is on an aggregate basis.

*Insurance facilities*

In Australia and Canada cover is arranged by a mutual scheme, provided by the profession itself, up to a compulsory limit. Cover above the compulsory limit is available through commercial insurers.

In Belgium, the local Bars contract collective policies for their members with local insurers. To obtain a higher level of cover, lawyers may take out supplementary insurance with either domestic or foreign insurers.

In Denmark, insurance is taken out with commercial insurers using a policy approved by the Danish Bar Association.

In England and Wales, the facilities for insurance for solicitors are policies issued by commercial insurers and a compulsory mutual scheme introduced by the Law Society, providing the first layer of cover. The compulsory insurance cover is arranged through a scheme of mutual insurance arranged by the profession itself. The compulsory first layer of cover for barristers is provided by the Bar Mutual Indemnity Fund. The cover is arranged through a scheme of mutual insurance managed by the Bar Mutual Management Company and any top-up insurance is available from commercial insurers.

In Finland, Germany, the Netherlands, Papua New Guinea and Singapore, commercial insurers are engaged.

A number of (major) Bars in France, such as the Paris Bar, take out collective insurance schemes which are compulsory for their members. In Ireland (i.e. for the 900 barristers), Luxemburg, Norway and Sweden, a group insurance is used as well.

In Scotland, there is one master insurance policy which is held by the Law Society of Scotland. Commercial insurance is obtained from insurers within the United Kingdom and primarily from within Scotland.

In the countries referred to above, insurance is often obtained from insurers from within the country and abroad. In Denmark, Germany, Finland and Sweden insurances are taken out only with domestic insurers (one insurer in Denmark — Codan — has a market share of approximately seventy per cent).

Another noticeable observation is that in Austria and Norway, foreign insurers are used more and more as a result of the fact that these countries have acceded to the European Economic Area Agreement. Under this agreement, insurers from EEA-countries may enter the markets of the other EEA-countries.

*Level of cover*

In Australia the compulsory level of cover ranges from USD373,000 (in Queensland) to USD820,600 (in New South Wales, the Australian Capital Territory, Victoria, Western Australia and Tasmania) (cover is a maximum for each claim). Normally a cover is taken out which varies between the compulsory minimum cover and USD74,600,000 (in the latter case cover usually applies to the total of all claims during a policy period).

In Austria the compulsory level of cover is USD50,000. Most firms maintain a cover which ranges from USD250,000 to USD550,000. In general, the cover is the maximum for each claim.

In Belgium, the cover of the collective Bar insurance policies is usually limited to USD160,000, USD320,000 or USD480,000 per claim. The level of cover for the Brussels Bar has a maximum of USD480,000 for each claim.

In Canada (Ontario, British Columbia, Alberta and Nova Scotia), the compulsory level of cover is USD736,700 per claim (in some Provinces a minimum cover applies for a total of claims of USD1.47 million). In excess of the limit the cover may vary from USD2.9 million to USD29.5 million.

In Canada (Quebec) the compulsory level of cover is USD1 million per claim. The cover in excess of the limit varies greatly (this cover then applies to the total of all claims in one policy period and with a maximum for each claim).

In Denmark the compulsory level of cover is USD166,000. Additional cover may be taken out, generally to USD1 million, and for large firms up to USD16.6 million (up to USD1 million the cover is a maximum for each claim, in excess thereof the cover is an aggregate for all claims in one policy period).

In England and Wales, for solicitors the compulsory scheme provides USD1.5 million cover for each and every claim, with an unlimited aggregate. For many smaller firms that is the only cover taken out. For the largest commercial firms involved in major transactions cover as high as USD300 million is taken up. For barristers, the compulsory scheme provides a minimum cover of USD375,000 and a maximum of USD3,750,000 for each barrister. Commercial Chambers no doubt take up substantial voluntary cover over and above USD3.75 million in the commercial market.

In Finland the compulsory level of cover is USD120,000 for each act resulting in damage. The cover for a medium-sized office is USD2.5 to USD3 million.

In France the compulsory level of cover is USD400,000 (cover is an aggregate for all claims within a year). The collective cover offered by the large Bar Councils is higher. The Parisian Bar, for example, offers collective cover of USD5 million for each claim. If required, lawyers may individually take out additional cover.

In Germany the compulsory level of cover is USD357,000. Policies often maintain a basic cover of approximately USD1.3 million for each claim, with a total maximum of USD28 million per insurance year (supplementary cover for each separate claim is possible). The maximum insurable level of cover is approximately USD53 to 57 million.

In Ireland, the compulsory cover limit for barristers is USD150,000. The average level of cover taken out by solicitors is USD390,000 for each claim. Supplementary cover is possible.

In Liechtenstein the compulsory level of cover is USD831,000 for each claim. The level of cover usually maintained varies between the minimum level and USD8.3 million. A minimum cover of USD1.6 million applies to lawyers concerned with patents.

In Luxemburg the compulsory level of cover is USD500,000 per claim. The collective insurance policy offers the option of taking out excess cover up to USD3 million per claim.

In the Netherlands the compulsory level of cover is USD570,000 for each claim. The cover usually maintained varies between the minimum level and USD57 million (cover is a maximum for each incident in which the total of claims permitted per policy period is usually restricted).

In Norway the compulsory level of cover is USD734,100 (the cover is an aggregate for all claims within a policy period). Lawyers who employ associates are required to take out a supplementary insurance up to USD440,500 minimum. Separate rules apply to lawyers in debt recovery. They should have a minimum cover equalling one-fortieth of the amounts collected by the lawyer by the end of the preceding fiscal year. Non-members of the Bar with a law degree may render legal advice but are also obliged by law to take out a professional indemnity insurance with a minimum cover of USD440,500 (if the non-lawyer works within a law firm, the cover is increased to USD734,100).

In Papua New Guinea the compulsory level of cover is USD420,000 (the total of all claims in the twelve-month policy period). Supplementary cover is possible (under the policy arranged by the Law Society or arranged independently).

In Scotland, the compulsory cover is USD1.5 million for each and every claim. Larger practices tend to purchase top-up insurance based on a calculation of risk.

In Singapore the compulsory level of cover is USD720,000 for each claim. Supplementary cover is possible (on the basis of the total of claims in a policy period).

In South Africa, the Professional Indemnity Insurance Scheme offers cover for a limit ranging from USD280,000 per year to USD560,000 per year, depending on the number of principals in each practice. The cover is an aggregate for all the claims in a policy period. An estimated fifteen per cent of all practices purchase cover in excess of the Scheme, up to a maximum cover of USD280 million.

In Sweden the compulsory level of cover is USD415,000, which is a maximum per claim per year. The same company contracted for the compulsory cover offers additional insurance cover of USD1.65 million.

*Cost of insurance*

The questionnaire also deals with the share of the annual expenditure of a (legal) practice taken up by professional indemnity insurance premiums. Many rapporteurs were unable to answer this question, as the percentage can vary from one firm to the next. The Canadian rapporteur indicated that

> the answer would be a broad range, depending on such factors as location (principal business centre or small rural community and where in Canada), and claims experience of the particular individual member of the profession.

Those rapporteurs that did provide an answer estimated that this premium does not take up more than 0.5 to two per cent of the annual expenditure. One remarkable exception is Kenya, where the professional indemnity insurance premium can represent approximately eight per cent of the annual expenses of the practice for firms with a level of cover of USD5 million (although most firms carry a significant lower level of cover). In the Channel Islands this share is also significantly higher, and is estimated to be approximately five per cent. Singapore estimates that on average this premium is less than five per cent of the annual expenditure.

*Deductibles*

In Australia the range of deductibles varies from state to state. The decisive factor is whether or not the lawyer practises in a partnership. In New South Wales, a sole practitioner's deductible is USD3,730. For a partner in a firm this deductible is USD2,238, up to a maximum of USD74,600, with a double penalty excess in respect of cases where the solicitor has acted for a borrower and a lender in a transaction or the claim is for damages for a personal injury action becoming statute barred. A similar system applies in most other states in Australia.

In Austria there is a great variety in the insurance policies taken out by the profession and the range of deductibles varies accordingly. Sometimes the deductibles are expressed in a percentage of the insured sum (often ten per cent) or in a fixed amount (usually they range between USD1,000 and USD10,000). Sometimes a combination of these two options is used.

In Belgium, policies often provide for substantial deductibles. For the members of the Brussels Bar, the first twenty-five per cent of a claim is self-insured by the lawyer, with a minimum of USD320 and a maximum of USD3,200. The maximum deductible increases in the case of legal delays to USD4,000 for the first claim, USD6,000 for the second claim and USD8,000 for further claims.

In Canada the range of deductibles varies per Province. Sometimes they are made conditional on the number of claims in a specific past period (in British Columbia the range is between USD3,600 and USD14,700).

In Denmark, the first ten per cent of a claim is borne by the lawyer himself, usually with a minimum of USD1,833 and a maximum of USD19,000.

In England and Wales, the range of deductibles for solicitors is from USD7,500 up to USD 225,000 for the largest firms. No deductibles are payable by barristers under the mutual scheme.

In Germany, insurance cover is always reduced by a deductible in the amount of the legal fees received by the lawyer in the matter. The General Terms and Conditions furthermore stipulate that the insurer of the first USD6,500 covers eighty per cent, and ninety per cent of the rest up to an amount of USD25,000.

In Finland the Bar Association requires that all its members arrange the deductible so that it does not exceed two per cent of the total payable amount of compensation for each act resulting in damage.

In France, deductibles never exceed ten per cent of the remuneration, up to a maximum of USD4,000.

In Ireland, generally, the first USD3,900 of a claim is payable by the insured solicitors themselves. However, where there are twenty or more solicitors in a firm, generally the first USD15,000 of a claim is payable by the insured solicitors themselves.

In Liechtenstein, the deductibles increase with the size of the law firm. Claims under USD10,000 are paid by the lawyers themselves.

In Luxemburg, the deductible is twenty-five per cent of the first claim, with a minimum of USD305 and a maximum of USD3,050. If the damage is caused by the violation of a time limit, the minimum deductible is USD1,500, while the maximum varies depending on the number of claims. In collective policies the bonus-malus varies with the number of claims of the entire Bar.

In the Netherlands deductibles are negotiable. For large law firms the maximum deductible is USD5,700 per insured *advocaat*, with a maximum of USD114,000 in total.

In Norway, under the collective scheme of the Norwegian Bar Association, the deductible for the first claim is USD7,340. In case of a second, third and fourth claim within a three-year period, the insured lawyer's own risk is increased to USD11,000, USD14,700 and USD22,000 respectively.

In Papua New Guinea, the deductible is USD850 per claim for sole practitioners. For partners this is the same, with a maximum of USD4,250 per partnership.

In Scotland, the deductible is based on the number of principals in a firm with an assumed maximum of ten principals. The excess is approximately USD3,000 per principal (or USD6,000 per principal at a reduced premium).

In Singapore, for large firms, for the first claim the deductible is USD108,000. For the second and further claims the deductible is USD111,000.

In South Africa, under the Attorneys Fidelity Fund Professional Indemnity Insurance Scheme, the deductible varies from USD1,690 to USD10,800, depending on the number of partners within a firm. If lawyers take out a supplementary insurance on the commercial market, the deductible is usually a minimum of USD14,000 and a maximum of USD50,400 per claim.

In Sweden the deductible is USD4,935 for the compulsory cover of USD415,000.

*Recent developments*

As mentioned above, Austria's entry into the European Union entails that insurers from other EU countries penetrate the Austrian market. This affects, among other things, premiums and insurance terms. Austrian insurers are considering differentiating the premiums by both the size of the insured sum and of the law firm. Another option mentioned is to limit the cover period upon termination of the policy for claims arisen while the policy was still in effect.

Some years ago the Austrian Bar Associations introduced a separate insurance system on behalf of clients who become victims of lawyers who embezzle the monies entrusted to them. These policies are taken out and the premiums paid by the respective Bars and not by the lawyers themselves.

In Ontario, Canada, the size of the cover was restricted to the minimum level between 1994 and 1995, while the costs of insurance have increased radically as a result of a major surge in the number of claims and their size.

In Denmark, professional indemnity insurance covers the lawyer in his capacity as a member of a Board of Supervisory Directors. Until recently, both the standard cover and the excess cover provided such cover. In the future, the liability of the lawyer acting in his capacity as member of a Board of (Supervisory) Directors will no longer be covered by the insurance with excess cover, but only under the standard cover (up to a maximum of USD1 million per claim). This restriction is caused by the increase in the number and level of claims for compensation from directors.

In the past few years, commercial insurers in Finland have been trying to reduce the risks under professional indemnity insurance. For example, they exclude liability for acts of lawyers acting as corporate board members. In view hereof, the Finnish Bar Association has instituted a working group to liaise between commercial insurers and the profession. In addition, the Finnish Bar Association has established a fund, out of which damage and losses which result from criminal acts of the Association's members may be compensated.

In France, the insurance premium tripled in 1995 due to an increasing number of claims. It is now being examined whether, and to what extent, a "no claim discount clause" may be introduced, or whether a deductible should be maintained higher than the maximum currently established by law (ten per cent of a claim with a maximum of USD4,000). The Bar Council is finally considering introducing an insurance system with one compulsory minimum cover for all lawyers. The Bar Council furthermore intends to adjust the level of insurance cover to the size of the law firm.

In Ireland the Law Society has indicated that compulsory indemnity insurance will be introduced on January 1, 1996 for all solicitors.

In Norway and Singapore there is also an upward trend in the number of claims. This could mean that in the near future the level of cover will increase.

Risk management is a subject which greatly concerns the Attorneys Insurance Indemnity Fund and the Attorneys Fidelity Fund in South Africa. For that purpose they have introduced risk-management programmes. It is foreseeable that in the future lawyers will have to contribute financially to the automatic cover provided by the Attorneys Fidelity Fund.

Sweden is also faced with an increasing number of claims, amongst other things as a result of the internationalization of the legal practice. In order to control increases in insurance premiums before they grow sky high, the Swedish Bar Association has proposed to establish its own insurance company in the form of a "captive". This proposal has been shelved for the time being because of ethical concerns and other doubts with respect to the financial power of a "captive" and the possibilities for reinsuring risks.

# Chapter 6

# Guidelines for Lawyers' Liability Indemnity Insurance Policies

## INTRODUCTION

This chapter analyses the most commonly used provisions in commercial professional liability indemnity insurance policies, cites examples of those provisions and, where appropriate, suggests alternatives. As with insurance in general, these policies vary widely from country to country because of language and cultural differences, making it impossible to suggest specific language that can be used universally. However, we will cite to exemplars from around the world.

The information for this chapter came primarily from the reports submitted by the national rapporteurs and the United States American Bar Association (ABA) compendium of lawyers liability indemnity policies. The examples are from specimen insurance policies used in the reporting countries as well as the ABA materials.

However, we must begin with several words of caution.

First, as noted in the preceding chapter, lawyers face liability from a variety of events — both from professional services and nonlegal activities. However, a lawyer's insurance policy attempts to limit coverage exclusively to traditional "legal services" (as that term is defined in the policy).

Having first restricted coverage to a lawyer's professional "legal services", the reviewed policies then include myriad exclusions — some found in almost every country; others, geographically exclusive.

It is imperative in evaluating a lawyer's insurance coverage to ascertain whether additional insurance may be needed to protect against potential liability both with respect to the lawyer's practice and region. For example, the following will typically not be covered by a lawyer's liability indemnity insurance policy:

- employment disputes or wrongful termination;
- business interruption insurance;
- nonlawyer business activities;
- automobile and personal injury;
- general liability;
- fiduciary or dishonest acts.

Second, as in many other areas of insurance, professional liability indemnity insurance is dynamic and ever changing. The market shifts constantly. Thus, exclusions expand and contract with changes in the law (such as, for example, a rise in employment discrimination suits). Lawyers should review their policies annually to determine if the cover is adequate for the practice in the light of various trends.

Third, a policy's coverage is negotiable. Lawyers can usually expand their cover to include boilerplate exclusions — but at an additional premium price.

## MUTUAL INDEMNITY ASSOCIATIONS

Several jurisdictions have enacted legislation authorizing the establishment of mutual indemnity associations of lawyers. The associations are funded and run by premiums paid by the members. There are, generally, no shareholders.

The most prominent association is the Solicitors Indemnity Fund of England and Wales, founded under the Solicitors Act 1974 (and as modified).

The mutual is most commonly used where there is compulsory insurance, and the mutual will only cover the minimum required. Its rules generally resemble the commercial policy terms — but with some notable differences. First, unlike a commercial policy, there is no application or proposal form. Everyone is in the programme. Second, high-risk insureds are not excluded. Third, mutuals have fewer exclusions, particularly in high risk practice areas. Fourth, because the programme is generally consumer oriented, it tends to be "fire proof" with no declinations of coverage.

The mutual is usually administered by the Bar or a specially created organisation and operates similarly to insurance companies in terms of reserves and claims handling.

For many specialist and commercial practices, mutuals do not provide enough coverage. Consequently, most firms must look to the commercial market for their excess coverage.

## THE APPLICATION AND ITS ROLE

Lawyers' liability insurance coverage begins with the completion of an Application. This document is critical (1) to determine the scope of cover and (2) to ensure that valid insurance exists when a claim is made. Pay careful attention to the completion of this document.

The Application, of course, varies from underwriter to underwriter. However, it usually seeks the following kinds of information: (a) name of the firm; (b) date established; (c) changes of the firm over a period of time (usually ten years or so); (d) the number of offices; (e) other businesses that the partners may be engaged in; (f) percentage of practice in various areas (e.g. corporate litigation, estate planning); (g) revenues for the past year; (h) whether the firm requires any special cover such as a partner's previous business, former partners, loss of documents, or libel and slander.

Two or three questions on the Application are particularly important. These questions seek information about past, present and potential claims. For example:

- Have any claims been made against the firm or any partner, director, consultant or employee for neglect, error or omission in relation to professional duties in the last five years? If yes, give details.
- Is any partner, principal, consultant or employee, after inquiry, aware of any circumstances which might give rise to a claim against the firm, its principals or partners or its predecessors? If so, please explain.
- Is there any claim outstanding or are there any circumstances which may give rise to a claim against the firm or any of its partners?
- Has the firm recently discharged or are you contemplating discharging any of your staff or employees for any omission, neglect or error? If yes, please give full details.

These questions attempt to elicit matters that will either be excluded from coverage or that will assist the underwriter in deciding whether to accept the risk. Inadequate completion of the Application may lead to rescission of the policy and the voiding of coverage.

The partners are almost always asked to sign the Application, asserting its truthfulness. Sometimes — and the trend is growing — the Application is attached to the policy or incorporated into the policy by reference.

Example: *Source: Lloyd's*

Application: By acceptance of this policy, the Insured agrees that the statements in the application are personal representations, that they shall be deemed material and that this policy is issued in reliance upon the truth of such representations and that this policy embodies all agreements existing between one Insured and the Underwriters, or any of their agents, relating to this insurance.

## COVERAGE LIMITS

### Generally

A policy's coverage amount raises three issues: (1) the policy limits "per claim" and in the "aggregate", (2) deductibles, and (3) applicability of defence costs to the reduction of policy limits.

Initially, review your policy limits: the international reports indicated both a general lack of insurance as well as the inadequacy of cover in many countries. A substantial claim will, by its very nature, exceed the coverage in most jurisdictions.

### Policy limits

Generally, each policy contains both a "per claim" and an "aggregate" limit. The "per claim" limit is often expressed as an occurrence limit, usually meaning that the underwriter will pay no more than that sum as the total amount for all claims arising out of the same act or omission, regardless of the number of claimants.

The "aggregate" limit is usually defined as the total limit of the underwriter's liability for all claims made within the policy period.

Most policies define the scope of a particular claim.

Example: *Source: Finland*

Events arising from the same occurrence or circumstance are considered a single event irrespective of whether they have been discovered during one or more insurance periods. If single losses under one insured event are discovered during different insurance periods, they are deemed to belong to that period during which the first event was discovered.

Example: *Source: Singapore*

All claims against the Insured or members of the same Firm (in accordance with Part Three, Clause 1 (iii)) arising:

(a) from one act or omission or series of acts or omissions attributable to the same or substantially the same underlying cause or source shall be regarded as one claim.

(b) acts of fraud, dishonesty or any criminal act or omission committed by one person acting alone or in collusion with others shall be regarded as attributable to the same underlying cause or source and accordingly will be deemed to constitute one claim.

Because multiple lawsuits can arise from one transaction, while the policy may have a single claim limit, analysing whether the per claim limit is sufficient to cover exposure for a particular engagement is critical.

## Deductibles

Almost every professional liability policy contains a deductible which is usually per claim, negotiable, and obviously affects the premium.

Deductibles appear to be rising in many nations. This is particularly true in certain high risk specialties (such as securities work) which may also require high premiums.

## Defence costs: applicability to coverage limits

The cost of defending claims can be substantial. For example, a claim in the United States relating to a failed bank may cost over USD1 million to defend. The question is whether the defence costs are to be deducted from the claim limit (a "sinking fund") or are in addition to the claim indemnity provisions.

Many lawyer liability policies do not deduct defence costs from the policy limits. (Although defence costs are frequently covered pro rata where the indemnity obligation exceeds policy limits.)

> Example: *Source: Denmark*
> Even if the sum insured is thereby exceeded, the Insurers will pay all reasonable costs and expenses incurred by the Insured in determining whether there exists a liability to provide indemnity and the extent thereof, and any interest on judgement amounts of indemnity coming within the scope of this Insurance. If the claim exceeds the sum insured, the Insurers are only obliged to pay a proportional part of costs and expenses.

> Example: *Source: Ireland*
> No grant of indemnity provided by the Company hereunder will exceed in respect of each such claim (including claimants' costs) the maximum sum specified in the Membership Certificate and in addition all costs and expenses incurred with the Company's consent in the defence or settlement of any such claim, provided that, if a payment in excess of the maximum sum is made by the member to dispose of any such claim and claimants' costs, the maximum amount which may be paid by the Company for any such costs and expenses incurred in defending and/or settling the claim will be limited to no more than such proportion thereof as the maximum sum bears to the amount of the total payment made to the claimant.

Some policies, however, require that defence costs be deducted from the policy limit.

> Example: *Source: Puerto Rico*
> It is further provided that the Company shall not be obligated to pay any claim, judgment, award or claims expenses, or to undertake or continue defence of any suit or proceeding after the applicable limit of the Company's liability has been exhausted by payment of judgments, awards, settlements, or claims expenses or after deposit of the applicable limit of the Company's liability in a court of competent jurisdiction, and that

in such case, the Company shall have the right to withdraw from the further defence thereof by tendering control of said defence to the Insured.

Thus, this issue needs to be carefully examined when selecting lawyer indemnity insurance.

## THE POLICY — MAJOR ISSUES

### Who is the insured?

Central to any insurance policy is "who is the insured?"

Every policy contains a definitional section that identifies the insured as well as a declaration page specifically naming the insured. There are a number of definitional issues that should be addressed when selecting a policy. These are:

- Does it include former partners?
- Does it include new partners?
- Does it include employees such as attorneys, secretaries, paralegals and other office personnel?
- Does it include lawyers retained in non-legal functions?
- What is the effect of the death of a named insured during the policy period?

The following are two examples of "insured" definitions.

Example: *Source: Papua New Guinea*

"The Assured" means the Firm and each partner of the Firm or the Sole Practitioner as the case may be shown in the Schedule and includes each person employed in connection with the Practice (including each Articled Clerk and each Solicitor who is a Consultant or Associate with the Firm) and the estate and/or the legal personal representatives of each of the foregoing and also includes each service or administration company or trust insofar as its activities are carried out in connection with the Practice, with the intent that each of the foregoing shall be severally insured hereunder.

Example: *Source: Lloyd's*

The Insured: The unqualified word "Insured", whenever used in this policy means:

a) the Named Insured firm or predecessor firm set forth in the Declarations;

b) any person who is not defined as Named Insured, but was, is now, or hereinafter becomes an employed lawyer or other employee of the firm or predecessor firms named in the Declarations solely while acting in a professional capacity on behalf of such firm or firms;

c) any former partner, officer, director or stockholder employee of the firm or predecessor firms named in the Declarations while acting solely in a professional capacity on behalf of such firms;

d) any partner, officer, director or stockholder employee of the firm or predecessor firms named in the Declarations who have retired from the practice of law, but only

for those professional services rendered prior to the date of retirement from the insured firm;
e) as respects the liability of each Insured as is otherwise covered herein, the heirs, executors, administrators, assigns and legal representatives of each insured in the event of death, incapacity or bankruptcy.

## The insured event

*Occurrence Policy Form.*
Initially coverage for professionals was on an occurrence basis. The insurable event that triggered coverage under such a policy was an act or omission during the policy period that would give rise to coverage. It was not a claim but the underlying act. There was coverage regardless of when the claim was made. This provision proved administratively difficult. In addition to the problem of determining the time of occurrence, underwriters had great difficulty in rating the potential risk because claims might not be made until many years after the policy expired. Additionally, defence costs and indemnity in the future were very difficult to quantify and reserve. This led to the demise of the pure occurrence policy. Thus, it is presently almost impossible to find an occurrence policy.

*Claims-Made Policy Form.*
Today, almost all policies are on a claims-made form. Claims-made policies require that a claim be made against the insured professional within the policy period. What is a claim? Although some policies (see below) define a claim, the following is certainly a list of accepted examples:

- A demand for damages, property or services
- The filing of a suit
- The threat of filing a suit

The following are examples of the claims-made form:

Example: *Source: New Zealand*
To indemnify the Insured against all claims (including claimants' costs and expenses arising as a result of any claim) which the Insured shall become legally liable to pay as damages up to the Limited of Indemnity stated in the Schedule in the aggregate in any one Period of Insurance stated in the Schedule or any period for which the Company shall have offered and the Insured shall have paid the premium for renewal of this Policy and which arise by reason of any negligent act error or omission on the part of the assured.

Example: *Source: Singapore*
The Underwriters shall indemnify the Insured up to an amount not exceeding the Limit of Liability for each and every claim which may be made against one or more Insured during the Period of Insurance in respect of any civil liability, whensoever or howsoever incurred in connection with the Practice.

*Hybrid Policy.*
An interesting combined claims made and occurrence cover is available in a Denmark policy:

Example: *Source: Denmark*
This Insurance covers primarily in accordance with the claims made Principle such losses as are ascertained and reported during the period of insurance, irrespective of the time of the act or omission giving rise to the loss, at the sum insured stated in the Policy when the loss is ascertained. Upon termination of the Policy, coverage will no longer be provided in accordance with the claims made Principle, but any loss ascertained and reported after this time will without any limitation as to time be covered in accordance with the occurrence Principle at the sum insured applying at the time of termination of the Policy, provided that the act or omission giving rise to the loss took place during the period of insurance.

*Discovery and Extended Reporting Period Option.*
A major problem arises when (a) the lawyer knows of circumstances that occurred within a policy period, but no claim has yet been made and (b) the lawyer wants to change insurance companies. Given the importance of the Application and the exclusion for known prior acts (see below), a gap in coverage may exist.

Claims-made policies often contain a discovery clause which covers an occurrence within the policy period that may not actually result in a claim until after the policy expires if a lawyer has given written notice of the occurrence before expiration of the policy. Discovery provisions are extremely important because subsequent policies usually exclude coverage claims arising for prior acts and omissions (if the insured should have reasonably foreseen that a claim would be made).

The following are typical Discovery and Extended Reporting Period provisions:

Example: *Source: Puerto Rico*
In the event of cancellation or non-renewal of this policy by the Company, the Named Insured shall have the right, upon payment of an additional premium of 90% of the total annual premium for this policy within 30 days of such termination, to have an endorsement issued providing a one year extended reporting period for all claims first made against the Insured and reported to the Company after the termination of the policy period arising out of any negligent act, error or omission occurring prior to the termination of the policy period and otherwise covered by the policy.

Example: *Source: United States*
Extended claim reporting period endorsement:
For the purpose of this coverage, claims-made relationship means that period of time between the effective date of the first claims-made policy issued by the Company and the termination of the last consecutive claims-made policy between the insured and the company, where there has been no gap in coverage, but does not include any hazard or any period covered by extended claim reporting period coverage.

With the exception of the 60 day automatic extended claim reporting period, the offering of the extended claim reporting period coverage will not apply if the claims-made relationship has been less than one year and the policy has been terminated for nonpayment of premium or fraud.
A. If this policy is terminated for any reason, a 60 day automatic reporting period extension will be granted to the Named Insured at no charge. In addition, the Named Insured has the option to purchase additional extended claim reporting period coverage.
B. Within thirty days after termination, we will notify the Named Insured, in writing, of the automatic extended claim reporting period and the availability of, and the premium for such additional extended claim reporting period coverage.
The Named Insured shall have the greater of sixty days from the effective date of termination of coverage, or thirty days from the date of mailing or delivery of the notice of the availability to purchase additional extended claim reporting period coverage, and to submit written acceptance of such extended claim reporting period coverage.

## The insuring clause

An insuring clause defines the policy's coverage. Generally, coverage is written for acts, omissions, or errors (though all errors are either acts or omissions) to the extent that they arise from the insured's professional activities as a lawyer.

The following are specific examples of the insuring agreements that limit liability to negligence arising from professional services:

Example: *Source: Australia*
On the terms and conditions herein contained the insurer shall indemnify the assured (...) in respect of any description of civil liability whatsoever incurred in connection with the Practice other than loss arising out of any circumstance or occurrence which has been notified under any other insurance attaching prior to the inception of this Certificate of Insurance.
The policy further defines "Practice" to include:
The practice means the business of practising as a solicitor undertaken by the assured or the assured's predecessors in business or loan or with others;
Including as acting as Trustee, Executor, Attorney-under Power, Tax Agent, Company Director, Secretary, Public Officer or Public Notary, or any activity declared by the Council of the Law Society of New South Wales to be undertaken as part of a solicitor's practice, which declaration of the Council of the Law Society of New South Wales shall be binding on the insured, provided that any fees or other income which accrue from any activities described above inure to the benefit of the Firm or sole practice of which the insured is or was a member.

Example: *Source: United States*
Subject to the limit of liability of any deductible, the company will pay on behalf of the insured all sums which the insured shall become legally obligated to pay as damages and all costs because of any claim or claims first made against the insured and reported to the company during the reporting period which claim or claims are caused by any

act, error or omission of the insured or any other person for whose acts, errors or omissions the insured is legally responsible, and which arise out of the rendering or failure to render professional service for the others in the insured's capacity as a lawyer.
The policy further defines key terms such as "lawyer" to include "A person in the profession of practising law pursuant to license" or "A person when acting in the capacity of an administrator, executor, trustee, conservator, guardian, or in any similar fiduciary capacity."

Example: *Source: New Zealand*
To indemnify the Insured against all claims (including claimants' costs and expenses arising as a result of any claim) which the Insured shall become legally liable to pay as damages up to the Limit of Indemnity stated in the Schedule in the aggregate in any one Period of Insurance and which are notified to the Company during the Period of Insurance stated in the Schedule (...) and which arise by reason of any negligent act error or omission on the part of
- the Insured or their specified predecessors in business.
- any person now or previously employed by the Insured or their specified predecessors in business.
- any other person(s) partnership company or firm acting for or on behalf of the Insured in the conduct of the Insured's business or occupation as specified in the Schedule.

Example: *Source: Finland*
To indemnify the Assured, up to but not exceeding the sum stated in Item 2 of the Schedule, against any claim or claims which may be made against them or any of them during the period specified in the Schedule
(i) for breach of professional duty as Solicitors, by reason of any wrongful act, whenever or wherever committed or alleged to have been committed, of
(a) the Assured or
(b) the predecessors in business of the said Firm, or
(c) any person at any time employed by, or any agent or consultant of, the Assured or such predecessors in business, in the conduct, by or on behalf of the said Firm or such predecessors, of any business conducted in their professional capacity as Solicitors, and
(ii) by reason of any wrongful act, whenever or wherever committed or alleged to have been committed, of any of the persons mentioned at (a), (b) and (c) above when acting as an Executor, Trustee, Receiver, Liquidator, Director, Company Secretary, Manager, or Administrator, provided the fees from such appointment form part of the income of the said Firm.

Example: *Source: Denmark*
This Insurance covers the liability which the Insured may incur as a lawyer working from a office in Denmark in respect of pecuniary losses inflicted on a third party by negligent acts or omissions attributable to the Insured or his staff.

Example: *Source: Puerto Rico*

To indemnify the Insured all sums which the Insured shall become legally obligated to pay as damages because of any claim or claims, including claim(s) for personal injury, first made against the Insured and reported to the Company during the policy period or extended reporting period, arising out of any act, error or omission of the Insured in rendering or failing to render professional services for others in the Insured's capacity as a Lawyer, Fiduciary or Notary Public, and caused by the Insured or any other person for whose acts, error or omissions the Insured is legally responsible, except as excluded or limited by the terms, conditions and exclusions of this policy.

The obvious focus is to limit liability to acts or omissions where the lawyer is hired to render legal services. Conversely, if the retention is principally non-legal — as in the case where a lawyer might serve on a board, serve as a public official, manage an estate unrelated to his position as a lawyer, or engage in business activities unrelated to retention as a lawyer (see following sections for examples of each) — then the performance of the services which could otherwise be considered legal are not treated as such. Typically, the "Exclusions" section of the policy will specifically enumerate those services (some of which are legal) which might ordinarily be considered professional services based upon the lawyer's knowledge and skill, but for purposes of the policy will not be covered.

## The policy territory

Many policies contain territorial restrictions and respond to claims and activities occurring or conducted only in a particular country. The following are examples of restrictive territorial provisions:

Example: *Source: Singapore*

This insurance applies to any civil liability which occurs anywhere in the world except in the United States of America and Canada.

The Underwriters shall have no liability to defend any suit against an Insured brought within the United States of America or Canada or to pay any judgment obtained thereby.

Example: *Source: New Zealand*

[Does not provide coverage] For any legal liability of whatsoever nature directly or indirectly arising out of any negligent act, error or omission committed outside the territorial limits of the Dominion of New Zealand or the Commonwealth of Australia.

The international practitioner must be extremely careful with respect to these kinds of provisions because they could completely void any cover for an international transaction. For example, if an Australian firm went to New York City to assist in negotiating a settlement concerning an Australian claim but on behalf of a United States client and gave erroneous advice concerning Australian law but the advice was given in New York City, it could lead to a claim in New York. This may not be covered.

The following is an example of expanded territorial coverage:

Example: *Source: Puerto Rico*

This policy applies to acts, errors or omissions occurring anywhere in the World:
(a) provided that those acts, errors or omissions occur any time prior to the end of the policy period, and
(b) further provided that claim is first made against the Insured within the United States of America, its territories or possessions or Canada and during the policy period or extended reporting period purchased in accordance with Condition VI, and
(c) further provided that the claim is reported to the Company during the policy period or an extended reporting period purchased in accordance with Condition VI.

Multinational law firms and international practitioners should be very careful of this issue and insist on the broadest type of coverage.

## Exclusions

In examining the various policies submitted from around the world, it appears that there are as many exclusions as there are fertile minds of underwriters. These exclusions range from the standard "personal injury" to the esoteric "insurance agent" exclusions. The following listing of exclusions simply highlight the general nature of the exclusion and, where appropriate, provides guidelines for the extension of cover over those matters.[1]

*Prior Acts.*

In its purest form, an occurrence policy does not cover acts or omissions committed before the policy period, even though a claim is made during the policy term. So, too, with a claims-made policy, the policy excludes coverage for acts or omissions occurring before the policy's effective date if the insured knew or could have reasonably foreseen the error would lead to claims. An example of such an exclusion is the following:

Example: *Source: Puerto Rico*

[Excludes] any claim arising out of any acts, errors, or omissions occurring prior to the effective date of the first policy issued to the Named Insured or any predecessor firm by this Company and continuously renewed and maintained in effect thereafter to the inception date of the policy period, if the Named Insured, any partner, shareholder or, where applicable, the Named Insured's management committee or any member thereof,

---

1 This section omits some standard exclusions such as war and nuclear hazard that are commonly used in all policies.

on such date knew or could have reasonably foreseen that such acts, errors or omissions might be expected to be the basis of a claim or suit.

Because policies exclude "prior acts" from coverage, they also include extended coverage and discovery provisions (see above section 2), which will extend coverage to claims made after the policy period has ended, even where the act occurred during the policy period.

*Libel, Slander and Defamation.*

Claims for libel, slander and defamation are routinely excluded from professional indemnity coverage. However, an extension of coverage may be obtained. The following are examples of the exclusion language:

Example: *Source: New Zealand*

This policy shall not indemnify the insured in respect of any claim against them alleging libel or slander.

And, as noted, here is an extension:

Example: *Source: New Zealand*

It is agreed that this Policy is extended to indemnify the insured against claims for Libel and Slander against any person.

*Intentional Acts, Gross Negligence and Fraud.*

There are a number of clauses whose aim is to exclude intentional acts, fraudulent or criminal conduct. Examples include intentional conduct such as malicious prosecution or abuse of process, or fraudulent conduct such as intentional misrepresentations, or criminal conduct such as embezzlement of trust funds. These exclusions attempt to differentiate merely negligent acts and those with a higher degree of culpability.

Example: *Source: Finland*

The insurance does not cover loss caused wilfully or by gross negligence by the policyholder or another person for whom the policyholder is liable for indemnification.

Example: *Source: Denmark*

Exclusion: because the insured has failed in his duties either intentionally or through gross negligence.

Example: *Source: Ireland*

The company will not indemnify the beneficiary in respect of any dishonest, fraudulent or criminal act or omission

Example: *Source: United States*

[Excludes] any intentional, dishonest, fraudulent, criminal, malicious or knowingly wrongful acts, errors or omissions committed by YOU or at YOUR direction or in which YOU acquiesce or remain passive after having personal knowledge thereof, or criminal conduct committed by someone for whose conduct YOU are legally liable.

There remains an issue of whether a firm or partners are liable due to the intentional, criminal or fraudulent act of one of their partners or employees. Under the exclusions set forth above, the firm and remaining partners do not have coverage.

However, an extension of coverage may be obtained for these kinds of acts.

Example: *Source: New Zealand*

It is agreed and declared that the Policy is extended to indemnify the Insured in respect of claims for damages made against them for breach of Professional duty arising out of or contributed to by the dishonest, fraudulent, criminal or malicious conduct of employees of the Insured.

*Personal Injury and Property Damage.*

Almost every lawyer's policy excludes damages for personal injury and property damage. These exposures are covered under other kinds of insurance.

Example: *Source: Lloyd's*

[Excludes] any liability for bodily injury, sickness, disease or death of any person, or injury to or destruction of any tangible property or loss of use resulting therefrom, except that this exclusion does not apply to mental illness or emotional distress or humiliation caused by personal injury.

*Punitive Damages, Penalties and Fines.*

Every policy excludes coverage where the lawyer is the subject of a penalty, fine, or punitive damages. In fact under most jurisdictions, insurance for punitive damages is not legal.

Example: *Source: Puerto Rico*

This policy excludes any losses from punitive or exemplary damages, fines, sanctions or penalties, for the return of or reimbursement for legal fees, costs or expenses.

However, in the United States, lawyers are sometimes subject to sanctions under Federal Rules of Civil Procedure, Rule 11 (and some state statutes, too). There are exclusions (and extensions) that cover these kinds of sanctions.

Example: *Source: United States*

[Excludes] any punitive or exemplary damages, fines, sanctions, penalties (other than those imposed under Rule 11 of the Federal Rules of Civil Procedure or any comparable state statute),[2] or other damages in addition to actual or compensatory damages.

*Public Official, Public Act Exclusion.*
Virtually all policies exclude liability for work, even legal work, as an elected public official. Extensions of cover may be obtained.

Example: *Source: United States*
This policy does not apply to any claim arising out of an insured's capacity as an elected public official or as an employee of a governmental body, subdivision, or agency thereof unless the insured is deemed an employee solely by virtue of rendering legal services to such government body, the remuneration for which services inured to the benefit of the Named Insured.

Many of these exclusions are broader than they first appear.

Example: *Source: Lloyd's*
A public official, an employee of a governmental body, subdivision or agency, an arbitrator or as a member of a bar group.

This clause excludes work as an arbitrator or for bar groups, making scrutiny of this provision important in an era where alternate dispute resolution is growing.

*United States Based Exclusions.*
Some exclusions apply only to U.S. areas of law practice. Primarily these involve the securities, banking, and tax areas.

Historically, all securities work has been excluded from cover in the United States.

Example: *Source: United States*
It is agreed that the company will not defend or pay under this policy for any claim:
A. Arising out of an actual or alleged violation of:
1. The securities act of 1933;
2. The securities exchange act of 1934;
3. The public utilities holding act of 1935;
4. The trust indenture act of 1939;
5. The investment company act of 1940;
6. The investment advisors act of 1940; and
7. Any state Blue Sky Laws;

or any rules, regulations or amendments issued in relation to such acts.

---

2 Federal Rules of Civil Procedure, Rule 11, allows the court to impose sanctions on lawyers and law firms for a variety of actions including failure to respond to discovery. If the sanctions are assessed against the firm, then each partner is personally liable.

B. Based upon common law principles of liability if made in connection with an actual or alleged violation of any law listed in A. above.
C. Arising out of professional services involving, directly or indirectly, any state or municipal financing or bonds.
D. Based upon or arising out of the formation, syndication, operation or administration of any limited partnership.

However, a securities extension may be obtained — but at a substantially higher premium.

Recently, there has been considerable litigation in the United States over failed savings and loan and banking institutions. In connection with that kind of litigation, the government has increasingly sued the professionals — including lawyers — who represented the failed institution. Accordingly, an exclusion now exists here, too.

Example: *Source: United States*

Any liability whatsoever based upon or arising out of any action or proceeding made or brought either directly by, or on behalf of, the Federal Deposit Insurance Corporation, the Savings Association Insurance Fund, any other depository insurance organization, Resolution Trust Corporation or any other National or State regulatory or supervisory entity or authority, or their successors or assigns, (each of the foregoing hereinafter referred to as an "Agency"), or any corporation or organization owned in whole or in part by an Agency, against any Insured including, but not limited to, any action or proceeding which such Agency, corporation or organization makes, brings or has the legal right to make or bring in its capacity as regulator, receiver, conservator, liquidator, shareholder, successor in interest, assignee or otherwise against any insured and regardless of whether such action or proceeding is made or brought in the name of such Agency, Corporation or Organization, or by or on behalf of such Agency, Corporation or Organization in the name of any other person or entity, or solely in the name of any other person or entity.

Another example of U.S. based exclusions are for matters based on the Racketeer Influenced Corrupt Organizations Act ("RICO"). RICO exclusions are growing.

Example: *Source: Lloyd's*

To any loss payments or claim expenses directly or indirectly brought about by arising out of, or attributable to any actual or alleged violation of the Racketeer Influenced and Corrupt Organizations Act, 18 USC Sections 1961 et seq., and any amendments thereto, or any rules or regulations promulgated thereunder.

Finally, most policies also exclude the advice relating to work that results in tax deductions that may be questioned by the government.

Example: *Source: Lloyd's*

To any claim based upon or arising out of professional services relating in any way to any offering, syndication, partnership, tax shelter, tax haven or tax avoidance arrangement, if an investment in any of the foregoing results in
(i) deductions in excess of income from the investment being available in any year to reduce income from other sources in the year, or
(ii) credits in excess of the tax attributable in any year to offset taxes on income from other sources in that year.
To any claim based upon or arising out of any tax opinion or analysis, or the performance of any professional services in relation to any offering, syndication, partnership, tax shelter, tax haven, or tax avoidance arrangement, organization or device where any Insured either directly or indirectly has an ownership interest, at any time, in the general partnership or controlling entity of any of the foregoing, or any of the Insured's fees, compensation or remuneration is based upon a commission or is related to the sale of shares or investment units or the profitability of the venture.

*Trading Debts; Fees and Disbursements Litigation.*
Virtually every policy excludes trading debts where lawyers are sued for debts related to the operation of their business.

Example: *Source: Singapore*

For the payment of trading debts incurred by the Insured.

However, a closely allied problem is when a lawyer sues for collection of outstanding fees and disbursements. They are often met with a claim covered under their policy. Therefore, many policies specifically exclude coverage for recovery on fees and disbursements.

Example: *Source: Papua New Guinea*

[Excludes claims] to repay any moneys charged as fees and disbursements or for costs incurred in relation to any dispute as to fees and disbursements.

Of course, these hybrid lawsuits raise major issues of apportionment in that the matter litigated is partially covered and partially noncovered.

*Business Pursuits.*
It is extremely common to exclude from coverage other business pursuits of the partners. What this means is that if a partner is sued regarding an error from a business activity — other than practising law — the claim is excluded from coverage even if those other business pursuits involved legal advice.

Example: *Source: Lloyd's*

To any claim made by or against any business enterprise, not named in the Declarations, which is owned by the Insured or in which the Insured is a partner or employee, or which is controlled, operated or managed by the Insured, either individually or in a fiduciary capacity, including the ownership, maintenance or use of any property in connection therewith; or to any claim made against the Insured solely because the Insured is a partner, officer, director or stockholder employee of any firm or corporation not named in the Declarations.

This exclusion, as noted in the example, may be avoided by proper disclosure and extensions of coverage.

*Loss of Documents.*

Traditionally, loss of documents in the course of a legal practice has been included under usual coverage. But exclusions do exist. The following is an example of a loss of documents exclusion:

Example: *Source: Sri Lanka*

This policy does not cover any claim or claims arising out of the cost of replacing documents which have been lost, mislaid or destroyed.

Example: *Source: New Zealand*

This policy shall not indemnify the insured in respect of any claim against them brought about or contributed to by loss or damage to documents.

Conversely, a growing recognition that document loss should be covered under the policy, has led to an extension — rather than an exclusion — of cover.

Example: *Source: New Zealand*

It is understood and agreed that if during the currency hereof the insured shall discover and shall within 7 days of the date of discovery give written notice thereof to Underwriters that any Documents (as hereinafter defined)[3] the property of or entrusted to the Insured or his predecessors in the business which now or hereafter are or are by him supposed or believed to be in his hands or in the hands of any other Party or Parties to or with whom such Documents have been entrusted, lodged or deposited by the Insured in the ordinary course of business have been destroyed or damaged or lost or mislaid and after diligent search cannot be found this policy shall indemnify the Insured for:

(a) any legal liabilities of whatsoever nature incurred to the Third Parties in consequence of such Documents having been so destroyed, damaged, lost or mislaid and

---

[3] In this extension "Document" includes:

(a) a book, plan, paper, parchment, film or other material on which there is writing or printing, or on which there are marks, symbols or perforations having a meaning for persons qualified to interpret them;

(b) a disc, tape, paper, film or other device from which sounds or images are capable of being reproduced; and,

(c) any other record or information.

(b) all costs, charges and expenses of whatsoever nature incurred by the Insured in replacing and/or restoring such Documents (...)

Example: *Source: United States*

It is hereby agreed that if during the period specified in the Schedule the Assured shall discover that any Documents (as hereinafter defined), the property of or entrusted to the Firm named in the Schedule or their predecessors in business which may now or hereafter be, or be supposed or believed to be, in the custody of the said Firm, or in the custody of any other person to or with whom such Documents have been entrusted, lodged or deposited by the said Firm in the ordinary course of business, have while within the limits of the Channel Islands or the United Kingdom or the Republic of Ireland been destroyed or damaged, or lost or mislaid and after diligent search cannot be found, the Underwriters will

(1) indemnify the Assured against

(a) legal liability of whatsoever nature which the Assured may incur to any other person in consequence of such Documents having been so destroyed, damaged, lost or mislaid, and

(b) costs and expenses of whatsoever nature incurred by the Assured in replacing or restoring such Documents, and

(2) in addition pay the costs and expenses incurred with the written consent of the Underwriters in the defence or settlement of any claim to establish liability as described in (1)(a) above, provided that, if a payment in excess of the amount of indemnity available under this Policy has to be made to dispose of a claim, the Underwriters' liability for such costs and expenses shall be such proportion thereof as the amount of indemnity available under this Policy in respect of that claim bears to the amount paid to dispose of that claim.

In this extension, "Documents" means deeds, wills, agreements, maps, plans, records, books, letters, certificates, forms and documents of any nature whatsoever, whether written, printed or reproduced by any other method (other than bearer bonds, coupons, bank-notes, currency notes and negotiable instruments).

This extension is terribly important if the lawyer handles any original legal documents such as patents, patent applications, copyrights, wills, contracts or declarations. The loss of any such document could be catastrophic and lead to tremendous damages. In an international practice this problem is multiplied as different legal systems commingle. For example, the loss of a certified patent application which is evidence in another jurisdiction at the time of trial can lead to a disastrously adverse result and lawyer liability.

*Officer and Director Liability.*

Frequently, attorneys are asked to serve as an officer or a director of a company. Activities as an officer or director of a company are generally not covered by insurance either because of the general insuring clause or a specific exclusion.

Example: *Source: Sweden*
The insurance does not cover liability for damages or debt liability which can rest upon the insured in his capacity as a member of a company board of directors to the extent that the liability is covered by another insurance up to the sum insured or more.

However, should a lawyer wish to extend cover for work as a director (as where an attorney serves as a legal officer of a company), this additional cover can be obtained either by an extension under the indemnity policy or by separate officers and directors policy. [Some policies include work as an officer or director as included in the definition of practice. See Section 4, C, above.]

*Losses Caused By Any Joint Venture Of The Assured.*
As the practice of law becomes more global in nature but the local bar regulations are still restrictive, law firms are increasingly engaging in joint ventures or associations with other law firms around the world. Often, it is possible that these joint ventures or associations will lead to potential liability. Usually, the application inquires as to any joint ventures or similar associations. In any event, some policies now exclude losses caused by any joint venture.

Example: *Source: New Zealand*
This policy shall not indemnify for any claim arising out of any activity which the insured is engaged as a joint venturer or as a partner unless the joint venture or partnership is described in the schedule as the insured.

*Miscellaneous Exclusions.*
In reviewing the various indemnity policies, there are many other exclusions which appear. These exclusions include:

- Payment or acceptance of cash.

Example: *Source: Finland*
The insurance does not cover loss due to miscalculations made in accepting cash or in making payments with it.

- Ownership of land, buildings or aircraft.

Example: *Source: New Zealand*
This policy shall not indemnify the insured in respect of any claim against them arising directly or indirectly from the ownership, possession, or use by or on behalf of the insured of any land, buildings, aircraft, watercraft, vessel, or mechanically propelled vehicle.

- Work as an investment advisor.

Example: *Source: United States*

Any claim based on or arising out of, in whole or in part, the rendering of investment advice by any Insured to any person in connection with the purchase or sale of any investment or property, including but not limited to, securities, real property, commodities or franchises, or based on or arising out of, in whole or in part, any Insured's services or capacity as a broker, dealer, investment advisor, accountant, real estate broker, or real estate agent.

- Discrimination and harassment.

Example: *Source: United States*

Any Claim based on or arising out of, in whole or in part, discrimination by the Insured involving sex, race, creed, age, national origin or religion.

Example: *Source: United States*

This Plan does not apply to any CLAIM based upon or arising out of harassment or discrimination by YOU on the basis of race, creed, age, sex, physical or mental handicap, or sexual preference unless such CLAIM arises out of YOUR professional service in an attorney-client relationship.

- Patent exclusions.

Example: *Source: United States*

This Plan does not apply to any claim based upon or arising out of professional services rendered or any act, error or omission committed in relation to the registration of patents.

**Notice requirements**

Each policy will require that the assured give underwriters prompt notice of any claim or, in the case of extended reporting, any potential claim. The policies often spell out the exact procedure. The following are several examples of notice requirements:

Example: *Source: Finland*

If the Policyholder wishes to use this Insurance, the Insurance Company must be notified of this in writing beforehand. The notification must state the Policyholder's jeopardized legal interest which might result in a claim.

The notification must be made within three years from the start of the dispute or the serving of summons in a criminal case. If notification is not made within this time, the Insured can no longer seek protection under this Insurance.

Example: *Source: Singapore*
Notice of Claims
The Insured shall give to the Insurance Broker, as soon as reasonably possible and practicable, notice in writing:-
a) of any claim made against them,
b) of the receipt of notice from any person of an intention to make a claim against them,
c)of any circumstance of which they shall become aware during the currency of this Policy which is likely to give rise to a claim against them.
Any subsequent claim or claims arising out of circumstances first notified to the Insurance Broker (whether such circumstances are notified as part of an actual claim made against the Insured or any intimation thereof or otherwise) during one Period of Insurance shall be deemed to have been made during the same Period of Insurance in which such notice was given irrespective as to whether such subsequent claim or claims are made after the expiry of the Policy.

This clause and strict adherence to it is important because most policies are claims-made policies. Additionally, it is essential under the Extended Reporting Clause to make sure that there is no gap in coverage.

## Defence of claims

Any claim against a lawyer strikes at his or her professional and personal integrity. It is no wonder then that when a claim is made the relationship between the insurer and the insured often becomes both tense and contentious. This manifests itself in the claims handling process. There are several issues with respect to how a claim is handled: (a) the requirement of the assured's cooperation, (b) the decision whether or not to actually contest the claim, (c) the determination of whose duty or right it is to defend the claim, (d) the choice of counsel to defend the claim, (e) the cost of defending a claim and (f) the control of any settlement.

There are a wide range of options with respect to these issues in the policies submitted by the national reporters.

*Cooperation Clause.*
All policies require that the assured cooperate with the underwriter in the investigation and defence of any claim. However, some clauses go further and give the assured the right to consent to and control any settlement. The following are examples of cooperation clauses:

Example: *Source: United States*
The Insured shall cooperate with the Company in the defence, investigation and settlement of any Claim. The Insured will assist the Company in effecting any rights of indemnity, contribution or apportionment available to The Insured or The Company. Upon the Company's request, The Insured shall: (i) submit to examination and interview by a representative of the Company, under oath if required; (ii) attend

hearings, depositions and trials; (iii) assist in effecting settlement, securing and giving evidence, obtaining the attendance of witnesses in the conduct of suits; (iv) give a written statement or statements to the Company's representatives and meet with such representatives for the purposes of determining coverage and investigating and/or defending any Claim, all without charge to the Company.

*Admission of Liability And The Decision to Contest a Claim.*

As soon as a claim is received it should be reported immediately to the underwriter. However, because a claim's defence is extremely sensitive, many Commonwealth country policies contain a provision that both prohibits the assured from admitting liability and protects the assured by requiring a Queen's Counsel opinion before a trial is required. These provisions should be carefully examined.

Example: *Source: Singapore*

The Insured shall not admit liability for or settle any claim or incur any costs or expenses in connection therewith without the written consent of Underwriters, who shall be entitled at any time to take over and conduct in the name of the Insured the defence or settlement of any claim.

Nevertheless, the Insured shall not be required to contest any legal proceedings unless a Queen's Counsel (to be mutually agreed upon by the Insured and the Underwriters) shall advise that such proceedings should be contested.

However, most other policies give the insurer the exclusive right to determine whether or not to contest a claim.

In most jurisdictions, a lawyer as an officer of the court is under an ethical obligation to inform the client of any circumstance under which the client should seek separate advice. Obviously great care must be taken when a lawyer learns of a mistake which may lead to a claim: he must tell his client to seek the advice of another lawyer but cannot admit that he did anything wrong. He is on quite a tight rope!

*Who Is To Defend The Claim — The Insurer Or The Insured?*

There are two kinds of clauses in this area: (a) The insurer has no duty to defend, but has a right to defend if it elects and (b) the insurer has a duty to defend. The following are examples of each of these clauses:

Example: *Source: Lloyd's*

Defence: With respect to the insurance afforded by this Policy, the Underwriters shall defend any claim against the Insured including appeal thereof seeking damages to which this insurance applies even if any of the allegations of the suit are groundless, false or fraudulent. It is further agreed that the Underwriters may make such investigation of any claim or suit as it deems expedient, but the Underwriters shall not be obligated to pay any claim or judgment or to defend or to continue to defend any suit or claim after the applicable limit of the Underwriters' liability has been exhausted by payments of judgments or settlements, and/or claim expenses.

Example: *Source: Sri Lanka*
The Insured shall not admit liability or settle or make or promise any payment in respect of any claim which may be the subject of indemnity hereunder or incur any costs or expenses in connection therewith without the written consent of the Corporation who if they so wish shall be entitled to take over and conduct in the name of the Insured the defence and/or settlement of any such claim for which purpose the Insured shall give all such information and assistance as the Corporation may reasonably require.

*Choice of Counsel.*
Again, since the decision is such a sensitive one, the choice of counsel is usually left to Underwriters but with the consent of the insured.

Example: *Source: Finland*
Taking into account their place of residence, the locality where the possible legal proceedings may be instituted, and the type of case, the Insured must employ as counsel a solicitor supervised by the Finnish Bar Association or a lawyer employed by such a solicitor, or some other competent lawyer suited to conduct the case.
The Insurance Company is entitled to appoint the counsel when the Insurance Company shares a common interest in the case with the Insured, or when the litigation, case or matter is conducted outside Finland.
If the Insured employs a counsel other than a person who holds a degree entitling to judicial office, this Insurance does not cover the resulting expenses.

*Cost of Defence.*
The cost of defence has been dealt with above in the section on Coverage Limits. Again, the issues are whether the costs of defence are deducted from the limits ("sinking fund" versus non-sinking fund policy) and what happens if the settlement exceeds the policy limits. This frequently requires a *pro rata* allocation of defence costs.

*Control of Settlement.*
Most policies require the written consent of the assured in order to effect settlement. If an insured refuses to consent to the settlement, then Underwriters are generally not liable by the terms of the contract for any amounts exceeding those which the insured would have been liable for if the settlement had been agreed to.

Example: *Source: Lloyd's*
Limit of Liability — Reduction for Refusal to Settle: The Underwriters shall not settle any claim without the consent of the Insured. If, however, the Insured shall refuse to consent to any settlement recommended by the Underwriters and shall elect to contest the claim or continue any legal proceedings in connection with such claim, then the Underwriters' liability for the claim shall not exceed the amount for which the claim could have been so settled including claim expenses incurred up to the date of such

refusal. Such amounts are subject to the provisions of the section Limits of Liability 1 and Limits of Liability 2.

Example: *Source: Puerto Rico*

Defence and settlement (Included in the limits of Liability)

The Company shall have the right and duty to defend, subject to and as part of the limits of liability, any suit against the Insured seeking damages which are payable under the terms of this policy, even if any of the allegations of the suit are groundless, false or fraudulent.

The Company shall have the right to make any investigation it deems necessary and, with the written consent of the Insured, any settlement of any claim covered by the terms of this policy.

If the Insured shall refuse to consent to any settlement or compromise recommended by the Company and acceptable to the claimant and elects to contest the claim, suit or proceedings, then the Company's liability shall not exceed the amount for which the Company would have been liable for damages and claims expenses if the claim or suit or proceeding had been so settled or compromised, when and as so recommended, and the company shall have no liability for claims expenses accruing thereafter and the Company shall have the right to withdraw from the further defence thereof by tendering control of said defence to the Insured.

## Defence of disciplinary proceedings

The typical lawyers liability indemnity policy applies to claims by clients for acts or omissions that have resulted in monetary damages. However, complaints to bar associations to investigate and punish can devastate one's professional integrity and practice. Additionally, such a proceeding may be binding in a subsequent liability claim in court.

Normally, lawyers insurance does not cover defending such claims. Extensions, though, are available.

Example: *Source: New Zealand*

It is agreed and declared that the Policy is extended to indemnify the insured for the reasonable costs and expenses incurred by or on behalf of Underwriters or by or on behalf of the Insured, with Underwriters' prior written consent, in respect to the investigation and defence of any complaint against the conduct of activities of the Insured by any committee or professional body which claims or has jurisdiction to inquire or adjudicate in any such matter.

## Other insurance clauses

On occasion, lawyers will have more than one professional indemnity insurance policy available and in force during the negligent act or omission. (Usually this occurs when the present policy is on a claims-made basis and there was an occurrence policy prior.)

To accommodate this situation, most policies provide for the contingency with a section called "other insurance." The clause can typically do any of the following: (1) prorate the loss between applicable policies by basing the loss and coverage upon the ratio of the limits of liability of the company's policy to the total limits of all other valid and collectible insurance against its loss; (2) the "other insurance" clause can limit liability to the amount by which the insurance exceeds that provided by other valid and collectible insurance; and, (3) the clause can seek to "escape" any liability if there is other valid insurance. Escape clauses are generally disfavoured by the courts. Examples of other insurance clauses include the following:

Example: *Source: United States*
The coverages provided by this policy, including endorsements hereto, shall be excess over any other valid and collectible insurance, available to the insured whether such other insurance is stated to be primary, pro rata, contributory, excess, contingent, or otherwise, unless such other insurance specifies in writing that its excess insurance over the limits of the liability provided in this policy.

Example: *Source: United States*
If the insured has insurance provided by other companies against a loss covered by this policy, the company shall not be liable under this policy for a greater proportion of such loss and claims expenses than the applicable limit of liability stated in the declaration bears to the total applicable limits of liability of all valid and collectible insurance against such loss; provided, however, with respect to acts, error or omissions which occur prior to the inception date of this policy, the insureds hereunder shall apply only as excess insurance over any other valid and collectible insurance and shall then apply only in the amount by which the applicable limits of liability of this policy exceed the sum of the applicable limits of liability of all such other insurance.

## CONCLUSION AND POLICY RECOMMENDATIONS

As noted at the beginning of this chapter, there can be no generalized lawyers liability indemnity policy that fits all situations. Each practice must be examined in the context of the partners, the country they are located in, the underlying potential lawyer liability, the cost of the coverage, and the risk to the partners.

### Practice-oriented conclusions

We are not able to provide general guidelines for policy wording because of language, cultural, and legal system differences. However, some basic advice is safe in any market.

1. Analyse the practice.
Each practice should be carefully analysed to determine what kind of coverage is needed. Is it an international practice? Is it likely to be involved with important documents? Is it likely that lawyers will either come or leave the partnership during the period? Are there any areas of particular concern such as patent law?
Obviously, all of these questions and many more need to be carefully considered when approaching your broker.

2. Analysis of your complete insurance programme.
The lawyers liability indemnity insurance policy is only one element of a comprehensive insurance programme that every law firm should have. Obviously, coverage for general liability, premises liability, automobile liability and worker's compensation should be put in place. Many of the exclusions that this chapter has dealt with are simply matters to be covered under other kinds of insurance.

3. The Application.
This document is central to obtaining valid coverage. It should be completed with great care and adequate documentation retained for inquiries to other members of the firm.

**Recommended provisions**

1. Who is insured?
The assured should insist on coverage for (a) all present partners, (b) all future partners, (c) all former partners for claims emanating from work as a partner, (d) all deceased partners, (e) all employees and (f) all consultants.

2. What is insured?
The short answer is that the lawyer should make sure that the definition of "practice of law" is sufficient to provide coverage for what that lawyer actually does in his or her practice. In many circumstances, it should include work as a notary, trustee, guardian, conservator, director, executor or public official. It is recommended that the scope of "practice of law" is spelled out rather than simply left as "work as a licensed lawyer."

3. The insuring event and extended reporting coverage.
This issue is market driven. While it might be desirable to have an "occurrence" or hybrid policy, the only type readily available today is a claims-made policy.
It is strongly recommended that every lawyer who has a claims-made policy also obtain extended reporting coverage. This provision should provide coverage for any subsequent claims if (a) the lawyer learned of circumstances during the policy period that could be reasonably foreseen to give rise to a claim and (b) the circumstances

were reported to the insurer during either the initial policy period or the extended reporting period.

4. What is a claim?
The concept of claim should be specifically defined and should include (a) lawsuits, (b) written demand for compensation, (c) written demand for return of files and (d) instigation of bar proceedings that may result in imposition of a monetary award.

5. Territorial limitations.
Given the growing globalisation of the practice of law, the lawyer should insist that the policy cover claims arising anywhere in the world. Some policies restrict coverage to lawsuits only in certain countries; these provisions should be scrutinized and, if possible, eliminated.

6. Exclusions and extensions of cover.
The policies examined contained a vast array of exclusions. The following are exclusions that are common and may be reasonably found in a policy:

- loss of documents
- libel, slander and defamation
- punitive damages and fines
- trading debts
- employment disputes
- prior disclosed acts
- dishonesty, intentional or gross negligence
- patent
- tax advice
- business pursuits
- officer and director liability
- bodily injury and property damage
- public official

Extended cover or separate insurance may be obtained for many of these exclusions. We recommend that a lawyer strongly consider extended cover for (a) loss of documents, (b) libel, slander and defamation, and (c) innocent parties exception to fraud. Specialised practice coverage can be obtained at a higher cost.

7. Control of defence.
It is very important for any lawyer to understand both how the cost of defence of a claim is treated in determining the amount of insurance available as well as who controls the defence. It is not at all unusual for lawyers to obtain coverage that gives them the right to concur in the appointment of counsel as well as the consent to any settlement. Since it is the lawyer's reputation that is at stake, these kinds of issues should be closely examined.

# Chapter 7

# Summary of Survey Results

## ARGENTINA

### The civil liability of legal advisers

*Basis of liability*

Within the Argentine legal system the standard of care and skill expected of a lawyer is that of a competent practitioner. The exact nature of liability is defined by statute although the courts ultimately adjudicate on the matter of liability. The issue may also be dealt with by way of arbitration if both client and lawyer agree.

Relief is restricted to compensation of those damages which are the direct result of the performance of lawyers and of those indirect damages which could be foreseen by the legal adviser. There are no financial limits on the compensation which lawyers may be ordered to pay.

*Restrictions on liability*

In principle, lawyers can enter into agreements with their clients to limit their liability. The agreement could relate to a particular matter or could be implemented through standard conditions. Under the Civil Code limitations to liability can be disregarded by the courts where such agreements are not made in good faith, although there is no judicial precedent which has tested the issue. The courts may also overrule any limitation which takes unfair advantage of the inexperience or the needs of the client.

In any event these types of agreement are rarely made in Argentina.

Any action a client wishes to bring against lawyers must be instigated within ten years.

*Liability to non-clients*

On rare occasions court decisions have made lawyers liable to non-clients for negligence. In principle, the following conditions should be present for a lawyer to incur personal liability:

- voluntary performance by a lawyer;
- the said performance should be against the law;
- the said performance should have caused certain damage;
- the lawyer's performance must be the cause of the damage inflicted.

For instance, lawyers have been found liable for damages caused to third parties who were not actual debtors and whose property had been wrongly attached by the lawyers. Argentine legislation also allows judges to declare both the losing party in litigation and its lawyer to be jointly liable for court costs.

*Recent developments with respect to liability*

In recent years an act unifying the Civil Code and the Argentine Commercial code was passed but vetoed by the National Executive. The act tried to introduce changes to the liability regime among which the following were included:

- excluding the possibility of agreeing a limitation on liability in contracts with standard conditions, except where the debtor establishes that such limitation allows him to provide a cheaper service to the creditor;
- in proceedings brought against lawyers they have the burden of proving that they have performed their job diligently.

The National Congress has not resumed the debate on the above mentioned act after the president's veto.

## Insurance

*Voluntary professional indemnity insurance*

Indemnity insurance for the legal profession is voluntary in Argentina, and only a small portion of the legal profession has such insurance.

*Insurance facilities*

Only commercial insurers within the country issue policies to lawyers.

*Level of cover*

The level of cover generally obtained by the legal profession is USD100,000. This covers an aggregate amount of USD200,000 for all claims within a policy period, with a maximum of USD100,000 for each single claim. It is very difficult to obtain a higher level of cover.

For a cover of USD100,000, the insurance premium due is USD270 plus tax.

*Deductibles*
For this level of cover, five per cent of a claim is payable by the insured lawyers themselves, with a minimum of USD1,000.

*Recent developments with respect to insurance*
Due to the high premiums that the international reinsurance companies are quoting for professional indemnity insurance, no local insurers are offering new policies to lawyers in the Argentine market at this time.

## AUSTRALIA

### The civil liability of legal advisers

*Basis of liability*
Liability is principally decided according to the degree of skill and care to be expected of a competent lawyer. In a limited range of circumstances liability is decided by reference to standards of commercial and professional conduct, for example, where a lawyer has engaged in misleading or deceptive conduct under the Trade Practices Act 1974.

The principles have evolved from decisions taken by the courts and the courts have sole responsibility for deciding liability.

Relief is restricted to compensation.

*Restrictions on liability*
Where a lawyer appears as a client's advocate he will be granted immunity. Lawyers appearing as advocates, whether they be barristers or solicitors in those states where the profession is divided or solicitors in states where the profession is undivided, enjoy immunity from liability for "in court" negligence as developed under the common law. The High Court of Australia, being the superior court in Australia, has applied English decisions. The courts have also held that there was no immunity for work done out of court that is unconnected with work done in court but immunity does apply to work done out of court which leads to a decision affecting the conduct of the case in court. In New South Wales, it was held that the immunity extends to court work intimately connected with or ancillary to the conduct of the case.

There are no statutory or regulatory restrictions on lawyers restricting liability to their clients by agreement or otherwise but generally lawyers do not seek such agreement. In any event, the common law principles as to excluding and limiting liability render such an approach difficult.

In relation to commencing an action, the time limit is generally six years from the date at which the cause of action first accrues. The issue as to when the cause of action against a lawyer first accrues is the subject of many Australian decisions. In cases involving lawyers the issue has been whether the cause of action arose at the date of the negligent act or omission or at the date of discoverability of damage. The trend in Australia is to adopt the first test and follow the line of English authorities rather than the discoverability test which has been applied in Canada.

*Liability to non-clients*
Lawyers can be liable to non-clients when a duty of care is established and the tests as to reasonable foreseeability and proximity are satisfied. This is based on common law principles. The proposition can be put broadly and the cases which have been decided on this issue very much depend on their own facts. Lawyers can also be liable to non-clients where they have breached the standards of commercial conduct referred to above and the non-client has suffered loss as a result.

*Recent developments with respect to liability*
The New South Wales Parliament has recently passed an act which will enable lawyers to put in place a scheme for a cap on damages. This trend may be adopted by other states but at the moment it is very much in the very initial stages and no detailed arrangements have been put in place.

## Insurance

*Compulsory professional indemnity insurance*
In Australia the position in each state varies with regard to the division of the profession but by and large the profession is "de facto" divided. The following will deal with the position of lawyers practising as solicitors.

Professional indemnity insurance is compulsory for solicitors. This is required by statute.

*Insurance facilities*
Insurance facilities up to the limits required by the compulsory insurance schemes are available in most states through a mutual scheme arranged by the profession with an additional "master" policy.

Cover above the limit of the compulsory insurance schemes is available through commercial insurers.

Commercial insurance is generally obtained through brokers within the country who place the cover with underwriters both within Australia and also through the London and United States markets.

*Level of cover*
The compulsory cover limit is USD820,600 in New South Wales, the Australian Capital Territory, Victoria, Western Australia and Tasmania. In South Australia and the Northern Territory it is USD558,000 and in Queensland it is USD373,000.

The level of cover generally taken up by the profession varies from firm to firm depending on the number of partners and the size of the practice. It varies from the compulsory cover limit to USD7.46 million or more.

Cover to the compulsory level is a maximum for each claim. Cover above that is generally an aggregate for all claims within a policy period. In some of the layers above the compulsory limit cover for a maximum for each claim is available.

The cost of compulsory cover may be 1.1 per cent of the annual expenses of a practice, although this varies from firm to firm. The cost of top up cover above the compulsory limit can amount to approximately 0,8 per cent of the annual expenses. Again, this figure is only an indication.

*Deductibles*

The range of deductibles payable by the insured solicitors varies from state to state. In New South Wales the deductible is USD3,730 for a sole practitioner, USD2,238 per partner up to a maximum of USD74,600 with a double penalty excess in respect of cases where the solicitor has acted for a borrower and a lender in a transaction or the claim is for damages for a personal injury action becoming statute barred. In Victoria the deductible is USD2,611 per partner up to a maximum of USD29,840, with a similar double penalty excess for transactions of the same nature as apply in New South Wales. The position in each of the other states is broadly similar, in particular in Tasmania, Western Australia and the Australian Capital Territory because the solicitors in those states have voluntarily joined the New South Wales scheme in order to comply with the compulsory requirements of their regulatory authorities.

*Recent developments with respect to insurance*

At the time of writing this book there are no new trends or potential developments in the area of insurance which may significantly alter the framework summarised above.

## AUSTRIA

### The civil liability of legal advisers

*Basis of liability*

The general law relating to the liability of professional people including lawyers (attorneys at law) is to be found in the Austrian General Civil Code. A lawyer is under the obligation to perform his work as stipulated. The contract between the lawyer and the client usually only specifies the main purpose of the agreement and does not either include a list of duties or set out how the retainer is to be performed.

A guiding principle of lawyers' liability to their clients in respect of advice given and the conduct of matters is that a client may expect the services to be carried out with the degree of skill and care of a lawyer with an average education and training. A lawyer is under a duty to carry out the mandate actively and honestly. Furthermore, in accordance with the Austrian Bar Act he is obliged to stand up for the rights of his client with enthusiasm, loyalty and conscientiousness.

The lawyer is liable for the quality of his services. According to the General Civil Code, instructions given to a lawyer constitute a contract of mandate. Under those provisions the instructed person is, in a very general way, obliged to carry out the mandate actively and honestly. As a lawyer is an expert within the meaning of the Code, he is liable and responsible to his client to a higher degree than a lay person who caused damage. According to these provisions the lawyer is also liable for detrimental advice he gave negligently. The liability of the attorney at law is put in more concrete terms by the Austrian Bar Act, but there is argument about the question whether and to what extent this statute is applicable to the civil law contract between lawyer and client.

Judgments by the various levels of courts are based on constitutional, statutory and regulatory sources and the principle of legal unity. Accordingly, the basis of lawyers' liability is also defined by court decisions. All civil law disputes between lawyers and clients fall within the jurisdiction of the ordinary courts. The Bar Association has disciplinary power over the members of the Bar.

The available relief is limited to compensation. The General Civil Code includes detailed regulations on compensation. There are no financial limits on compensation lawyers may be ordered to pay.

*Restrictions on liability*

The liability of a lawyer for damages depends on the individual case. There are no general restrictions as to the circumstances under which lawyers may be held liable to their clients. Under the General Civil Code, the damage must have been caused both wrongfully and culpably.

Lawyers may, for a particular case, limit their liability by agreement with their client insofar as the agreement does not conflict with national policy and public morals. Such agreements are, however, concluded rarely in Austria. There are no specific restrictions, except for national policy and public morals, preventing lawyers from restricting their liability to their clients. However, some lawyers are of the opinion that it is against professional ethics for an attorney at law to conclude a general agreement with a client restricting his liability. This is a contested issue.

The statutory period of limitation is three years from the time the person having sustained damage becomes aware of the damage and knows the identity of person who caused it. There is also a thirty year absolute time bar from the date of the breach of duty.

*Liability to non-clients*

Generally, non-clients can neither demand the performance of a lawyer's duty nor make a lawyer liable for breaching his duties. This basic rule might, however, not apply in some cases. The lawyer has protective duties for persons who are closely connected with the contractual relationship between lawyer and client. These duties might become relevant in cases of contracts for the benefit of a non-client. When a lawyer drafts a contract he has to be objective, in that he is not only responsible to his client but also to the other party to the contract if the latter is neither his client nor assisted by a lawyer in the negotiations.

*Recent developments with respect to liability*
There is increasing concern amongst law firms engaged in high-risk, high-volume or international business regarding ruinous professional liability claims. Various strategies against such tendencies are being discussed in this context, such as:

- formal admission under the professional rules of agreements by attorneys at law with clients regarding the limitation of liability with respect to the type and the amount of damages to be claimed;
- recognition by the Bar Associations that limitation of liability may be provided for in General Terms and Conditions used by lawyers;
- introduction of new types of legal entities providing for limited liability (such as the company with limited liability — *GmbH*) for professional associations of lawyers;
- higher insurance cover.

No preferences have yet emerged.

**Insurance**

*Compulsory professional indemnity insurance*
In Austria the legal profession is divided in the sense that there are attorneys at law (*Rechtsanwälte*), notaries (*Öffentliche Notare*) and tax advisers (*Steuerberater*). There are no essential differences between these groups regarding the basic insurance.

Indemnity insurance for the legal profession is compulsory in Austria. This is required by Statute (Article 21a of the Austrian Bar Act).

*Insurance facilities*
The usual facility used by lawyers is a policy issued by commercial insurers.

In addition, a lawyer may make use of a special group insurance scheme negotiated by the Austrian Bar Associations for its members. This collective scheme is offered by two commercial insurance companies and provides for a policy covering damages over and above the compulsory minimum cover up to a maximum amount of USD2.25 million. Between seventy per cent and one hundred per cent of the members of the various Austrian Bar Associations participate in this voluntary collective insurance scheme.

A number of the larger Austrian law firms have taken out additional policies for higher cover.

Due to a high insurance tax on foreign policies commercial insurance was, until recently, obtained from insurers within the country. This higher tax has, however, been abolished under the impact of EEA/EU regulations so that insurance coverage is increasingly obtained from abroad.

*Level of cover*

The minimum compulsory cover limit is USD50,000. A number of the smaller firms take out policies for the minimum cover only. Most firms take up a cover of between USD250,000 and USD550,000. Larger firms (five to six partners and more) also take out higher amounts.

The cover is generally a maximum for each claim. Some policies provide, however, for a maximum amount of coverage per year.

The insurance premium ranges between approximately 0,5 and one per cent of the annual expenses of a practice.

*Deductibles*

There is a great variety amongst the insurance policies taken out by lawyers and the range of deductibles payable by the insured lawyers varies accordingly.

The deductibles are sometimes defined in a percentage of the insurance sum (frequently ten per cent of the basic insurance) or a fixed amount (usually in the range between USD1,000 and USD10,000 — occasionally even more) or a combination of these two alternatives.

*Recent developments with respect to insurance*

Austria's entry into the European Union opens the Austrian insurance market to insurers of other European Union member states. Austrian insurers are considering varied insurance premiums for professional indemnity insurance not only by covered amounts, but by the turnover of the respective law firm, which would significantly alter the premiums to be paid by a number of firms.

Also, there is a tendency to limit the term of insurance cover under a policy that has expired for cases which were handled by a lawyer while such a policy was still in force.

Some years ago, the Austrian Bar Associations introduced an insurance scheme for the indemnification of clients who have become the victims of attorneys who defrauded monies entrusted to them. These policies are taken out and premiums for them are paid by the respective Bar Associations and not by individual lawyers.

Notaries have recently introduced a special trust register in which sums of money which they hold in trust are registered. A special mutual insurance scheme was introduced for the protection of such trust monies by the Chamber of Notaries.

## BELGIUM

### The civil liability of legal advisers

*Basis of liability*
The relationship between the lawyer and his client is of a contractual nature. The contract is "mixed" since there may be aspects of different contracts such as mandate, the supply of services, or deposit that form together the whole contractual relationship between lawyer and client. The rules governing the liability of a lawyer are the general rules with regard to contractual liability which are laid down in the Civil Code. Specific rules may be applicable to a specific type of contract, for example a mandate.

With regard to the contractual obligations of the lawyer, a distinction is made between two types of obligations: obligations to achieve a specific result, such as the filing of written pleadings or the lodging of an appeal within a legal term (these are the so-called *obligations de résultat*) and obligations to use one's best efforts without guaranteeing a specific result, such as giving advice or pleading a case (these are the so-called *obligations de moyens*.

In case of an *obligation de résultat* the fault, and consequently the responsibility of the lawyer, will be presumed from the absence of the specified result. In case of an *obligation de moyens*, the client will have to prove that the lawyer did not act in the way a normally careful and reasonably cautious lawyer would have acted when placed in similar circumstances. Whether the degree of specialisation or the degree of skill will be taken into account, is a rather difficult question. A cautious lawyer should not accept a matter or a case for which he lacks sufficient knowledge or expertise.

Questions of liability of lawyers are decided by the civil courts. Arbitration is possible but is rather rare in practice.

The lawyer would normally be held liable for damages which compensate for the losses and costs incurred by the client. The determination of damages might be difficult if they are to compensate for the "loss of chance", for example the loss of a chance to win an appeal. In theory relief is not restricted to financial compensation as, under the principles of contractual liability, compensation should be "in kind" whenever possible. This, however, never occurs in practice.

*Restrictions on liability*
Financial compensation should cover the total loss suffered by the client, which means that in theory compensation should put the client in a situation as if the error or fault of the lawyer had not occurred. Compensation must be restricted to the damages that are a direct consequence of the fault of the lawyer. The liability of the lawyer may be reduced to the extent the client himself has caused the loss. Of course, no liability will be incurred in case of force majeure or to the extent that a loss has been caused by the sole fault of a third party. Further, a lawyer might point

out the particular circumstances under which he was to act, for example extreme urgency of the matter. Lawyers enjoy, under certain conditions, an immunity which covers the written and oral pleadings but this does not relieve them of their contractual responsibility towards the client.

As a general principle of contract law, a lawyer is entitled to limit or exclude his contractual liability except for intentional fault. However, such a restriction or disclaimer of liability clause must not have the effect of frustrating the object of the contract. Such agreements are extremely rare.

A claim based on professional liability of a lawyer to his client is statute barred five years from completion of the work performed by the lawyer.

*Liability to non-clients*

Liability towards non-clients is non-contractual. A lawyer may be liable to third parties under the general rules of civil liability laid down in the Civil Code. Under these rules a third party has to establish that it has incurred a loss which was caused by a fault of the lawyer. The time limit is thirty years for claims based on non-contractual liability towards third parties.

*Recent developments with respect to liability*

At the time of writing this book there have been no such developments.

**Insurance**

*Compulsory professional indemnity insurance*

Indemnity insurance for the legal profession is compulsory in Belgium. All lawyers are required by statute to be members of the Bar, and the Belgian Bars take out collective insurance policies for their members.

*Insurance facilities*

The Belgian Bars contract with commercial insurers for their collective insurance policies. On top of these collective insurance policies, individual lawyers or law firms may purchase additional insurance policies to cover higher amounts.

*Level of cover*

The cover of the collective bar insurance policies is limited to:

- USD500,000 per claim based on contractual liability;
- USD8 million (for bodily damage) or USD800,000 (for other damage) per claim based on non-contractual liability.

The insurance premium is paid by the Bar and is included in the professional contribution paid to the Bar by each lawyer. In 1994, the annual insurance premium amounted to USD200 for each lawyer.

*Deductibles*
For the members of the Brussels Bar, the first twenty-five per cent of a claim is self-insured by the lawyer, with a minimum of USD320 and a maximum of USD3,200.

The maximum deductible increases in the case of legal delays to USD4,000 for the first claim, to USD6,000 for the second claim and to USD8,000 for further claims.

*Recent developments with respect to insurance*
There are no recent developments or trends in this area.

## BERMUDA

### The civil liability of legal advisers

*Basis of liability*
The liability of legal advisers is decided according to the degree of skill and care to be expected of competent lawyers. In both contract and tort the duty owed by a lawyer to his client is to use reasonable care and skill in giving such advice and taking such action as the facts of the particular case demand. The standard of care is that of a reasonably competent lawyer.

Those principles are defined by court decisions. The principles of lawyers' liability to their clients are established by the English common law (i.e. court decisions), both in contract and in tort.

The adjudication of civil liability of lawyers to their clients is a matter solely for the courts. Although lawyers may become subject to disciplinary proceedings before the Bar Council for improper conduct toward their clients, this does not constitute civil liability.

An award of damages is the principal remedy and in most cases the only remedy which the court will grant when a breach of duty has taken place. However, where the breach of duty by the lawyer takes the form of breach of fiduciary duty (e.g. making a secret profit or failing to disclose an interest that the lawyer may have in a particular transaction) the remedies available are at the discretion of the court and are not necessarily limited to compensation. The court may direct accounts to be taken and, in appropriate cases, may order the lawyer to replace property improperly acquired from the client. The amount of damages will be decided in accordance with the normal principles relating to contractual and tortious remedies.

*Restrictions on liability*
A lawyer enjoys a special immunity against actions in both contract and tort in respect of his conduct and management of a cause of action in court. This principle is based on public policy. The immunity extends not only to the conduct of a case in

court but also to pre-trial work that is "intimately connected" with the conduct of that case. It does not extend to matters not closely connected with litigation.

It is not the practice in Bermuda for lawyers to seek to restrict their liability to clients for breach of duty. In any case, if a lawyer seeks to restrict his liability, he must ensure that the contractual term was expressly incorporated into the contract of engagement, was brought to the client's attention and is sufficiently clear to apply to negligence. The term should be accepted by the client, preferably in writing. There are no statutory provisions in Bermuda which prevent lawyers from restricting their liability to their clients.

The limitation period is six years for both contract and tort actions. Where the lawyer is being sued for breach of contract, the limitation period will begin to run on the date of the breach (i.e. the day the lawyer breached his duty of care by some act of omission). In tort actions, such as negligence, proof of damage is required, so the cause of action accrues when the damage actually occurs. In an action against a solicitor for negligent advice, the plaintiff must have suffered actual damage and he has a complete cause of action when the advice is acted on by the plaintiff, for example, when he executes a document such as a mortgage.

*Liability to non-clients*

Lawyers can be held liable to third parties in tort. There are two bases of liability.

First, lawyers can be held liable to non-clients for negligent mis-statements when it is established that the lawyer knew or should have known that reliance was being placed on his advice. In that situation the claimant must prove financial loss resulting from such reliance.

Second, a liability can arise where a duty of care is owed to a non-client in particular circumstances, for example to an intended beneficiary when the lawyer draws up a will.

*Recent developments with respect to liability*

There are no recent developments which affect the liability of lawyers in relation to their relationship with clients.

**Insurance**

*Voluntary professional indemnity insurance*

Indemnity insurance for the legal profession is voluntary in Bermuda.

The majority of the small law firms in Bermuda, to the best of our knowledge, do not have professional indemnity insurance. There are probably only three large firms that do.

*Insurance facilities*

Insurance is available from commercial insurers abroad.

*Level of cover*
The level of cover ranges from USD5 million to USD26 million.

It is estimated that lawyers spend on an average four per cent of their annual expenses on professional indemnity insurance.

*Deductibles*
The range of deductibles payable by the insured lawyers themselves is between USD150,000 and USD250,000.

*Recent developments with respect to insurance*
At the time of writing this book there are no new trends or potential developments in the area of insurance which may significantly alter the framework summarised above.

## BOLIVIA

### The civil liability of legal advisers

*Basis of liability*
The issues of a lawyer's liability are generally decided according to the degree of skill to be expected from a competent lawyer. A careless following of the law, the procedure, or ignoring the Bolivian Code of Ethics are the three ways by which negligence, incompetence, deceit or any other inexcusable fault can be proved.

These principles are defined by statutes, being the Bolivian Code of Ethics and the Bolivian Civil Code. The Honor Tribunal of the Bolivian Bar Association is the only competent judicial entity entitled to handle civil liability cases, or any other matter concerning a violation of the Code of Ethics. Once the Honor Tribunal has rendered its decision the matter can be taken up to an ordinary court of justice.

The relief given to a client may be by way of compensation, but can also be satisfied by other means, depending on the Honor Tribunal's decision. There is no general financial limit for compensation, rather it is set on a particular basis depending on the amount of damage inflicted upon a client. The compensation is decided on by the Honor Tribunal after a careful assessment of the damage caused to the client and his case by the actions of his lawyer.

The Civil Code requires the use of diligence in any type of professional activity. A lawyer can only be held responsible for his actions when there has been negligence, deceit or any other inexcusable fault, but he is immune from liability if the client has chosen an inappropriate lawyer for a specific case.

*Restrictions on liability*
Lawyers by agreement with their clients may limit their liability only on a particular basis. This is due to the fact that lawyers' liability cases in Bolivia are very rare,

and therefore, if a client would like this kind of security he would have to agree with his lawyer on a particular basis and not expect any kind of general standard conditions.

The financial relationship between a lawyer and a client is strictly personal. Therefore there are no restrictions to the financial limits of the liability or to the lawyer's fees. However, if abuse or deceit has taken place this matter may be taken up to the Honor Tribunal, and thereafter, to an ordinary court of justice.

As for any other action that generates a liability, a client has up to three years to make a claim, from the time the action was verified.

*Liability to non-clients*

Under Bolivian law there is no principle which provides a client outside a contract with a right to sue.

*Recent developments with respect to liability*

To date there have been very few cases concerning the civil liability of legal advisers, especially on the grounds of negligence or incompetence. There is no specific procedure that can be found in the Civil Code concerning the responsibility of the lawyer to his client, rather the matter is included as part of the "responsibility in professional activity", which in itself does not constitute an important procedure.

However, as professional malpractice claims in general come more frequently before the Bolivian courts of justice, the liability of the legal profession will become more significant.

### Insurance

*Professional indemnity insurance*

There is no professional indemnity insurance available for the legal profession in Bolivia.

## BRAZIL

### The civil liability of legal advisers

*Basis of liability*

Attorney liability in Brazil is based on contract. Lawyers are held liable for malpractice, negligence and errors committed during the performance of their mandate, including errors involving ordinary fault (*culpa levis*).

As a general trend in Brazil, legislation creates more and more cases of strict liability, such as on environmental matters and product liability. The recently enacted Consumer Protection Code provides for strict liability of service renderers, which would include lawyers. However, a specific provision was inserted into that statute to provide that the civil liability of professionals such as doctors, lawyers and members of other regulated professions is not strict. The civil liability of such professionals therefore depends on the demonstration by the prejudiced party that the professional in question acted with fraudulent intent or fault.

The Brazilian Civil Code adopts fault as the principal basis for liability. The "duty of reparation" is set out in the Civil Code. Also a recent statute regulates the Brazilian Bar Association and the legal profession, establishing that a lawyer will be held "liable for any acts in the course of his/her profession which are performed with fraudulent intent or fault".

Case law, which in Brazil does not bind future decisions of the courts, confirms the contractual nature of the civil liability of legal advisers. Civil liability is a matter of court jurisdiction. The Brazilian Bar Association is in sole charge of ruling on disciplinary matters and breaches of the Code of Professional Ethics and Law within the legal profession.

There is no limit to the compensation which lawyers may be ordered to pay as a result of damage incurred by their clients. However, this compensation cannot exceed the sum total of the following:

- the value of the loss incurred by the client, as fixed by the courts;
- any loss of profits;
- court costs;
- six per cent interest per annum; and
- lawyers' fees due to the attorneys acting for the client on his claim (not exceeding twenty per cent of the total indemnity).

Relief for losses is restricted to loss and damage that actually result from an error of the legal adviser. They include any loss (both actual loss and pain and suffering), and any reasonable profits that were not made due to such error.

Other consequences may also result from professional malpractice on the part of the lawyer, such as administrative sanctions by the Bar Association, which may vary from a simple warning up to the disqualification of the professional to practise as a lawyer. Criminal sanctions may also apply in cases where crimes are committed. Such sanctions, however, do not assist the client except as evidence to support a civil claim for damages.

*Restrictions on liability*

The law does not provide any immunity for lawyers with regard to their duty to make good damages suffered by their clients. Clauses limiting or excluding liability are not prohibited under Brazilian law, and are even contained in the regulations applicable to certain types of contracts. Although not prohibited, the use of such clauses has been gradually restricted under more recent legislation, for example the Consumer Protection Code. Recent case law has also tended not to accept the validity of limitation or exclusion clauses on the grounds that such clauses contravene the principles of public policy. Although there has been no specific case law on this subject in relation to the provision of legal services, it may be concluded that the courts will not recognize the validity of any such clause.

Any action on the part of a client or third party seeking reimbursement for damage caused by a lawyer would come under the usual statute of limitations for personal litigation: twenty years as from the date on which filing of the case was first possible.

*Liability to non-clients*

Liability of lawyers vis-à-vis third parties is exceptional. As the mandate is the contractual basis linking the attorney to the client, any acts performed by the attorney in the performance of his or her duties are considered to be acts of the client (the principal), unless abuse or misuse of power can be shown. If the act of the lawyer (at the behest of the client) were to harm any third party in any way whatsoever, reparation for this damage would in theory fall to the client who gave the order.

In the event of a frivolous suit, the lawyer will be held jointly liable with the client, provided the lawyer has acted in connivance with the client in order to harm the opposing party.

*Recent developments with respect to liability*

Civil claims for professional malpractice are not a trend in Brazil. There are actually very few cases in which a client has taken the lawyer to court in Brazilian case law, and even medical malpractice is not usual in the Brazilian courts.

Furthermore, it is often very difficult, and sometimes impossible, to produce enough evidence to prove a lawyer has been negligent or at fault to any extent.

## Insurance

*Voluntary professional indemnity insurance*

Indemnity insurance for the legal profession is voluntary in Brazil. It is very rare to take out professional indemnity insurance cover.

*Insurance facilities*

Policies issued by commercial insurers are available for insurance. The insurance policies are taken out with local insurers, as it is forbidden to contract with insurers abroad.

*Level of cover*

Statistics are not available to indicate the level of cover generally obtained by the legal profession.

*Deductibles*
Statistics are not available on the range of deductibles payable by the insured lawyers.

*Recent developments with respect to insurance*
There are no new trends or potential developments in the area of insurance which may significantly alter the framework summarised above.

## CANADA
## Provinces of Ontario, British Columbia, Alberta and Nova Scotia

### The civil liability of legal advisers

*Basis of liability*
The standard of care and skill which can be demanded from a lawyer is that of a reasonably competent and diligent solicitor. It is not enough to prove that the lawyer has made an error of judgment or shown ignorance of some particular part of the law; it must be shown that the error or ignorance was such that an ordinarily competent lawyer would not have made or shown it.

These principles are defined by court decisions. A court may look to the ethical and professional codes of conduct established by the Law Society governing the profession in each province for assistance in defining the standard of care in any particular case.

The civil liability of lawyers is a matter decided solely by the courts. Lawyers are, however, subject to disciplinary action by their governing societies for breaches of ethical and professional rules of conduct. Negligence will not necessarily expose a lawyer to disciplinary action, and ethical breaches will not always raise a civil cause of action.

Relief is not restricted in any way. There is no financial limit on the compensation which a lawyer may be ordered to pay. Subject to independent fiduciary and tort duties, and the doctrine of fundamental breach, the scope and terms of the solicitor-client retainer determine the extent to which a lawyer will be liable to the client in contract for a particular matter.

*Restrictions on liability*
There is less scope for a finding of liability against a lawyer acting in the capacity of a barrister. A barrister is not immune from civil liability in respect of the conduct of litigation, but liability will not be imposed for mere errors in judgment. The error must be egregious in order to find liability.

The Ontario Solicitors Act states that a provision in an agreement between a solicitor and client which exempts a solicitor from liability for negligence is void. British Columbia and Nova Scotia have similar provisions. In Alberta, while the point is not addressed specifically by legislation, it is thought such agreement would likely be unenforceable under common law principles.

The limitation period for actions generally is six years from the date when the breach of duty was or ought to have been discovered, whether the action be for breach of contract, tort or breach of fiduciary duty. The limitation period for actions founded in negligence is six years from the date the negligence was discovered or ought to have been discovered by the exercise of reasonable diligence. A claim against a lawyer for negligence is founded in both contract and tort, and so the limitation period does not start to run until the breach or negligence has been discovered or ought to have been discovered by the exercise of reasonable diligence.

The limitation period in Nova Scotia is also six years, but a defendant must show prejudice in order to enforce the limitation period as a defence, unless the action has been brought more than four years outside the limitation period (i.e. ten years after the commencement of the limitation period), in which case the bar is absolute.

*Liability to non-clients*

General principles of proximity, foreseeability and detrimental reliance, as in the tort of negligent misrepresentation, govern the liability of lawyers to third parties. A lawyer may also be liable to an opposing party in a real estate transaction, for example, in circumstances in which the lawyer knew the other party would rely on some act of the lawyer and it was foreseeable that carelessness on the part of the lawyer would cause damage to the other party.

Lawyers can be liable to opposing parties for the failure to perform an undertaking. Lawyers can be liable to third parties for breach of trust and breach of fiduciary duty, quite apart from any contractual and tort duties.

*Recent developments with respect to liability*

There appear to be no significant trends or incipient developments which are likely to change this information.

## Insurance

*Compulsory professional indemnity insurance*

Professional indemnity insurance is compulsory up to a primary level in the provinces of Ontario, British Columbia, Alberta and Nova Scotia. This is required by statute and the requirements of a professional body.

*Insurance facilities*

Compulsory insurance to the primary level is available through a collective or mutual self-administered programme introduced by professional body.

Excess insurance in one or more layers is purchased in commercial markets by lawyers themselves, generally from abroad.

*Level of cover*

The compulsory level of cover is approximately USD736,700 per claim. There is an aggregate primary limit of approximately USD1.47 million in some provinces, and no aggregate limit in other provinces.

The primary layer of insurance is reinsured to a substantial extent with commercial reinsurers.

Typically, the excess insurance layers would be approximately USD2.9 million as first excess, approximately USD3.7 million as second, third and fourth excess, up to total limits to the order of approximately USD29.5 million.

The insurance premium for the primary level of cover may represent the following percentage of the annual expenses of a law firm:

- roughly four per cent in Toronto, Ontario, but may be higher because of very recent developments (see below);
- roughly four per cent in Vancouver, British Columbia; and
- roughly two per cent in Calgary, Alberta.

These are rough estimates and the exact figures vary per practice and depend on such factors as location (principal business centre or small rural community and where in Canada) and claims experience of the particular individual member of the profession.

*Deductibles*

Deductibles (per claim) vary depending on the particular province of Canada, and in some provinces depending on the claims experience of the particular individual member of the profession.

Example ranges of deductibles are:

- in Ontario, from approximately USD4,500 if no claims paid in last five years to approximately USD11,000 if five claims paid in last five years, plus approximately USD1,800 for each additional claim beyond five;
- in British Columbia, from approximately USD3,600 to approximately USD14,700;
- in Alberta, a standard deductible of approximately USD3,600; and
- in Nova Scotia, a standard deductible of approximately USD3,600.

*Recent developments with respect to insurance*

In Ontario, significant changes have taken place very recently between 1994 and 1995, in that the scope of the primary layer coverage has been narrowed and its cost has increased drastically as a result of it having been determined that the accumulated deficit position of the self-insured portion of the self-administered programme is much greater than was previously understood to be the case. The very substantial increase in the deficit over the last several years appears to be attributable to rapid increase in the number and size of claims, corresponding increase in defence expense, and worsened overall loss experience, whereas the cost of the coverage was not increased at a comparable rate. Such developments appear to have had greatest impact in Ontario, which is the province with the largest lawyer population and, as among the provinces which have the greatest economic activity, is the one on which the recent economic recession has had most impact.

## CANADA
## Province of Quebec

### The civil liability of legal advisers

*Basis of liability*
The standard of care owed by a lawyer is decided according to the degree of skill and care to be expected of a competent lawyer. Those principles are defined by statute and court decisions. The latter also take responsibility for deciding on the liability of lawyers. The relief available is restricted to compensation and there are no restrictions as to the levels which can be awarded.

*Restrictions on liability*
Lawyers in Quebec enjoy a relative immunity only when acting as lawyers *ad litem*. Otherwise there are no restrictions. The Code of Ethics prevents a lawyer from restricting his liability. An action must be instituted against the lawyer within three years from the date of the knowledge of the client or non-client of the act of negligence committed by the lawyer.

*Liability to non-clients*
Lawyers can be held liable to non-clients if they commit a professional act of negligence which causes prejudice to non-clients. The non-client is obliged to prove that the lawyer's act or omission was of such a degree that it constitutes professional negligence, that he suffered damage and that the damage resulted directly from the professional negligence of the lawyer.

*Recent developments with respect to liability*
The frequency and severity of claims against lawyers are increasing. However, the Quebec experience is not as bad as that which prevails in the United States and some of the common law provinces of Canada.

### Insurance

*Compulsory professional indemnity insurance*
Professional indemnity insurance is compulsory in the Province of Quebec, as this is required by statute.

All lawyers take out professional indemnity insurance cover, unless they obtain an exemption from the Quebec Bar Insurance Fund. Exemptions are granted to lawyers if they are not practising law and for other reasons which are set forth by statute. Generally, if the employment of the lawyer does not represent a risk to the public, insurance coverage will not be required of him.

Notaries are separately covered in Quebec. They have their own mandatory professional liability scheme.

*Insurance facilities*
All lawyers of the Province of Quebec must be insured with the Quebec Bar Insurance Fund.

The excess insurance provided by commercial insurers is generally obtained from Canadian commercial insurers. However, it is also available from US and UK insurers. The wordings of these excess insurance policies do not need to be approved by the Quebec Bar.

The insurance premium can vary from one firm to another depending on the amount of excess insurance purchased by each firm and the insurer's assessment of the risk. It is unlikely that the insurance premium would represent more than five per cent of the annual expenses of a firm.

*Level of cover*
The Quebec Bar Insurance Fund provides primary limits of approximately USD720,000 per claim. The fee is approximately USD865 per lawyer, per annum.

The level of excess insurance coverage varies. The excess insurance is usually an aggregate for all claims within a policy period and a maximum for each claim.

*Deductibles*
The deductible under the Quebec Bar Insurance Fund is approximately USD3,680.

*Recent developments with respect to insurance*
There are no recent developments in the area of professional indemnity insurance.

## CHANNEL ISLANDS
## Guernsey

### The civil liability of legal advisers

*Basis of liability*
Broadly, the position is similar to that in England. Liability is founded upon contractual and tortious duties to use reasonable care and skill in the provision of services. Liability is not strict. Liability is determined by the degree of care and skill to be expected of a reasonably competent advocate (lawyer). The duty does not extend to lawyers acting as advocates in and about the conduct of the client's case in court.

Liability may be owed:

- to clients in contract or tort or both;
- to persons not in a contractual relationship with the lawyer who have been led by him to rely on his special skill and judgment;
- to third parties to whom he owes a duty of care (for example beneficiaries under a will).

The principles of liability are determined by jurisprudence and by order of the Royal Court of Guernsey (of which all advocates of the Guernsey Bar are officers). Liability is determined by the Royal Court of Guernsey. The Guernsey Bar Council has no jurisdiction in respect of matters of professional misconduct or negligence save to make rules relevant to the professional conduct of advocates. Professional misconduct is dealt with by a *Chambre de Discipline* established by the Royal Court of Guernsey.

The client's remedies are pecuniary. The Royal Court of Guernsey / *Chambre de Discipline* may separately discipline the advocate. There are no limits on compensation, other than in accordance with general principles that damages should be reflective of loss sustained.

*Restrictions on liability*

When appearing as advocate in or about the conduct of the case in court, an advocate is subject to immunity. In other circumstances there are no specific statutory or other restrictions preventing lawyers restricting or limiting their liability to clients. The extent of a lawyer's liability to his client is simply one of contractual negotiation. There are no restrictions on the limits of financial liability that may be agreed, save that in certain circumstances it is possible to envisage such agreements being declared void as a matter of public policy if, for example, unfair advantages were being taken of a client.

Agreements limiting financial liability are sometimes agreed, particularly in relation to the giving of formal written legal opinions.

Claims are prescribed six years after the date the cause of action arose.

*Liability to non-clients*

Lawyers may be liable to non-clients in two circumstances:

- to persons other than their clients who have been led by them to rely on their special skill and judgment;
- to other persons who, by reason of the nature of the matter the subject of the lawyer's retainer, the lawyer owes a duty of care (for example beneficiaries under a will).

*Recent developments with respect to liability*

At the time of writing this book there have been no developments or trends in this area.

### Insurance

*Voluntary professional indemnity insurance*
Indemnity insurance for the legal profession is voluntary in the Channel Islands.

It is likely that all independent advocates in private practice carry some level of professional indemnity insurance cover. Of the advocates employed in industry it is believed that none carry individual cover.

*Insurance facilities*
Firms either negotiate individual policies with commercial insurers or take out insurance direct with underwriters.

The insurance is generally obtained locally, in England, or is negotiated direct with Lloyds.

*Level of cover*
The level of cover is wholly within the discretion of the individual firm. The largest firms typically maintain cover of between USD7 to USD15 million for all claims within a policy period.

The insurance premium payable is estimated to be approximately five per cent of the annual expenses of a practice.

*Deductibles*
There is limited information available to indicate the range of deductibles payable by insured lawyers. The likely range is between USD15,000 and USD90,000.

*Recent developments with respect to insurance*
There are no recent developments or trends in this area.

## CHILE

### The civil liability of legal advisers

*Basis of liability*
Unless otherwise agreed, lawyers' liability is decided according to the degree of skill and care to be expected of an average competent lawyer. The basic principles regarding this matter are established by law although the judges have power to interpret or broaden the meaning and application of the law.

When it comes to bringing out an action against a lawyer such action should be brought in court. Upon bringing the complaint to court, the plaintiff usually obtains only monetary compensation. If the action of the lawyer may result in further damage for the claimant, an injunction or provisional remedy may be sought. In addition, the claimant may file a complaint with the Chilean Lawyer Association with a view to disciplinary measures being taken against the lawyer. However, that is only possible if the lawyer concerned is a member of the Association and membership is not mandatory.

There are no financial limits on the amount of compensation that the lawyer may be ordered to pay. The amount of the compensation will be based on the value of the damage caused to the plaintiff.

*Restrictions on liability*
Lawyers can limit their liability for a particular matter or generally, by way of standard conditions. Those agreements are uncommon. The disclaimer of liability is not valid in regard to wilful misconduct. Otherwise there are no restrictions, by statute or otherwise, which prevent lawyers from limiting their liability to clients.

Pursuant to Chilean law, the time limit for the client to claim contractual malpractice or negligence on the part of the lawyer is five years; the statute of limitations for negligence (in tort) is four years.

*Liability to non-clients*
Lawyers may be liable to non-clients only if they are responsible for criminal or tortious actions.

*Recent developments with respect to liability*
Many claims have been filed in court seeking monetary compensation, but for injuries caused by medical malpractice.

**Insurance**

*Voluntary professional indemnity insurance*
Indemnity insurance for the legal profession is voluntary in Chile.

*Insurance facilities*
Insurance is generally obtained from local commercial insurers.

*Level of cover*
Statistics are not available to indicate the level of cover generally obtained by the legal profession.

But, as for medical practitioners, the insurance policies provide a maximum level of cover of approximately USD120,000, which is an aggregate amount for all claims within the policy period.

*Deductibles*
There are no statistics available on the range of deductibles payable by the insured lawyers.

*Recent developments with respect to insurance*
At the time of writing this book there are no new trends or potential developments in the area of insurance which may significantly alter the framework summarised above.

## CHINA

### The civil liability of legal advisers

*Basis of liability*
There is currently no legislation in force governing lawyers' liability to their clients in the People's Republic of China (PRC). The PRC promulgated "Provisional Regulations on Lawyers" which were made effective as of January 1, 1982. Unfortunately, the Law is silent on the liability of lawyers.

Recently, there have been a number of discussions by the authorities to promulgate a revised "Legal Profession Law" which will not only regulate the admission of lawyers but also their conduct and duty to their clients. Until such time as that law is promulgated there will continue to be a void in the PRC legal system.

Legal practice in the PRC is based on principles of equality, mutual benefit, honesty, fairness and justice. A lawyer enters into a contract of engagement with his client, in which the terms of service and liability are mutually agreed. There is an implied understanding that the lawyer will use legal means to protect and further the interests of his client and will not compromise his duty to the client for personal self-gain. Above all the lawyer has a duty to protect the interests of the State. It is often the case that a client does not consider what recourse he can take if a lawyer that he instructs does not carry out his duties properly. Liability is, however, based on what is considered fair and just in the circumstances of the case.

These principles are implied generally in PRC legislation although it contains no specific reference to the conduct of lawyers. Such principles can also be gleaned from court decisions and government directives.

The liability of lawyers is in most instances decided solely by the courts or by arbitration tribunals if a dispute is so referred. No other body has power to adjudicate on liability although it is possible in some instances that power may be delegated to a state organisation which has lawyers under its charge. It is nonetheless still open to the complainant or the lawyer to seek recourse in the courts. Administrative sanctions may be imposed by officials of state-run organisations (law offices) and in some instances by officers of the judicial bureau in the locality where the lawyer is registered. There is, however, no separate and independent investigation into a complaint by any state designated or legal/professional body.

Relief is usually provided in the form of monetary compensation, although specific performance where applicable may be ordered. Mandatory orders are imposed with a view of achieving fairness, usually providing benefit to the client. Financial compensation from a law office which enjoys the status of a legal entity is limited to the assets of the law practice. Otherwise, the liability of lawyers who do not constitute a legal entity will be borne personally and will be limited to the assets of the organisation of which the lawyer is a member.

Most financial compensation is awarded by the courts in the PRC and as it is relatively low, it may be substituted by or made alongside punitive sanctions such as cancellation of a practice licence or imprisonment.

*Restrictions on liability*

There are no restrictions as to the circumstances where lawyers may be held liable to their clients. Arguably a lawyer would be exempt if he shows that the complaint raised was caused through no fault of his own or was the result of compliance with PRC law.

Lawyers can by agreement limit their liability in all of the circumstances described. Where liability can be limited, almost any form of financial restrictions can be agreed; for example loss or damage which is remote can be excluded. Such agreements at present only occur sometimes.

There are no restrictions on lawyers limiting their liability, although in practice any attempt to do so where it is clearly unfair to the client may be struck out as being void.

Proceedings against lawyers must be instituted within two years from the time the action arose or at the time the client should have known he had a claim.

*Liability to non-clients*

Lawyers cannot be made liable to non-clients, but there is a rule that lawyers in the PRC have a duty to treat as confidential any state or personal secrets which might come to their knowledge in the course of work. This could raise an actionable breach of confidence in non-client situations.

*Recent developments with respect to liability*

As mentioned above, the PRC is currently drafting legislation on lawyers' liability.

## Insurance

*Professional indemnity insurance*

There is no professional indemnity insurance available for the legal profession in the People's Republic of China.

## COLOMBIA

### The civil liability of legal advisers

*Basis of liability*
In accordance with the principles of Colombian law, primarily the Colombian Civil Code, and the jurisprudence of the Colombian Supreme Court, the liability of a lawyer towards his client is a contractual liability based in the first place on the rules contained in the Civil Code regulating the Mandate which the Code defines as "a contract whereby a person entrusts the handling of one or more of his affairs to another one who will handle such affairs for the account and the risk of the first person". The Code expressly provides that:

> The services of professionals and those whose careers require lengthy studies, where the capacity to represent and obligate a given person in respect to third parties exists, are subject to the rules of the Mandate (..), when such services are remunerated, the attorney will be liable for slight negligence in the performance of his duties.

In accordance with such rules, the attorney must fulfil his obligation in good faith with special care and diligence and in accordance with the instructions and terms of the Mandate. His liability will extend to the acts required for the fulfilment of the obligations.

In the case of attorneys, the statute that regulates the profession establishes specific ethical guidelines for the practice of law. The statute requires that attorneys must perform their duties with dignity and decorum, cooperate with the administration of justice, respect public officials and assistants, act with loyalty and honesty, maintain confidential the information obtained from their clients and attend with utmost diligence to their professional duties.

In summary, the liability of an attorney will derive from a "slight negligence" in the performance of his duties based on the general principles that govern the mandate in the Civil Code and the ethical provisions contained in the statute that regulates the profession.

The liability is decided by a court of law as distinct from any disciplinary actions decreed by the "Disciplinary Tribunal" of the legal profession which extends from public admonition to the partial or total suspension of the attorney's licence.

Under the Colombian system, the plaintiff can be awarded material and moral damages, the former being "direct damages" and "loss of revenue" as duly evidenced in court. Moral damages are imposed by the judge but limited to the equivalent of one thousand grams of gold. The Colombian system does not provide for punitive damages.

There are no limits other than the direct damages and loss of revenue that the plaintiff can evidence to the court's satisfaction. The damages are assessed in the proceedings by court-appointed experts but it is ultimately up to the judge, taking all facts into consideration, to decide on the level of damages including any moral damages.

*Restrictions on liability*

In certain cases, such as when an attorney is to appear on behalf of a client to answer questionnaires produced in court proceedings or when attorneys act as directors in a Board meeting representing the client, he may request an indemnity letter giving him a specific immunity.

Although there are no legal obstacles to limiting liability in the general rules of the Civil Code governing "mandate agreements" and "contractual liability", such agreements are extremely rare. Along the same lines the parties could pre-determine in a contract the maximum amounts for losses direct and loss of revenue damages, or provide for fines in lieu of such damages. Any attempt to limit liability for gross negligence or wilful misconduct would be void.

The Statute of Limitations for damages based on the general rules of the Colombian Civil Code imposes a twenty year limit; the disciplinary sanctions that may be imposed by the Disciplinary Tribunal have a limitation of two years.

*Liability to non-clients*

The attorney will be liable for damages caused in the performance of his duties in the case of tortious conduct to third parties including the opposing party.

*Recent developments with respect to liability*

At this date, there is no development taking place which may significantly alter the position.

**Insurance**

*Voluntary professional indemnity insurance*

Indemnity insurance for the legal profession is voluntary in Colombia.

It is very rare for the legal profession to take out professional indemnity insurance.

*Insurance facilities*

As stated above, the statute of limitations for taking action against a lawyer is twenty years while the statute of limitations for actions derived from insurance policies is two years. This makes it extremely difficult to find a system that effectively protects the insured.

The matter is further complicated by the fact that the Colombian system provides that in such policies the damage occurs at the time the underlying incident occurs, whereas the prevailing system today in common-law countries is to consider that the loss occurred when it was discovered, even where the incident took place at an early date.

Under these circumstances, and due to the fact that Colombian insurance companies offer an extremely limited cover, only for specific judicial actions, the Superintendency of Banks (the official entity that supervises all matters related to insurance companies) has authorised Colombian law firms to contract direct with foreign insurance companies, waiving the requirements that insurance must be obtained from domestic insurance companies and that a specific policy must be authorized by the Superintendency of Banks.

*Level of cover*
There are no statistics available to indicate the level of cover obtained by the legal profession.

*Deductibles*
There are no statistics available on the range of deductibles payable by the insured lawyers.

*Recent developments with respect to insurance*
There are many groups in Colombia interested in finding a solution for the insurance difficulties. Due to the fact that an adequate solution would require adoption of a specific law regulating the liability of the legal profession, we do not expect a solution in the near future.

## CYPRUS

### The civil liability of legal advisers

*Basis of liability*
There are no legal principles which specifically govern lawyers' liability to their clients for advice rendered and for the conduct of their cases. Consequently, lawyers' liability is governed by the general principles of negligence.

Lawyers' liability towards their clients is not strict, but like other forms of negligence, is judged according to the degree of skill and care which is expected of a reasonably prudent person qualified to practise the profession.

The basic principles of the law of negligence are set out in the Civil Wrongs Law but in interpreting and applying this statute the courts will also be guided and be bound to follow precedents established in prior court cases. Under certain conditions, the Cyprus courts will follow or be guided by English court decisions.

The liability of lawyers is a matter solely decided by the courts and professional bodies have no jurisdiction in this respect. The relief available is not restricted to compensation but could take the form of mandatory or other orders. There are no financial limits on the compensation which lawyers may be ordered to pay.

*Restrictions on liability*
There are no restrictions as to the circumstances in which lawyers may be held liable to their clients.

In principle, lawyers may limit their liability towards their clients by means of an appropriate agreement reached between themselves and the clients. The effectiveness of any limitation or exclusion clause will, however, be subject to the rules of interpretation governing such clauses generally. The agreement limiting liability may be for a particular matter or generally and would not be affected by way of standard conditions, statute or the directive of any professional body. Since the limitation of liability is a matter for agreement between the two parties, there are no financial restrictions on the limitation that can be agreed. Such agreements are rarely made, if at all.

There are no restrictions by statute or otherwise which prevent lawyers restricting their liability to their clients. All time limits for making civil claims or instituting proceedings in Cyprus have been suspended and there is therefore no time limit within which claims or actions against lawyers must be instituted.

*Liability to non-clients*
According to the Civil Wrongs Law, a person, exercising a profession or rendering a service, whether for reward or otherwise, owes a duty not be negligent to any person upon whom, or upon whose property, or to whom he is exercising his profession or rendering a service. It is therefore very unlikely that a situation will arise whereby a lawyer will be liable to non-clients.

*Recent developments with respect to liability*
There are no current trends or developments in Cyprus which will modify the framework summarised in the above answers.

**Insurance**

*Voluntary professional indemnity insurance*
Indemnity insurance for the legal profession is voluntary in Cyprus.

A very small proportion of the legal profession (estimated as being only one per cent of all lawyers) takes out professional indemnity insurance.

*Insurance facilities*
Available for insurance are policies issued by commercial insurers. The available insurance is very limited as it is offered by few insurance companies.

The insurance may only be obtained from local authorised insurers.

*Level of cover*
There are no statistics available to indicate the level of cover generally obtained by the legal profession. The level of cover is estimated to be in the region of USD100,000.

*Deductibles*
There are no statistics available on the range of deductibles payable by the insured lawyers.

*Recent developments with respect to insurance*
At the time of writing this book there are no new trends or potential developments in the area of insurance which may significantly alter the framework summarised above.

## DENMARK

### The civil liability of legal advisers

*Basis of liability*
In Denmark, lawyers' liability is based upon the normal rules relating to liability for negligent acts or omissions. When deciding whether an act or omission is negligent it will be taken into consideration whether the lawyer has acted with the degree of skill and care to be expected by a competent lawyer.

Strict liability exists for the lawyer with respect to his staff, that is the lawyer is liable for negligent acts or omissions committed by the staff.

The principles for liability are defined by court decisions and only the courts have jurisdiction. All Danish lawyers are required by legislation to be members of the Danish Bar Association. The Danish Bar Association may issue statements as to what it considers to be good conduct of a lawyer. Such statements are, however, not binding on the courts.

The only relief available to a client is compensation. A client may, however, also make a complaint to the disciplinary committee of the Danish Bar Association, which may punish the lawyer in question. However, the disciplinary board cannot grant any relief to the client.

*Restrictions on liability*
In principle no financial limits exist with respect to the compensation but as a general rule liability may be limited or even waived if it is considered especially burdensome or other reasons may make this reasonable. The decision is left to the courts. The factors to be taken into consideration will be the size of the compensation, the degree of negligence, the interest of the tortfeasor, the interest of the claimant, the insurance position and any other relevant circumstances.

A lawyer cannot limit his liability for matters of law. In cases where the relevant law is unclear the lawyer may qualify his opinion and thereby limit any possible liability. Otherwise a lawyer cannot by agreement limit any liability he may have to his client.

The normal time limit for commencing an action is five years, calculated from the day when the act or ommission took place. Normally the error will not be detected until some time after it has been made. The five year limitation period, therefore, in practice, starts when the error is detected or ought to have been detected. Irrespective of when the error comes to light, liability expires twenty years after the act or omission took place.

*Liability to non-clients*

Normally the lawyer is not liable towards non-clients. The lawyer may, however, be held liable to non-clients in certain cases where the lawyer is deemed to act on behalf of both parties. Examples might include a lawyer who prepares a mortgage deed which is not as agreed between the parties, a lawyer who handles a sale of real estate in a wrong manner so that the other party suffers a loss, a lawyer who does not take the appropriate steps to secure an assignment of a receivable. The cases in which a lawyer can be held responsible to non-clients are characterized by the fact that the lawyer has an obligation to secure the interests of both parties in the matter, which he has undertaken.

*Recent developments with respect to liability*

There are no special trends which may alter the framework summarized above. The only tendency which can be mentioned is towards a more aggressive climate for claiming compensation from lawyers.

## Insurance

*Compulsory professional indemnity insurance*

Indemnity insurance for the legal profession is compulsory in Denmark. All lawyers are required by statute to be members of the Danish Bar Association, and the Danish Bar Association has decided that indemnity insurance is compulsory for its members.

*Insurance facilities*

Indemnity insurance is taken out with commercial insurers according to policies approved by the Danish Bar Association.

For lawyers who cannot take out an insurance with a commercial insurer — for example, because of non-payment of premiums or because of a history of many previous liability cases — the Danish Bar Association operates a scheme to secure the clients. The lawyer pays a premium equal to the premium he would have had to pay a commercial insurer.

Insurance may be obtained from insurers within Denmark or abroad. Normally the insurance is obtained from insurers within the country. One insurance company (Codan) has a market share of approximately seventy per cent.

*Level of cover*

The standard commercial policy insures only the liability a lawyer incurs in his capacity as a lawyer working in Denmark. Both intentional acts and acts of gross negligence are excluded.

The minimum obligatory cover is approximately USD166,000. Additional cover may be taken up, generally to about USD1 million. Large law firms take out a cover of USD16.6 million or more.

Up to approximately USD1 million, the cover is a maximum for each claim. For cover exceeding this, it is an aggregate for all claims within a policy period.

The insurance premium for a small practice ranges between one and two per cent of the annual expenses of a practice and is less than one per cent for large law firms. The insurance premium for the compulsory cover is approximately USD4,100 per year per lawyer.

*Deductibles*

The first ten per cent of a claim is self-insured by the lawyer, usually with a minimum of USD1,833 and a maximum of USD19,000. The lawyer may take out insurance with a higher deductible and pay less insurance premium.

*Recent developments with respect to insurance*

As something unique to Denmark, indemnity insurance covers the lawyer in his capacity as a member of a board of directors.

Until recently, such cover was insured under the standard cover and under the excess cover. In future, the liability for a lawyer acting in his capacity as a member of a board of directors will no longer be covered by the excess cover but only by the standard cover (up to a maximum of approximately USD1 million per claim). This restriction is caused by the increase in the number and level of claims for compensation from directors.

To obtain full cover for liability as a member of a board of directors, it is now necessary to take out a special excess-policy or insurance which covers the directorship of a specific company.

## ECUADOR

### The civil liability of legal advisers

*Basis of liability*

The concept of strict liability does not exist in Ecuadorean legislation and thus is not applicable to lawyers' advice or conduct. Lawyers' professional liability is governed by general principles of civil responsibility pursuant to the Ecuadorean Civil Code since there are no provisions which refer specifically to lawyers' duties and liabilities except for regulations of the National Federation of Lawyers that have the force of law. According to the Civil Code, a duty arises either:

- by a meeting of the minds of two or more persons, as in a contract;
- by a voluntary act of one person who assumes a duty, as in the case of an heir or in quasi-contracts;
- as a result of an act that has caused injury or harm to another person, as in an offence, an illicit act done with the intent to harm, or a quasi-offence, an illicit act but with no intent to harm; or
- by operation of law, as between parents and children.

The Civil Code establishes degrees of care for persons with certain duties. Within the express or implicit service contract between a lawyer and his client, and considering the fiduciary relationship that is established and the degree of trust and responsibility given by the latter to the former, a lawyer would be responsible under the Ecuadorean system, not only for serious fault or negligence but also for anything constituting mild fault or negligence, which constitutes "fault in or lack of the extraordinary care that a prudent man uses in the management of his most important business."

In addition to the above standards of care and responsibility set forth in the Civil Code, the Organic Law on the Judiciary prohibits lawyers from engaging in any of the following:

- disclosing their clients' secrets, documents or instructions;
- abandoning, without just cause, the cases they are representing;
- guaranteeing their clients success in a suit;
- representing one side after having represented the other or acted as a judge;
- authorizing by means of their signature documents prepared by others.

The Supreme Court has the power to order the suspension of a lawyer in his professional capacity wherever the law so permits. In those cases, the decision reached by the Supreme Court is not subject to appeal.

Case law is not binding precedent under the Ecuadorean legal system, except where the Cassation Court, the highest court, reaches the same holding three times on a particular matter. Nonetheless, cases are used as references especially those decided by higher courts. In any event, there are no cases on lawyers' liability for advice given for the conduct of matters. In addition to the courts, which have the power to determine lawyers' civil or criminal liability, each provincial law bar

(*Colegio de Abogados*) possesses an Honor Tribunal made up of lawyers and charged with judging its members' professional conduct in the event of a written complaint. This professional control mechanism is without prejudice of additional civil and criminal actions .

A Tribunal's decision may be appealed to the Central Board of Directors of the national Federation of Lawyers.

*Restrictions on liability*

Relief available in cases of lawyers' liability, as in civil responsibility claims generally, is restricted to compensation. There is no relief by way of mandatory or other orders imposed for the benefit the client. Ecuadorean law contains no monetary limits on the compensation which lawyers may be ordered to pay. Nonetheless, the Civil Code limits the remedies any person may recover for breach of duty to direct damages and lost profits. In some circumstances, the law will grant remedy for emotional distress when such remedy is justified by the seriousness of the damage or of the breach.

There are no restrictions as to the circumstance under which lawyers may be held liable to their clients. Lawyers could by agreement with their clients limit their civil liability for a particular matter or by way of standard conditions. According to law, however, lawyers and their clients cannot agree to limit liability arising from any future intent to harm or from criminal liability.

The statute of limitations applicable to ordinary civil claims is ten years.

*Liability to non-clients*

A lawyer will be liable not only to his client but to third parties who benefit from, live in or use a client's harmed property in cases where a lawyer has committed a tort (*quasi-offence*) or a criminal offence which harmed that property. Under Ecuadorean law a *quasi-offence* occurs where there was fault but no intention to harm.

*Recent developments with respect to liability*

At the time of writing this book there are no new trends or potential developments which may significantly alter the framework summarised above.

**Insurance**

*Voluntary professional indemnity insurance*

Indemnity insurance for the legal profession is voluntary in Ecuador. Until this date, no lawyer or law firm has taken out professional indemnity insurance.

*Insurance facilities*
Available for insurance are policies issued by commercial insurers from abroad. Obtaining insurance from abroad requires prior authorization from the Superintendency of Banks.

*Level of cover*
Local insurance brokers offer foreign policies with a maximum per claim coverage of USD200,000, USD500,000 or USD1 million. This cover is significantly in excess of any compensation likely to be claimed in an Ecuadorean court.

*Deductibles*
A typical foreign professional liability insurance policy available through insurance brokers in Ecuador contains a USD50,000 deductible payable by the insured lawyers.

*Recent developments with respect to insurance*
At the time of writing this book there are no new trends or potential developments in the area of insurance which may significantly alter the framework summarised above.

## EGYPT

### The civil liability of legal advisers

*Basis of liability*
A lawyer is to be judged by the standards of a reasonably competent professional man. Lawyers' liability to their clients in respect of advice given and the conduct of matters is decided according to the degree of skill and care to be expected of a competent lawyer. The client expects his lawyer's advice to be given carefully and in accordance with the particular skill or knowledge that the lawyer holds himself out as possessing.

The guiding principles of lawyers' liability to their clients are defined by the Civil Code, the Code of Advocacy, the by-laws and Internal Regulations of the Bar Association. To his clients the lawyer owes duties of care both in contract as an implied term and in tort as a duty imposed by law. The duty between a professional and his client is not of a purely contractual nature. For breach of that duty he is liable in damages, and they are the same, whether he is sued in contract or in tort. A lawyer may thus be sued in contract by a client who suffers loss or damage from the failure of the professional to provide the agreed degree of skill and care.

The liability of a lawyer is a matter that is decided by courts in the civil actions brought by his client regarding the lawyer's contractual duties.

The disciplining of lawyers comes under the jurisdiction of a council made up of the President of the Cairo Court of Appeal or his deputy and two of the counsellors of the court appointed by its general meeting every year and two members of the board of the Bar Association, one of whom is selected by the lawyer against whom the disciplinary action is raised and the other by the board of the Bar Association.

The relief available, for the benefit of the client, is restricted to compensation. There are no financial limits on the compensation which lawyers may be ordered to pay, but such compensation should be compatible with the damage suffered. There are no mandatory or other orders to be imposed on the lawyer. A lawyer who violates the Code of Advocacy or the by-laws of the Bar Association, who is in breach of the duties of his profession, who performs an act demeaning to the honour of the legal profession or who commits a shameful act which derogates from its prestige may be subject to various disciplinary penalties.

*Restrictions on liability*

With the exception of cases of gross negligence and misconduct, lawyers may by agreement with their clients limit their liability generally in accordance with statutes and financial restriction may also be agreed upon by the parties. However, such agreements are rarely made.

The only limitations which prevent lawyers restricting their liability to their clients are those governed by the general principle of law regarding specific performance. The Egyptian Civil Code provides that:

> Subject always to any provision of the law or agreement to the contrary in the case of an obligation to do something, a debtor who is required to preserve a thing, to manage it or to act with prudence in the performance of his obligation, satisfies his obligation if he brings to the performance thereof the care of the reasonable person, even if the object in view is not achieved. The debtor always remains liable for fraud or gross negligence.

The time limits for making claims or instituting proceedings against lawyers are governed by the general rule in the Egyptian Civil Code regarding the prescription of actions for damages. If the damage arises from the lawyer's breach of his contractual obligations, an action for damages is prescribed after fifteen years. But an action for damages arising from a tortious act is prescribed after three years from the date upon which the victim knew of the injury and the identity of the person who was responsible. An action for damages is prescribed in any case after fifteen years from the date on which the act was committed. When a claim arises out of a penal offence and the penal action is not prescribed after the aforementioned delays, the action for damages is only prescribed when the penal action itself is prescribed.

*Liability to non-clients*

A lawyer owes both a contractual duty of care to his clients and a tortious duty of care to clients and others that may be expected to rely, or do rely, on the skill and judgement he possesses. A lawyer may be liable to non-clients by breaching his tortious duty of care and causing damage by his act, his negligence or his imprudence in observing the principles of probity and rectitude in his professional and personal conduct, imposed on him by the provisions of the Code of Criminal Procedures, the Code of Civil and Commercial Procedures and the Code of Advocacy.

*Recent developments with respect to liability*
In Egypt there are no general developments which may significantly alter the position as set out above.

**Insurance**

*Voluntary professional indemnity insurance*
Indemnity insurance for the legal profession is voluntary in Egypt. Only a small proportion of the legal profession takes out professional indemnity insurance.

*Insurance facilities*
Available for insurance are policies issued by commercial insurers. Generally, insurance has to be obtained from insurers within the country. An exception is made when it is impossible to obtain insurance locally. In that case, the Egyptian Insurance Supervisory Authority may authorize insurance policies from foreign insurance companies.

*Level of cover*
There are no statistics available to indicate the level of cover generally obtained by the legal profession.

The cover may either be an aggregate for all the claims within the policy period or a maximum for each claim.

*Deductibles*
There are no statistics available on the range of deductibles payable by the insured lawyers.

*Recent developments with respect to insurance*
According to information from the Egyptian Insurance Supervisory Authority a draft is being prepared for a new insurance law. If the law is passed, it will no longer be prohibited to obtain insurance from abroad for matters which can be insured locally. This new law will make it possible to obtain commercial insurance either from insurers within the country or from abroad.

## ENGLAND AND WALES

### The civil liability of legal advisers

*Basis of liability*
If a solicitor breaches the terms of his retainer (the contract of engagement with his client), then he will be liable to his client for any loss suffered by reason of the breach. The duties owed by a solicitor to his client under the terms of his retainer include a duty to exercise reasonable skill and care in performing the retainer. In the absence of any express provision, this duty is implied into the retainer by statute. The extent of that duty is defined principally by decided cases.

It is now also generally accepted that, in addition to his contractual obligations, a solicitor owes a duty of care in tort to his client to exercise reasonable skill and care in advising the client or performing services on the client's behalf. If a solicitor breaches his tortious duty of care to his client, and as a result his client suffers foreseeable loss, the solicitor will be liable to his client for such loss. The standard of skill and care which the court will apply is that of the "reasonably competent solicitor". A solicitor is not to be judged by the standard of a particularly meticulous and conscientious member of the profession. The question of whether a solicitor has failed in his duty to exercise reasonable skill and care will depend on the facts of each particular case. A number of general obligations may, however, be identified. For example, a solicitor must keep his client informed of and advise him on all matters relevant to his retainer, to the extent reasonably necessary. He must protect his client's interests and carry out his client's instructions by all necessary means.

As his agent, a solicitor owes fiduciary duties to his client. In general, this means that a solicitor cannot do anything which abuses the special position in which he is placed by virtue of his relationship with his client. More specifically, the fiduciary duties owed by a solicitor to his client include duties, in respect of any matter upon which he is advising, to account for client's property which comes into his hands, not to make a secret profit, and to make full disclosure of any interest that he may have in that matter.

There is no contract between a client and his barrister nor, by convention, is there a contract between a barrister and the solicitor who has instructed him. (Thus, for example the barrister cannot sue the solicitor for his unpaid fees.) Claims against barristers are therefore generally framed in tort rather than in contract, in many instances with the initial claim made against the solicitor who then joins in the barrister for a contribution or indemnity. The immunity from suit of the advocate in court, referred to below, is of course particularly important for the barrister.

Although the liability of solicitors to others is principally a matter for the courts, the professional practice and conduct of solicitors is regulated by their professional body, the Law Society, and governed by the Solicitors' Practice Rules. They are supplemented by the Guide to the Professional Conduct of Solicitors published and updated from time to time by the Law Society. Together, they set out, *inter alia*, specific principles governing a solicitor's relationship with his client and impose obligations, for example, to set up a proper complaints procedure, to avoid conflicts of interest, and to keep clients' affairs confidential. These principles provide useful guidance to the courts in determining whether, in certain cases, a solicitor should be held liable to his client.

Professional misconduct on the part of a solicitor may render him liable to disciplinary proceedings. The court has an inherent disciplinary jurisdiction over solicitors which is confirmed by statute. Disciplinary powers are more commonly exercised, however, by the Solicitors' Disciplinary Tribunal. Disciplinary powers which may be exercised by the court and the Tribunal include powers to remove or suspend a solicitor from practice, or to fine him. They also include a power to direct a solicitor to rectify any error, omission or deficiency on his part, or to take such other action in the interests of the client as may be necessary.

In addition, where any person has suffered loss or hardship in consequence of a solicitor's dishonesty, the Law Society may grant compensation to that person out of the Solicitors' Compensation Fund. The Compensation Fund is funded by levies on the profession.

In any claim founded upon the tort of negligence or upon breach of contract, the client's usual remedy will be an award of damages. Damages will be awarded to place the client in the position he would have been in had the breach not taken place (i.e. to compensate the client for the foreseeable loss caused to him).

The remedies available to a client for breach of fiduciary duty by a solicitor are in the discretion of the court, and are not necessarily limited to compensation. For example, if a solicitor acting on a transaction fails to disclose to his client facts material to that transaction, then he may be liable for any loss suffered by the client on the transaction, regardless of whether, had he known such facts, he would still have entered the transaction. Under "Recent developments with respect to liability" below we refer to the attempt to claim against solicitors for breach of trust.

Where a solicitor's services are such that, as matters turn out, they are of no value to his client, then the solicitor will be prevented from recovering his professional fees (or ordered to repay any such fees received from the client).

Where damages would be an insufficient remedy for the client, then alternative remedies may be available. For example, if a solicitor has omitted to take certain steps in breach of his duty to his client, and the client has thereby suffered loss which cannot adequately be compensated by damages, then specific performance may be available. Similarly, if a client suspects that a solicitor is about to breach his duty of confidentiality, damages will be an insufficient remedy, and the client may be able to obtain an injunction to restrain the anticipated breach.

There are no financial limits on the damages which a solicitor may be ordered to pay to his client.

*Restrictions on liability*

A solicitor will have an absolute defence to any claim for breach of duty and/or contract arising from the conduct of his client's case in court as an advocate. This principle extends to any pre-trial work which is "so intimately connected with the conduct of the cause in court that it can fairly be said to be a preliminary decision affecting the way that a cause is to be conducted when it comes to a hearing". It has been expressly confirmed by statute that a solicitor's immunity from suit in this respect is the same as a barrister's.

Any claims which may properly be considered an abuse of the court process will not be upheld. In the case of solicitors, claims have been held to be an abuse of process where they would involve a re-examination of the final decision of another court. This would be the case, for example, where a convicted client claims that, had he been advised properly by his solicitor, he would not have been convicted.

Where a solicitor has acted in accordance with a barrister's advice, he will not be held liable to his client for any wrong advice given by counsel. There are a number of exceptions to this general principle :

- a solicitor will be liable if, on counsel's advice, he acts contrary to his client's express instructions;
- a solicitor will be liable if he fails properly to instruct counsel, or if his choice of counsel is clearly not competent:
- recently, the courts have recognised that a solicitor should not be entitled merely to accept counsel's advice without question. A solicitor may therefore be liable where it is, or ought reasonably to be, clear to him that counsel's advice is misconceived.

Where a client suffers loss by reason of a solicitor acting on his express instructions, he will have no claim against the solicitor, provided that the solicitor has properly advised him on the consequences of his chosen course of action and ensured that such advice has been understood by him.

The Law Society's Statement on Limitation of Liability by Contract disapproves of any attempt by a solicitor to exclude altogether liability to his client. The Statement considers it acceptable, however, for a solicitor to seek to limit his liability to his client, provided that such limitation is not less than the minimum level of cover required from time to time by the Solicitor's Indemnity Rules, currently USD1.5 million per firm per claim. Any such limitation of liability must, however, be brought to the client's attention and be understood and accepted by him (preferably in writing).

Any attempt by a solicitor to limit his liability to his client is subject to the general position in law. In particular, liability for fraud or reckless disregard for professional obligations may not be limited and existing legal requirements for solicitors cannot be varied or abrogated by agreement with the client.

Furthermore, any limitation by a solicitor of liability is subject to the provisions of the Unfair Contract Terms Act 1977. Under that Act, a contract term will be of no effect unless it satisfies the "reasonableness test". The contract term must be fair and reasonable having regard to all circumstances known to the parties, or which ought reasonably to have been in their contemplation, when the contract was made. Where a contract term seeks to limit liability to a specific sum, such circumstances include the resources which the person seeking to impose the limitation might expect to be available to him to meet any liability and the availability of insurance to cover such liability.

Where a solicitor undertakes any work involving proceedings before a court or arbitrator, any attempted complete exemption by the solicitor in his retainer of liability for negligence or breach of duty is void and unenforceable.

Claims based upon both the tort of negligence and breach of contract will be statute-barred if not brought within six years from the date upon which the cause of action accrued. By an amending statute an additional time limit of three years from the date of "discovery" has been added, but with a long stop maximum of fifteen years from the date of the negligent act or omission.

*Liability to non-clients*

The doctrine of privity of contract, whereby only parties to a contract may sue upon it, prevents claims by non-clients founded upon breach of the retainer between the solicitor and his client. In certain circumstances, however, a solicitor may owe a duty of care in tort to a non-client and may therefore be held liable to that non-client for breach of such duty. Where a solicitor negligently gives incorrect advice which is relied upon by a non-client to his detriment, then he may be held liable to that non-client for any loss suffered. A duty of care will only arise, however, where the solicitor is aware that the advice is required by the non-client for a specific purpose, and that such advice is likely to be communicated to the non-client and relied upon by him for that purpose. A duty of care will only be imposed in such circumstances where the non-client has acted reasonably in relying upon the solicitor's advice. Reliance will not be found reasonable, for example, where the non-client has sought independent advice himself, or where he has a remedy against the solicitor's client.

A solicitor will in some circumstances owe a duty of care to a non-client, notwithstanding that there is no reliance upon the solicitor's advice by the non-client, where the solicitor is instructed by his client to undertake work which is intended to confer a benefit on an identifiable non-client. In such circumstances, it is foreseeable to the solicitor that, if the work is performed negligently, then the non-client will suffer loss. The only decided case on this concerns a solicitor instructed by his client to prepare a will and, owing to his negligence, loss is suffered by the beneficiaries under the will. It remains to be seen whether liability to non-clients (who also do not rely on the solicitor) will be established in actions other than those of a disappointed beneficiary.

A solicitor who is negligent in the conduct of litigation may be held liable to the opposing party for any wasted costs caused by his negligent conduct. The courts have tended to take the view, however, that the solicitor's liability in such circumstances arises not from a breach of any duty to the opposing party, but from a breach of the solicitor's duty to the court.

A solicitor may be liable to his client's opponent in litigation for any loss caused to that party by reason of his negligent performance of a court order. Again, liability here arises from a breach of the solicitor's duties as an officer of the court. A solicitor may, however, owe a duty of care to the other side if he is negligent in performing an arrangement voluntarily agreed between the parties.

*Recent developments with respect to liability*

One recent development is the establishment of a solicitor's liability to intended beneficiaries under his clients' will (or intended will).

In a 1995 decision the House of Lords held that the intended beneficiaries may recover damages, amounting to the value of their legacies, from the solicitors who, through delay, negligently failed to carry into effect the testator's instructions to draw up a new will. The liability of the solicitor arises because of the breach of a special duty of care owed to intended beneficiaries to act with due expedition and care in effecting the testator's instructions. The House of Lords' decision by a majority, found a way of making negligent solicitors liable in tort to intended beneficiaries for having breached the contract of retainer between the solicitor and the testator. The court avoided establishing any right for a third party beneficiary to a contract to sue under the contract because of the lack of privity. It remains to be seen how far the Courts will extend this duty, if at all, in future cases.

A further recent trend has been an attempt to hold solicitors liable for breach of trust rather than for negligence where client's money has been paid away not in accordance with instructions. This approach avoids argument about contributory negligence and the foreseeability of damage that would otherwise arise. Whether the breach of trust authorities will be upheld on appeal will shortly be known.

## Insurance

*Compulsory professional indemnity insurance*

Professional indemnity insurance is compulsory for solicitors and barristers in England and Wales.

For solicitors, compulsory cover is required by rules made by the Council of the Law Society, which is in turn given the power to do so under statutory authority.

For barristers, compulsory cover is required by the Rules of the professional body, the Bar Council.

*Insurance facilities*

The facilities for insurance for solicitors are policies issued by commercial insurers and a compulsory mutual scheme introduced by the Law Society, providing the first layer of cover. The compulsory insurance cover is arranged through a scheme of mutual insurance arranged by the profession itself.

The compulsory first layer of cover for barristers is provided by the Bar Mutual Indemnity Fund. The cover is arranged through a scheme of mutual insurance managed by the Bar Mutual Management Company. Any top-up insurance is available from commercial insurers.

*Level of cover*

*Solicitors:* the compulsory scheme provides USD1.5 million cover for each and every claim, with an unlimited aggregate. For many smaller firms that is the only cover taken up. For the largest commercial firms involved in major transactions cover as high as USD300 million is taken up. To that level there are a variety of different terms. It would be unusual to have cover provided to this level on an each and every claim basis, without an aggregate. It is estimated that the cost of insurance cover represents five per cent of the annual expenses of a solicitor's practice.

*Barristers:* the compulsory scheme provides a minimum cover of USD375,000 and a maximum of USD3,750,000 for each barrister. The amount of cover taken is a matter for the choice of the individual member. Commercial Chambers no doubt take up substantial voluntary cover over and above USD3.75 million in the commercial market.

*Deductibles*

The range of deductibles for solicitors is from USD7,500 up to USD225,000 for the largest firms. To protect insureds against multiple claims these deductibles can only be applied three times in any one year.

No deductibles are payable by barristers under the mutual scheme.

*Recent developments with respect to insurance*

We expect no such developments for solicitors in the short term. There was a very substantial increase in premiums in the commercial market two years ago. The cost of obtaining adequate professional indemnity cover is now one of the major overhead expenses of a commercial firm. An issue that may develop over the next few years is whether the high cost of insurance, driven by an increased level of claims, will provoke a move towards increased use of contractual limitation of liability by solicitors.

There are no significant developments taking place at the present time for barristers.

## FINLAND

### The civil liability of legal advisers

*Basis of liability*

The responses stated in this report are reflective only of the practices and regulations adhered to by the members of the Finnish Bar Association. This report does not purport to be representative of other individuals that are engaged professionally or as non-professionals in the practice of law in Finland.

In Finland, lawyers, law firms, and law corporations are liable for damages arising from a breach of their contractual obligations to their clients. Seldom, however, are these obligations committed to precise terms when legal advice and assistance is rendered to clients. Normally lawyers are commissioned only orally, and aside from a description of the task with which lawyers have been entrusted the commissioning contracts do not record other terms.

In the absence of specific contractual terms, the lawyer's obligations arising from the contractual relationship with the client are defined by, among others, the rules of good professional conduct adopted by the Finnish Bar Association and the Advocates Act, which obligates members of the Association to abide by these rules of conduct. Members of this professional body are required by law to perform with integrity and conscientiously the tasks with which they have been entrusted as well as abide by good professional conduct in all of their activities. In general, Finnish courts have accepted the Bar Association's rules of good professional conduct as the professional standard of lawyers, even though these rules are not binding norms on the court.

In legal literature, the liability faced by a lawyer has been described as a mix of contractual liability and a form of professional liability defined by both lawyers' knowledge of the law and the confidential relationship established between the lawyer and the client. The public trust and stature enjoyed by lawyers generally entitles the client to rely on the professional abilities of individual lawyers.

The liability of a lawyer commissioned directly and specifically by the client is based on culpable negligence, which comprises a breach of contract. Generally, the point of departure in evaluating a lawyer's liability is not the results achieved or not achieved by the lawyer's performance of the commission entrusted to him or her, but the manner in which the lawyer performed the commission. Whether or not a lawyer has performed a commission in the correct manner is determined objectively on the basis of how a reasonable lawyer with the same qualifications and experience would have performed the commission. When the qualification requirements and supervision of the Finnish Bar Association are taken into account, a high degree of professional knowledge and diligence can be expected from a lawyer.

The distinction between law firms in the form of partnerships and law corporations is important for determining partner liabilities. All partners in a law firm partnership are jointly and severally liable for economic loss resulting from a contractual breach committed by themselves, their co-partners, or their assistants.

The liability of partners (i.e. shareholders) in a law corporation, however, varies depending on whether or not the partner (i.e. shareholder) is responsible directly or indirectly for the contractual breach. Since the concept of a law corporation is relatively new to the legal profession in Finland, a brief description is warranted.

As of April 1992, lawyers are permitted to establish limited liability companies ("law corporations") through which as sole shareholders they may offer legal advice and assistance to clients. To maintain a lawyer's personal responsibility for his or her activities, individual shareholders in such a law corporation are jointly and severally liable with the law corporation for activities falling within their sphere of responsibility. The area of responsibility for shareholding lawyers includes their own activities as well as the supervision and instruction of their assistants. Even though such "responsible partners" are not considered to be parties to the contract between the client and the law corporation, their liability is nevertheless, as a matter of law, the same as if they were parties to the contract. Additionally, all shareholders are jointly and severally liable with the law corporation for damage resulting from a contractual breach that cannot be attributed to a responsible partner or his or her assistants. This liability is referred to as anonymous liability.

Under the general law governing liability in contractual relationships, the liability of lawyers commissioned by the client includes an obligation to compensate the client for economic loss caused by a contractual breach, whether committed by themselves or their assistants. Due to the nature of the activities performed by lawyers, the extension of liability to lawyers for economic loss seldom presents a problem. Under the general law, lawyers' liability is in a sense quite strict since clients only need to demonstrate that damage has been caused as a consequence of the lawyer's act or omission. Once this has been established, to exculpate themselves the lawyer must prove that the damage did not result from his negligence.

In theory, a client may file for a mandatory injunction to compel a lawyer to perform an act required by a court order granted to the client against the lawyer. The likelihood of such a situation occurring is, however, remote, and, therefore, in practice, there is no other relief available to clients aside from compensation.

*Restrictions on liability*

The difference theory is adhered to when determining the amount of damages suffered by the client as result of a lawyer's negligence. According to this theory, a lawyer is liable to pay compensation only for damage that would not have occurred if the lawyer had not been negligent. If, for instance, a lawyer submits an application late and the application would not have been successful regardless of when it had been submitted, the lawyer would not be liable to pay compensation to the client since no damage has occurred according to the difference theory.

Compensation for injuries or loss suffered by a third party may be subject to the adjustment mechanism found in the Damages Act, which is not generally applicable in respect of contractual liability. According to this mechanism, compensation may be adjusted if the compensation is considered to be unreasonably severe in light of the financial status and other circumstances of both the responsible party and the party suffering the damage. If, however, the injury or loss was deliberately caused, compensation may not be adjusted unless special circumstances exist. There is open opinion that this compensation adjustment mechanism should also be applicable to compensation for damages arising from a contractual relationship. Though there is no statutory authority to directly support this opinion, recent trends in the courts and in legislation indicate that the application of the adjustment mechanism in contractual relationships may find support in the courts. However, in determining whether or not to adjust compensation, the nature of the lawyers' liability must be taken into account.

Lawyers' relationships with their clients are defined by the nature of the commission and the requirements of the profession. Any restrictions on lawyers' liability towards their clients must be interpreted within these seminal obligations. The use of contractual clauses restricting a lawyer's liability is not looked upon favourably. Though there are no statutory provisions prohibiting the use of such clauses, their use has traditionally been viewed within the profession to be unethical. Lawyers' statutory obligation to adhere to good professional conduct may not be contractually restricted.

Additionally, the Contracts Act contains a provision allowing courts in special circumstances to contravene the binding obligation of a contract. This provision may be used to mitigate or nullify a contractual clause restricting a lawyer's liability. Under the Act, Finnish courts are empowered, giving consideration to the objective and subjective circumstances prevalent during and after the conclusion of a contract, to mitigate or nullify contractual clauses that are inequitable or the fulfilment of which would result in inequities. If the court considers that the entire contract is inequitable as a result of a mitigated or nullified clause, the court may mitigate other provisions in the contract or terminate the entire contract.

The general limitation for making a claim for compensation is ten years, unless another statute *lex specialis* provides otherwise. This ten-year limitation applies to both claims for damages arising from a contractual relationship and for damages suffered by a third party. There exists a host of special statutes providing for periods of limitation shorter than the general ten years, for instance, the one-year protest period for accounts rendered.

*Liability to non-clients*

Lawyers are often appointed to such functions as bankruptcy estate or reorganization administrator, legal guardian, estate executor or executrix, member of a corporate body, liquidator, and arbitrator. These functions are considered essentially to constitute the activities performed by lawyers, and therefore members of the Finnish Bar Association appointed to these functions are required to adhere to the rules of good professional conduct.

Since lawyers appointed to a function by a corporation are considered to have entered into a contractual relationship with the relevant corporation, the professional liability of these lawyers is defined by the same general principles that determine the liability of lawyers commissioned by the client. Lawyers appointed to civil law functions by a court, however, are not considered to have entered into a contractual relationship, and therefore their liability is defined by the provisions in the law governing third-party liability. Many of these functions entail an increased standard of liability that often includes compensation for economic loss suffered by third parties.

Lawyers' liability towards non-clients is based primarily on the third-party liability rules established in the Damages Act and court rulings. Lawyers appointed to a special function are additionally subject to the relevant liability rules governing damages arising from an act or omission while performing the function. According to the Damages Act, which applies to non-contractual liability, a lawyer is liable for compensation for injury, whether to person or property, suffered by a non-client if the injury resulted from the lawyer's actions. The standard of negligence is based on both the lawyers' obligation to act in good faith and their obligation to adhere to good professional conduct in all their activities.

In contrast to the liability of lawyers towards their clients, a lawyer may be liable for pure economic loss suffered by a non-client only if the damage resulted from a punishable act or the use of government power, or other particularly pressing reasons exist for awarding such compensation. If a lawyer commits a punishable crime, the awarding of economic loss is not problematic. In other situations, the prospect of compensation for economic loss depends on the court's interpretation of "particularly pressing reasons", since membership in the Finnish Bar Association precludes the use of government power.

A clear and concise interpretation of "particularly pressing reasons" has only recently been defined by the courts. In a 1992 Supreme Court decision, an estate administrator was held liable for economic loss caused to an heir when the administrator liquidated estate property on the basis of an invalid testament. By neglecting to investigate the validity of the testament, the administrator had failed to act conscientiously and to safeguard impartially the rights of a legal heir. The Supreme Court stated that the heir was entitled on the basis of the public trust enjoyed by the profession of lawyers to rely on the administrator's ability and diligence to investigate the validity of the testament. The legal grounds for the decision were the "particularly pressing reasons" fostered by this position of public trust enjoyed by lawyers.

Lawyers are also liable under the Damages Act for their actions that result in suffering to third parties. However, compensation for suffering may not be awarded unless the responsible lawyer has committed a criminal act such as libel, slander, perjury, or false denunciation.

*Recent developments with respect to liability*

The recent developments in Germany concerning lawyers' ability to restrict their liability contractually have sparked a lot of discussion in Finland. There is presently, however, no intention to act officially on the concern expressed during these discussions.

## Insurance

*Compulsory professional indemnity insurance*

Indemnity insurance is compulsory for all members of the Finnish Bar Association. The Finnish Bar Association is a statutorily-recognized professional body entrusted with the supervision of its members. Indemnity insurance was made compulsory at a 1982 Assembly of the Finnish Bar Association.

Besides the members of the Finnish Bar Association, there are a great many other individuals who either professionally or on a non-professional basis give legal advice and assistance to clients. It can be said that any individual who professionally gives legal advice and assistance to clients is insured in one form or another against liability, regardless of his or her status as an Association member.

*Insurance facilities*

The indemnity insurance required by the Finnish Bar Association is offered by commercial insurers. Although the market is also open to foreign insurance companies, all members of the Bar Association are insured by Finnish commercial insurers, except in those instances where a reinsurer is required.

Members are, in principle, free to insure themselves in any appropriate manner, provided that they comply with the minimum amount of coverage required by the Bar Association.

The Finnish insurance market is very competitive since there are at least four large domestic commercial insurers offering insurance policies tailored to meet the demands of lawyers.

*Level of cover*

The compulsory cover limit is USD120,000 for each act resulting in damage.

According to information from an expert in the insurance business, the level of cover of an average-sized Finnish law firm is approximately USD2.5 to 3 million.

Some of the large Finnish law firms maintain altogether different types of policies than what the average Finnish lawyer requires. These policies may include coverage sums nearing USD12 million and require a foreign reinsurer since the Finnish reinsurance market is not large enough. These insurance policies are typically modelled on the professional indemnity insurance policies used on the London insurance market.

It is estimated that lawyers spend on an average two per cent of their annual expenses on professional indemnity insurance.

*Deductibles*
The Finnish Bar Association requires that all its members arrange the deductible so that it does not exceed two per cent of the total payable amount of compensation for each act resulting in damage.

*Recent developments with respect to insurance*
Recent efforts by commercial insurance companies to reduce their risks under indemnity insurance policies have led to some interesting developments during the past couple of years.

One of the most debated issues has been the assertion by insurance companies that indemnity insurance covers only damage resulting from acts considered to fall within the ambit of the activities performed by lawyers. It was the contention of the insurers that acts performed while serving in an appointed function are not covered by lawyer's indemnity insurance. In a 1992 decision, however, the Damage and Personal Insurance Board stated that lawyers' indemnity insurance does in fact cover damage resulting from an act performed by a lawyer while serving as a corporate board member. It was reasoned that it is common practice for business lawyers to serve as corporate board members and, insofar as a lawyer in the capacity of board member performs tasks related to giving legal advice and assistance to a client, these acts do fall within the ambit of the activities performed by lawyers.

Consequently, commercial insurers have tried to eliminate this risk by contractually excluding liability for acts performed while serving as, among others, a corporate board member. In response to this, the Finnish Bar Association has established a liability work group to serve as a liaison between the commercial insurers and lawyers.

Mention is also deserving of the compensation fund established in 1989 by the Finnish Bar Association. The purpose of the fund is to indemnify damages caused by the criminal actions of the members of the Association or their assistants. Awarding of compensation from the fund is decided by the Association Board. The Board is free in its discretion to award compensation. Therefore, it cannot be claimed that the compensation fund is a form of indemnity insurance, but rather a private fund administered for the benefit of the profession.

## FRANCE

### The civil liability of legal advisers

*Basis of liability*
Lawyers' liability to their clients is a contractual liability. Pursuant to a reorganization of the legal profession, in effect as of 1991, the two former professions *avocat* and *conseil juridique* merged in one profession known as *avocat*. The role of a lawyer now consists of different services such as:

- to render advice and assistance to his client in connection with legal issues relative to commercial, civil and criminal matters;
- to oversee litigation and submit written pleadings to all courts on behalf of his client, as well as to make oral arguments before these courts (except before the *Cour de Cassation* and the *Conseil d'Etat*);
- to draft acts, contracts and other legal documents on behalf of his client;
- to give legal consultations.

A French lawyer has three general obligations towards his clients who can hold him liable if the lawyer does not respect them:

- diligence and care: he must conduct the proceedings with care;
- advice: he must advise his clients on all relevant legal and judicial procedures regarding their problems;
- case conduct for the defence at court: a lawyer who refuses to plead, or forgets a hearing or a time limit, is committing a professional misconduct.

The principal basis is that the liability is not strict but is decided according to the skill, diligence and care brought by the lawyer. The client who asserts he has suffered damage because of his lawyer must prove misconduct according to the degree of skill and care to be expected of a competent lawyer for the matter in question. Although a lawyer normally gives no undertaking as to the result of his acts, the lawyer who drafts acts and legal documents is considered to give an undertaking of result as to the validity and efficiency of the said legal documents; however, courts continue to require evidence of a lawyer's fault. The client must also prove that he has suffered a material or a moral damage, which can be a caused by the loss of case that might have otherwise been won. Finally, the damage must be a direct consequence of the lawyer's professional misconduct.

These principles are defined by the Civil Code in relation to contractual liability generally and statutes specially dealing with the legal profession, as well as court decisions.

The civil liability of lawyers is a matter solely decided by the courts, but lawyers can also be sued before a professional disciplinary body, the *Conseil de l'Ordre*. A disciplinary fault is not necessarily a civil offence, but the client who has suffered a loss due to his lawyer can bring a claim before the professional body. Clients cannot obtain damages from the professional body which only imposes disciplinary sanctions.

The relief available is always restricted to compensation. There are no financial limits on the compensation which lawyers may be ordered to pay. The amount of the compensation must correspond to the importance of the damage suffered by the client. Courts of first instance and courts of appeal have full powers to assess the damages.

*Restrictions on liability*

A lawyer can always be held liable to his clients for his faults. He is free to choose his method of working and his argumentation provided that he has explained them to the client. The lawyer's liability can be limited when the client has a legal knowledge or experience, or, when the lawyer has committed a fault which is the cause of the damage the client has suffered.

There are no court decisions and no statutes about restricting liability clauses. The law of contract, generally speaking, allows these clauses, but under some restrictions, such as public policy. Authors think that lawyers have a mission of public service which prohibits this kind of clauses. French lawyers are representatives of the law and give access to a public service, so that authors believe that judges would not apply such clauses, if ever a lawyer was audacious enough to assert that these clauses are applicable to his liability. Courts have already decided that notaries' liability cannot be restricted because of their mission of public service.

The Civil Code provides for a time limit of ten years for claims made against lawyers who represent and assist their clients before courts. The limitation period begins from the end of the retainer. No legal texts provide for a specific time limit in the case of a lawyer's liability for negligence in drafting a document. In that situation the time limit depends on a general civil law which provides a time limit of ten years for contractual liability and thirty years for liability on tort. The courts have not yet clarified the nature of the lawyer's liability for negligence in drafting work and jurisprudence is divided on the point.

*Liability to non-clients*

Lawyers can be held liable to opponents and to third parties under liability in tort.

Lawyers have an obligation of moderation towards opponents, particularly when they give statements to the press: they must not use excessive words. Also, lawyers must be moderate when they attach real estate. It might be considered a professional misconduct to attach real estate for a small debt.

Lawyers have to be prudent towards third parties. That means that they can be held liable to third parties if they commit serious professional misconduct or if their fault does not come from their attorney power. If that is the case, the client will be held liable to third parties. But he would probably afterwards seek indemnity from the lawyer. A lawyer who attaches a real estate instead of another because he did not verify its street number has committed a fault towards the third party who owns the real estate.

*Recent developments with respect to liability*

The number of liability actions against lawyers has appreciably increased for a few years. In 1994 there were fifty-six per cent more law suits than in 1993 and the incidence of losses increased by sixteen per cent. The Paris Bar Council is currently thinking about making the negligent lawyers more aware of their responsibilities.

## Insurance

*Compulsory professional indemnity insurance*

The following information only regards professional indemnity insurance for lawyers. The professional insurance system of the other branches of the legal profession is different to that of the lawyers, because their professional organization and the rules governing their liability are totally different.

Indemnity insurance for the legal profession is compulsory in France. Law no. 71-1130 of December 31, 1971 provides that lawyers must be insured for their professional liability.

*Insurance facilities*

Some important Bars, such as the Paris Bar Council, take out collective schemes which are compulsory for their members.

Generally, this insurance is issued by a leading insurer in the name of co-insurers. Usually, it also covers other risks connected with the profession.

Other Bar Councils do not offer these schemes. Their members can take out collective or personal policies. These policies do not have to be approved by the professional body.

*Level of cover*

The compulsory cover limit is USD400,000. Cover to the compulsory level is an aggregate for all claims within a year.

The Bar Councils which offer a collective cover to their members generally take out a higher insurance cover. The Paris Bar Council has taken out a cover of about USD5 million for each claim. The insurance premium for professional liability for lawyers practising in Paris ranges between USD684 and USD930 in 1995.

The insurance premium of the Paris Bar is relatively low compared to other French Bars (approximately USD1,489) and other legal professions, such as notaries (approximately USD8,510).

Lawyers can individually take out additional cover over the cover taken out by the Bar.

*Deductibles*

The Decree of November 17, 1991 provides that the deductibles cannot be higher than ten per cent of the compensation, with a maximum of USD4,000.

Generally, the amount of the claim payable by the insured lawyer himself is equivalent to the maximum provided by law.

*Recent developments with respect to insurance*

As a result of the increasing number of liability actions against lawyers, the insurance premium has tripled in 1995 and will become even higher in 1996. In

1994 the insurance premium was USD247 and in 1995 the premium ranged from USD684 to USD930.

The creation of a no-claim discount clause is now being examined, as well as the possibility of providing insurance with a higher deductible than the maximum currently provided by law (ten per cent of a claim with a maximum of USD4,000).

The Bar Council is at present contemplating the creation of one insurance system for the whole country, with the same compulsory amount insured for all lawyers.

The Council is also trying to adapt the level of insurance cover according to the size of the law firm.

## GERMANY

### The civil liability of legal advisers

*Basis of liability*

A distinction exists in Germany between those lawyers practising as attorneys, who are admitted to practise law at court (*Rechtsanwalt*), and other lawyers. The latter group falls under the general principles of professional liability whilst attorneys are subject to special standards set forth in the Federal Regulations for Attorneys (*Bundesrechtsanwaltsordnung — BRAO*). The focus of this chapter will be on the standards of liability imposed on attorneys.

Principally, an attorney will be liable on a contractual basis if he does not meet his professional obligations with due care. In a situation where liability is an issue the client must prove that the attorney either negligently, grossly negligently or wilfully violated these duties. An attorney acts negligent if he disregards the necessary diligence which he should have used from the perspective of an objective observer. An act of gross negligence would be committed if the attorney disregards due care on an aggravated level. The principle of due diligence in the performance of professional obligations of an attorney has been extensively developed in the courts. As a general standard, an attorney must advise his client comprehensively. This includes advising a client on the potential risks involved in concluding a commercial deal or bringing a lawsuit. The duty even extends to advising a client on the risk that a court might overrule earlier decisions which might have supported the client's case. An attorney cannot excuse himself by relying on a wrong opinion if a correct opinion is published elsewhere.

Any liability claims against attorneys are litigated at courts competent for civil law cases. Lawyers' professional bodies only have jurisdiction on the questions of professional codes of conduct and admission to the local bar. They have no authority to rule on damages by financial losses. In making a claim, the client's main aim will be to secure full financial relief. The German Civil Code states as a general rule that a person who has caused damage to another person is liable to put him in the position he would have been in, had that damaging event not occurred. Any financial damage thus will be fully compensated. Also, clients may seek mandatory orders.

*Restrictions on liability*

A client wishing to initiate an action against his attorney must commence proceedings within three years after the damage occurred if the attorney was acting within the core area of his profession. In claims arising from other activities of an attorney, such as tax advice, the regular limitation period of thirty years applies. Time will start to run from the moment the client suffers financial loss as a result of that wrong legal advice, irrespective of the fact whether the client has positive knowledge of the financial damage at that time.

By statute the limitation period is imposed that any claim must be brought not later than three years after the termination of the contract between client and attorney. If an attorney, however, knows of a mistake and the likelihood of financial damages and fails to inform the client that there may be a case of liability against him, the initial period of three years is extended by another three years which directly follows the primary period of three years. If after six years (at the longest) no claim is made, any action will be time barred.

Although for attorneys it is possible to limit their liability by way of prior agreement it is not clear to what extent such restrictions are valid.

This has been taken further by a new regulation in the *BRAO*. An attorney may seek to limit his liability for damages arising from bad professional conduct in the following ways:

- He may now enter into an individual written agreement with a client excluding liability above the mandatory minimum malpractice liability insurance of USD357,000. Such an agreement limits liability in cases involving grossly negligent malpractice. Previously this was not possible. Also any individual agreement which purports to go beyond the general standard of the statute will be declared invalid.
- An attorney may also limit his liability by general terms and conditions. The scope of such clause, however, is not as extensive as an agreement since the exclusion only relates to liability incurred as a result of ordinary negligence. Such a clause is only valid if the attorney's insurance is at least four times the mandatory minimum of USD357,000, i.e. USD1,428,000.
- A law firm can now restrict its liability by way of a general clause in its terms and conditions so that any liability will fall upon the individual attorney who worked in the matter. This limitation is only valid if the client has agreed to that limitation in a clear written statement. It is uncertain how this principle will work in practice since large cases will involve several partners and associates and it might be very difficult to decide who actually worked on the matter. Also the risk of shifting the responsibility pertains.

In summary, it must be considered questionable whether the new *BRAO*-provisions really bring satisfactory relief for lawyers since many problems arising in practice remain open and unsolved, for example whether conduct is ordinary or gross negligence.

The limitation of liability in General Terms and Conditions for ordinary negligence will leave legal practices unprotected in most areas of potential liability. German courts on all levels have established standards over many decades and in most cases any mistakes of lawyers would be considered to be gross negligence.

Until enactment of the regulations lawyers seldom entered into agreements limiting their liability, because of the commonly-known legal uncertainties. Lawyers avoided the often unpleasant discussions with their clients on potential mistakes and liability and preferred to cover the risks connected with their practice by insurance. Only in exceptional cases with high financial risks would lawyers choose to limit their liability by individual agreement. Such agreement would include a limitation of liability for gross negligence and it would offer financial coverage up to the insured amount. As an option the attorney would offer to increase the insurance amount if the client reimbursed him for the additional insurance premium. The legality and practicality of such agreements has not yet been tested and the validity of such clauses may fail by reason of weak drafting.

*Liability to non-clients*

Generally, a lawyer can only be liable to his client, because of the principle of privity of contract. However, an attorney can become liable in exceptional cases to a non-client by way of statutory regulation, for example in the case of a trustee or executor of a will, where contractual obligations have been extended beyond the client.

*Recent developments with respect to liability*

The Superior Court of Bavaria has recently established that a law firm, under qualified and restricted circumstances, may form a German limited liability company thereby limiting the personal and comprehensive liability of individual lawyers.

In its edge-breaking ruling that a firm may practise as a legal entity it clarified the restrictions since there has been no statutory intervention. It held that a law firm could only be set up as a legal corporate body if:

- An attorney assumed the position of a managing director.
- The shareholders' assembly (contrary to the law) has no right to give directives to attorneys (employees of the legal entity) with regard to their professional activities.
- Only attorneys working for the company may bear capital investment in it, that is no external capital investment is permitted.
- Liability insurance is in place for a significantly higher figure than the minimum cover of USD357,000 for an individual attorney.

It is not yet clear how many law firms will adopt this new option or indeed whether other German courts will corroborate or supplement it. Notwithstanding the obvious advantages of sheltering-off personal liability of lawyers, the organisational structure of a limited liability law firm is subject to tax disadvantages, such as corporation tax and trade tax, which law firm partnerships do not need to pay at present.

**Insurance**

*Compulsory professional indemnity insurance*
Indemnity insurance is compulsory for all attorneys, as required by law (article 51 of the *Bundesrechtsanwaltsordnung*).

*Insurance facilities*
Professional indemnity insurance is offered by large German insurers either individually, or, depending on the amount of coverage, by way of a consortium of insurers.

Indemnity insurance must be obtained from an insurance company authorized to conduct business in Germany. The General Terms and Conditions which apply to professional indemnity insurance need to be approved by the German Supervisory Body for Insurance Companies (*Bundesaufsichtsamt für das Versicherungswesen in Berlin*). Accordingly, commercial professional indemnity insurance generally is obtained from insurers within Germany.

The annual premium for professional indemnity insurance amounts to approximately 7/1000 of the aggregate amount covered.

*Level of cover*
The minimum insurance coverage is USD357,000. The attorney is obliged to render proof to the local bar that he is properly insured.

Level of coverage depends on the size of the law firm, its kind of business and potential of liability.

Policies usually grant a base coverage (e.g. USD1.3 million) for each single case with a cap on the aggregate of damages in one insurance year (e.g. USD28 million). Additionally, insurance policies provide for supplemental coverage (e.g. USD13 million) for each single case, up to an annual maximum of an aggregate amount (USD53 to USD57 million).

The law explicitly allows insurers to limit the aggregate for all damages within one year to four times of the minimum insurance coverage of USD357,000, i.e. USD1,428,000.

Coverage may be extended for individual matters with additional premium. The maximum insurable (and reinsurable) level of cover is approximately USD53 to USD57 million.

*Deductibles*
Insurance coverage is always reduced by a deductible to the amount of the legal fees received by the attorney in the matter.

General Terms and Conditions provide further that of any incurred damage the insurer bears only eighty per cent of the first USD6,500 and only ninety per cent of any further damage up to an amount of USD18,500. Any damage in excess of USD18,500 will be fully covered by the insurer up to the contractually agreed coverage limit.

*Recent developments with respect to insurance*
At the time of writing this book there are no new trends or potential developments in the area of insurance which may significantly alter the framework summarised above.

## GREECE

### The civil liability of legal advisers

*Basis of liability*
The lawyer, who in Greece is considered to be a non-salaried civil servant, is subject to civil, criminal and disciplinary liability. The civil liability, is basically of the mandatory performing his mandate together with liability in tort.

The liability principles are defined by the Civil Code. The disciplinary liability is defined by the Code of Lawyers. The findings of the Disciplinary Council of the Bar are not binding on the findings of the Civil Court and vice versa. However, there is a degree of influence of one procedure upon the other. Disciplinary and/or Civil Court decisions form precedents in the application of civil or disciplinary justice, but in Greece, the *stare decisis doctrine* is not as stringent in its applicability compared to other countries, for example common law jurisdictions. The civil liability includes the *culpa levis in abstracto*. This degree of negligence is the lack of care required in dealings from a prudent and diligent person. The liability therefore does not take into consideration the particular lawyer, his/her skills etc, but is applicable in an "objective" manner, *in abstracto*.

Although the relief is usually restricted to compensation, other orders for a specific act or omission cannot be excluded under the general provisions.

*Restrictions on liability*
There are no financial limits on the compensation which lawyers can be ordered to pay. Likewise, there are no restrictions as to the circumstances in which lawyers may be held liable to their client. Of course, a client is responsible for the information provided to his lawyer.

In principle, (and theoretically, because in practice it is unlikely to happen) lawyers may limit their liability under the general freedom to contract, but not to limit liability caused by fraud or gross negligence.

The time limit for civil liability actions is twenty years.

*Liability to non-clients*
There may be a case against lawyers in such situations in tort liability.

*Recent developments with respect to liability*
So far in Greece civil claims against lawyers are rare and insurance cover is not usual.

A recent development that should be noted is a very recent law which came into effect in December 1994 and concerns the protection of consumers. The law does not specifically include lawyers, but one could assume that lawyers are covered by the law. The service provider is liable for any damage caused by his/her fault.

The claimant must prove the damage and causation of the damage. The service provider has the burden to prove the lack of fault. The Minister of Commerce may impose fines from approximately USD2,250 to USD90,000.

Presently, however, the prevailing view of scholars on said law is that it should be inapplicable to lawyers because of the nature of the lawyer's position as a civil servant.

**Insurance**

*Voluntary professional indemnity insurance*
Indemnity insurance for the legal profession is voluntary in Greece. Only a very small proportion of the legal profession takes out professional indemnity insurance cover.

*Insurance facilities*
Available for insurance are policies issued by local commercial insurers.

*Level of cover*
There are no statistics available to indicate the level of cover generally obtained by the legal profession.

*Deductibles*
There are no statistics available on the range of deductibles payable by the insured lawyers.

*Recent developments with respect to insurance*
At the time of writing this book there are no new trends or potential developments in the area of insurance.

## GUATEMALA

### The civil liability of legal advisers

*Basis of liability*

Lawyers should render their services with dedication and diligence. They are liable for damage caused by deceit, negligence, inexcusable ignorance or by disclosure of secrets and confidences of a client. The lawyer is liable for damages if, without notice, he abandons a case and fails to appoint another competent attorney.

The principles governing lawyers' liability are defined by statute. Only the courts have jurisdiction on matters relating to liability of lawyers. It should be noted that the Guatemalan Bar Association imposes disciplinary sanctions based on ethical misconduct.

The relief available is restricted to compensation. But the client has the right to file criminal charges against the lawyer if his conduct constitutes a criminal offence. The punishment could include prison, fines and disbarment.

*Restrictions on liability*

There are no pre-established financial limits on the compensation lawyers may be ordered to pay. The court determines the compensation according to the circumstances of the particular case or may require expert opinion on the amount of the damages. There are no restrictions provided as to the circumstances in which lawyers may be held liable to their clients.

Lawyers can by agreement with their clients limit their liability for a particular matter and restrict the amount of compensation for which they may be liable. Such agreements are rarely made.

There are no restrictions, by statute or otherwise which prevent lawyers limiting their liability to their clients. Criminal responsibility may not be limited.

The time limit for clients to make claims or institute proceedings against their lawyers is generally five years.

*Liability to non-clients*

The law does not provide for particular circumstances where lawyers can be liable to non-clients.

*Recent developments with respect to liability*

There are currently no trends or developments which may significantly alter this framework.

### Insurance

*Professional indemnity insurance*
There is no professional indemnity insurance available for the legal profession in Guatemala.

## INDIA

### The civil liability of legal advisers

*Basis of liability*
In the discharge of their professional duties, a high standard of conduct, care, caution and diligence is expected from the members of the Indian Bar as in the other jurisdictions.

In India the canons of professional conduct for lawyers are embodied in the rules framed by the Bar Council of India. Any violation of these canons on the part of a lawyer is treated as professional misconduct. Where misconduct is proved, the penalties which may be imposed on the lawyer concerned by the Bar Council of the concerned State include reprimand, suspension, or removal of the advocate's name from the roll.

An action taken by the Bar Council of India or the State Bar Council is liable to be reviewed by the Supreme Court of India.

The principles regarding lawyers' liability towards their client and the conduct of matters can be traced to statutes and court decisions.

Under the Indian Contract Act, the lawyer may be held liable for a breach of contract with his client depending upon the terms contracted between the two, which are subject to the rules of professional conduct. The damages recoverable are required to be traced to consequences "arising naturally, that is according to the usual course of things" from the breach or such as may reasonably be supposed to have been in the contemplation of both the parties at the time they made the contract as the probable result of the breach.

Under the Consumer Protection Act a complaint may be made in respect of any deficiency in services rendered. The term deficiency, with reference to any service has been defined as

> any fault, imperfection or shortcoming or inadequacy in the quality, nature and manner of performance which is required to be maintained by or under any law for the time being in force or has been undertaken to be performed by a person...

Services rendered by lawyers for consideration have been brought within the ambit of the Consumer Protection Laws and compensation to clients has been awarded by courts under the Act and in exercise of their inherent jurisdiction through the extension of common law rules of equity.

Generally a lawyer's liability to his client in respect of advice given and conduct of a legal matter in particular is decided according to the degree of skill and care to be expected of a competent lawyer.

The courts and *quasi-judicial* bodies can grant compensation in proportion to the loss and injury caused to the client due to the fault and negligence of the lawyer. The Superior Courts, however, in the exercise of their discretionary powers can always pass such other orders which are deemed necessary to effect complete justice on the facts of a given case.

The guidelines as regarding the quantum of compensation have been laid down in various court decisions. Compensation awarded depends upon the facts of each case. It is an established principle of law in India that compensation awarded must have a rational relation to the nature and extent of injury, inconvenience or physical and mental suffering caused to the complainant by action or omission of the opposite party.

*Restrictions on liability*

Lawyers can by agreement limit their liability for a particular matter or by way of general agreement. This is not restricted by either statute or a regulatory body. They cannot agree upon exemption clauses exempting their liability for negligence. These agreements are very rarely made in India. There is also The Indian Contract Act which invalidates any agreement that is in restraint of legal proceedings. Thus, a lawyer may not lawfully enter into an agreement with his client precluding the latter from initiating any legal action against the lawyer where such cause of action has arisen.

The Law of Limitation for initiating proceedings against a lawyer is as follows:

- in a complaint under the Consumer Protection Act for deficiency in services the limitation is two years;
- in a suit for damages at common law the limitation is one year;
- in a suit for damages under the Contract Act for breach of contract the limitation is three years; and
- in a complaint for initiating the disciplinary proceedings against the lawyer, the limitation is one year.

*Liability to non-clients*

The duty of lawyer is not limited to his client. It extends to the court, the profession and society at large. A lawyer is accordingly responsible for his conduct as an officer of the court. Failure to observe proper decorum in court in conduct of litigation can render a lawyer liable for contempt of court under the Contempt of Courts Act.

At common law a lawyer is not immune from actions against him for negligence. In the field of tort negligence has come to be recognized as the most important tort. The measure of its importance is attested by the fact that negligence litigation today overwhelmingly occupies the attention of courts across the world. In India too, the number of cases in this regard is increasing. The law of torts as administered in India has generally followed common law principles. It is evident that although the standard is uniform, the degree of care required in different situations will vary. The principles applicable are more or less the same for all professional persons including advocates. The person concerned has to show the care and skill not of an ordinary layman but of a member of his class. Where the person concerned represents himself to be a specialist or an expert, such as an advocate, the standard is to be modified accordingly.

*Recent developments with respect to liability*
With the emergence and formal recognition of the utility of concept of public interest or social action litigation, the development of consumer laws and growing awareness of public rights, the number of cases filed against lawyers holding them liable for their advice given or conduct of matter is increasing.

**Insurance**

*Voluntary professional indemnity insurance*
Indemnity insurance for the legal profession is voluntary in India. It is very rare to take out professional indemnity insurance cover.

*Insurance facilities*
Available for insurance are policies issued by commercial insurers. Since professional indemnity insurance is not common, there is not much market competition and the policy is presently available on uniform rates, terms and conditions.

*Level of cover*
There are no statistics available to indicate the level of cover obtained by the legal profession.

*Deductibles*
There are no statistics available on the range of deductibles payable by the insured lawyers.

*Recent developments with respect to insurance*
The Indian Government has decided gradually to de-regulate the insurance sector. It is expected that indemnity insurance for the legal profession will be promoted and popularised in the near future.

## IRELAND

### The civil liability of legal advisers

*Basis of liability*

Liability is decided according to the degree of skill and care expected of a competent solicitor. The Irish courts have laid down the following tests in deciding whether a solicitor or other professional person has been negligent:

- was a duty of care owed in the particular circumstances by the solicitor to the client?
- if so, did the solicitor in the performance of that duty fall short of the standard of care imposed by the law?

The Irish Supreme Court has stated the following:

> The General duty of care created by the relationship of solicitor and client entitles the client to sue in negligence if he has suffered damage because of the Solicitor's failure to show due professional care and skill, notwithstanding that the client could sue alternatively in contract for breach of the implied term in the contract of retainer that the solicitor will deal with the matter in hand with due professional care and skill.

The Supreme Court has held that a solicitor does not discharge his duty of care to the client by following instructions blindly. He must consider not only his instructions but also the legal implications of the facts presented to him by his client and advise the client accordingly. Where pending legislation affects advice already given in a current matter, there is a duty on the part of the solicitor to justify or correct that advice as soon as possible.

The guiding principles of lawyers liability to their clients is defined by both statute and court decisions. The Irish courts tend to be influenced by court decisions in other common law countries, for example England and the United States, in the whole area of professional negligence. The Civil Liability Act 1961 also legislates for certain areas affecting claims for negligence, such as contributory negligence.

The liability of lawyers is a matter solely decided by the courts and not by any professional body. The Incorporated Law Society of Ireland is the professional body which is responsible for the solicitors profession in Ireland. The Society sets, maintains and where necessary improves professional standards, deals with complaints and where appropriate initiates disciplinary action. If a client complains about both their solicitor's behaviour and his or her negligence the Society will normally suggest that the client seeks legal advice on whether or not they have a claim but may also investigate the matter from the conduct aspect.

The relief available for professional negligence of solicitors is restricted to compensation. There are no financial limits on the compensation which lawyers may be ordered to pay. The limit is determined by the actual damage suffered. In order for the client to recover financial loss arising as a result of the solicitor's negligence it is necessary to establish that the solicitor owed a duty of care and that the economic loss was reasonably foreseeable because of the negligence of the solicitor. However, it is a fundamental principle of Irish law that the client must take all possible steps to mitigate his losses and if he fails to do so then he will be penalised by having to pay any additional costs or expenses incurred as a result of failure to take such steps.

*Restrictions on liability*

As a general rule if a solicitor acts in accordance with the advice of a barrister, whom he has properly instructed, then usually he will not be held liable in negligence, even if the barrister's advice proves to be mistaken or misconceived. Similarly, if a barrister acts as an advocate on the instructions of the solicitor, that solicitor cannot be held liable in negligence from actions arising out of advocacy in court.

Lawyers can by agreement with their clients limit their liability for a particular matter and by way of standard conditions. Financial restrictions can be agreed but it is a matter of contract between the solicitor and client, subject to Irish and European Law. Such agreements are made only rarely.

The time limit for making claims or instituting proceedings against lawyers is six years in contract and six years or more, in negligence depending on the circumstances. The Irish Statute of Limitations Act 1957 provides that an action in contract or in tort, which includes negligence, must be taken within six years of the date on which the cause of action accrued, that is, the date of the breach of the contract or the date of the action which caused the negligence. However, the Irish Supreme Court has held that the six year time limit in a negligence claim cannot begin to run until the actual damage happens or occurs. This may extend the six year time limit in certain cases involving professional negligence.

It is normal that where a client intends bringing an action against a solicitor for negligence that there will be two separate claims within the one action, namely breach of contract by the advisor for failure to exercise reasonable care and skill in the provision of advice in accordance with the contract of appointment, and secondly an action for professional negligence.

*Liability to non-clients*

There are certain circumstances where lawyers can be liable to non-clients. The Supreme Court has decided that

> the solicitors liability in tort under the general duty of care extends not only to a client for reward, but to any person for whom the solicitor undertakes to act professionally without reward, and also to those (such as beneficiaries under a Will, persons entitled under an intestacy or those entitled to benefits in circumstances such as a claim in respect of a fatal injury) with whom he has made no arrangements to act but who, as he knows or ought to know, will be relying on his professional care and skill.

In 1988 the Court set out the following principles in deciding whether a professional person owed a duty of care to another person:

- the proximity of the party alleging the loss to the professional adviser, that is whether the advice was tendered for the purpose of a particular transaction or type of transaction and the advisor knew or ought to have known that it would be relied on by a particular person or class of persons in connection with that transaction;
- the foreseeability of the damage i.e. that the professional adviser could clearly be expected specifically to anticipate that the client alleging the loss would rely on the advice or information given by the professional adviser for the very purpose for which he did in the event rely on it; and
- that public policy supports the claim being made, that is, where there is a duty to act with care to the other person, public policy in general demands that such damage should be made good to the party to whom the duty is owed by the person owing the duty.

*Recent developments with respect to liability*

There are no trends appearing or developments taking place which would significantly alter the above. The long established rule that solicitors never owe a duty to persons other than their clients has now been discarded by the court decisions. The courts in Ireland, England and elsewhere are gradually defining the situations in which such a duty of care arises. Irish courts will be influenced by developments in England and elsewhere where such a duty of care is extended gradually over the years by decisions of foreign courts.

## Insurance

*Voluntary professional indemnity insurance*

Indemnity insurance for solicitors is voluntary in Ireland. Present statistics indicate that out of 3.877 practising solicitors only fifty-one members do not have professional indemnity insurance.

For barristers, indemnity insurance is compulsory, with a minimum level of cover of USD150,000. Barristers are forbidden to practise in partnership and they are all sole practitioners. There are approximately nine-hundred barristers practising in Ireland and they are all insured under a group scheme.

The following report will deal with indemnity insurance for solicitors.

*Insurance facilities*

Available for insurance are policies issued by commercial insurers and a mutual voluntary scheme for professional indemnity insurance which was arranged by the Law Society. This scheme is provided by the Solicitors Mutual Defence Fund Limited, which is a company limited by guarantee and not having a share capital.

As mentioned above, in 1994 there were 3.877 practising solicitors in 1.795 firms. In 1994 the total membership of the Solicitors Mutual Defence Fund Limited comprised 1.149 firms representing 2.454 solicitors. The Solicitors Mutual Defence Fund therefore provides professional indemnity insurance cover for the vast majority of solicitors in Ireland.

Professional indemnity insurance is generally obtained from insurers in Ireland. However, a substantial amount of reinsurance is carried out with institutions in the United Kingdom and elsewhere.

*Level of cover*

The level of cover generally taken up by members of the profession is up to a maximum figure of USD390,000 for each claim. There is a provision to increase this level of cover by paying additional premiums.

The professional indemnity insurance premium amounts to approximately two to three per cent of the annual expenses of a practice.

*Deductibles*

Generally, the first USD3,900 of a claim is payable by the insured solicitors themselves. However, where there are twenty or more solicitors in a firm, generally the first USD15,000 of a claim is payable by the insured solicitors themselves.

*Recent developments with respect to insurance*

Section 26 of the Solicitors (Amendment) Act 1994, which came into law on November 4, 1994, provides that the Law Society may, by regulations, make provision for a compulsory indemnity insurance.

The Law Society has indicated that compulsory indemnity insurance will be introduced on January 1, 1996 for all members of the profession. It is anticipated that the regulations made by the Law Society will provide for compulsory professional indemnity insurance cover for 1996 and all succeeding years.

The Law Society has provisionally agreed a scheme of approved insurers to provide compulsory insurance cover. The Society is hoping to negotiate a standard policy with all approved insurers including the Solicitors Mutual Defence Fund.

The Society is considering introducing a minimum cover of USD550,000 for the first two years of the compulsory insurance scheme. It is hoped that this level of cover will be increased to USD780,000 two years later and to USD1.5 million after six to eight years. This level of cover is dependent on the rates quoted for the appropriate premiums.

## ISRAEL

### The civil liability of legal advisers

*Basis of liability*

Under Israeli law, the guiding principles of lawyers' liability to their clients in respect of advice given and the conduct of matters is decided according to the degree of skill and care to be expected of a competent lawyer, having regard to the nature of the legal profession the practice of which gives rise to special duties of loyalty and devotion to the interest of the client.

Those principles are defined by a combination of statute and judicial decisions. The general principles of professional liability derive from the law of tort, which is codified in The Civil Wrongs Ordinance. The breach of a contract made between the lawyer and the client will also fall under the civil statutes on contract law. The Chamber of Advocates Law, ("The Law") and the Rules of Professional Ethics enacted by virtue thereof ("the Rules") provide statutory framework definitions of the special professional duties of the lawyer to act loyally and devotedly on behalf of the client. The Chamber of Advocates (Bar) is a statutory body charged with the function of promoting and preserving the dignity of the legal professional. The Bar National Committee enacted the Rules with the approval of the Minister of Justice, with the full effect of subsidiary legislation. In the rulings of the courts, the loyalty of the lawyer to the client has been enunciated as the duty to be truthful and honest with the client; the devotion as a requirement for diligence and attention to the client's interest.

The liability of lawyers is decided by the courts and the disciplinary tribunals of the Israel Bar established under the Chamber of Advocates Law, comprising judges selected by the National and District bodies from among members of the profession. The jurisdiction of both a civil court and a disciplinary tribunal can be invoked. A disciplinary tribunal in each district has jurisdiction over the lawyers practising in the district. Judgments of the District Disciplinary Tribunal are appealable to the National Disciplinary Tribunal of the Bar, and from the National Disciplinary Tribunal to the Israel Supreme Court. Proceedings in a disciplinary tribunal may be instituted by the Bar Central Committee or District Committee, or by the State Attorney or Attorney General.

The relief available against a lawyer in a civil court proceeding is congruent with the availability of remedies in civil proceedings generally. This includes monetary relief such as compensation, restitution and costs, as well as mandatory or prohibitive injunctions, subject to the rule that a contract for personal services will not be the subject of an order of specific performance. In disciplinary proceedings, the disciplinary tribunal of the Bar, in addition to having the power to convict a lawyer of a disciplinary offence, may order restitution of fees, payment of costs and special compensation to a complainant or any other person whose interests were damaged by the disciplinary offence of the lawyer.

A disciplinary tribunal of the Israel Bar, upon conviction of a lawyer for a disciplinary offence, is empowered to order payment of compensation to a person aggrieved by such disciplinary offence, in an amount which shall not exceed the equivalent of approximately USD9,000. An order for refund of fees may be for all or part of the fee. Orders for payment of legal costs of the proceeding have no limits save for the discretion of the tribunal. Any such order for payment of compensation, restitution or costs has the same effect for execution purposes as a money judgment of a Magistrates' Court The limitation of liability as imposed by the disciplinary tribunal of the Bar is without derogation from the full extent of general civil liability of the lawyer, which remains enforceable by the courts.

*Restrictions on liability*

The law does not restrict by way of immunity the circumstances in which lawyers may be held liable to their clients. However, as a matter of judicial policy in the application of the law it is generally held that a mistake in judgment by the lawyer in the conduct of a legal proceeding does not per se constitute breach of duty toward the client. Lawyers cannot limit their liability for breach of professional duty by agreement with their clients. This general principle applies in respect of any matter being handled by the lawyer on behalf of the client, as opposed to any particular matter for which the lawyer may be specifically released from duty while continuing to act for a client.

It is generally perceived that the law prevents lawyers from prospectively restricting their liability to clients, on grounds of public policy. The import of the Chamber of Advocates Law and the Rules of Professional Ethics appears to be that the professional duties of a lawyer or the consequences of their breach cannot be stipulated against in a contract, unless the same will be allowed by an amendment of the Law or the Rules.

The time for instituting a civil proceeding for enforcement of a civil claim against a lawyer is subject to the general statute of limitations of seven years from the accrual of the cause of action, as well as the statutory exceptions to the rule.

The time for the institution of disciplinary proceedings is generally within ninety days from the day of the service of the complaint by the disciplinary prosecutor to the lawyer. The Bar institution or prosecutor handling the complaint must decide within that time whether or not to institute proceedings, unless special circumstances justify an extension. A decision not to prosecute is notified to the complainant.

*Liability to non-clients*

Lawyers can be liable to non-clients who are aggrieved by the commission of a disciplinary offence of the lawyer, or by the commission of any tort by the lawyer toward such non-client, including the negligent rendition of advice or information where it is foreseeable that such person will rely upon it.

*Recent developments with respect to liability*

The jurisdiction of the disciplinary tribunals of the Israel Bar occasionally creates public controversy over the question whether members of the legal profession ought to be in charge of trying and judging their fellow members, or whether an outside body should handle such matters. No particular alternative to the present arrangement appears to be forthcoming, however. In principle, a patently unreasonable decision of a public prosecutor not to institute disciplinary proceedings against a lawyer following a complaint from an aggrieved person is subject to the residual power of judicial review vested in the Israel Supreme Court Sitting as a High Court of Justice.

Within the Bar there is discussion about whether lawyers should be allowed to limit their liability, with no significant developments to date.

## Insurance

*Voluntary professional indemnity insurance*

Indemnity insurance for the legal profession is voluntary in Israel. The vast majority of the legal profession take out the professional indemnity insurance cover.

*Insurance facilities*

Indemnity insurance is generally taken out with commercial insurers within the country.

The Bar pursues collective insurance arrangements on behalf the members and annually concludes an agreement with an insurance company on the basic premiums for lawyers after negotiations with the competing insurers.

*Level of cover*

A basic insurance cover negotiated between the Bar and an insurance company provides each insured with a USD75,000 cover for a single claim, and USD150,000 coverage as an aggregate for all claims during the policy period. Beyond the basic cover, individual lawyers usually insure themselves.

The insurance provides for indemnity to the insured, being a lawyer and member of the Israel Bar, or insured's successors or executors, on a claims-made basis, against claims for breach of professional duty emanating from negligence, mistake or oversight of the insured, the insured's business predecessors or persons engaged by the insured, in relation to matters conducted by them as lawyers, within the last seven years.

Coverage does not generally apply to publication of libel, infringement of privacy unless unintentional and in good faith, dishonest acts, such as embezzlement, or crimes, liability in respect of issue of a prospectus, or liability to return fees to a client. Coverage can be broadened to libel, fidelity insurance and liability insurance for prospectuses.

The arrangements for professional indemnity insurance differ according to the risk of the activity. Land practice is considered a higher risk and therefore has a higher deductible. Prospectus practice requires special insurance for a separate premium.

*Deductibles*
The professional insurance cover will generally involve a deductible of USD3,500 to USD6,500 for non-land matters, and USD5,500 to USD9,000 for matters related to land.

*Recent developments with respect to insurance*
There are no developments in the indemnity insurance area in Israel.

## ITALY

### The civil liability of legal advisers

*Basis of liability*
The guiding principle for assessing a lawyer's liability to his clients in respect of advice given and the conduct of matters is, in general, that of simple negligence by reference to the standard of care and the nature of the services rendered. Only in the case of technical problems of particular difficulty, is the principle of gross negligence required to establish liability. Those principles are defined by the Italian Civil Code, enacted by Royal Decree 1942.

The liability claims of clients against lawyers are decided by the courts. The professional bodies have jurisdiction for disciplinary measures.

In general, the relief available is restricted to compensation, but other forms of relief may be occasionally granted, like specific performance.

*Restrictions on liability*
There are no financial limits to the compensation which lawyers may be ordered to pay and there are no restrictions as to the circumstances in which lawyers may be held liable to their clients.

Lawyers, by agreement with their clients, can limit their liability both for a particular matter and even by way of standard conditions. The limitation of liability will be excluded in cases of gross negligence or fraud on the part of the lawyers. The Italian Civil Code deals with limitation of liability clauses. The lawyers can also agree with their clients to limit their financial exposure in matters where they can limit their liability. Both kinds of agreements are rather rare in Italy.

The time limits for making claims or instituting proceedings against lawyers are those provided in general, by the Civil Code, namely ten years for the claims in contract and five years for the claims in tort.

*Liability to non-clients*
Limitation agreements are a matter of privity between the parties and have no effect whatsoever on the liability of the lawyers in tort, i.e. when they commit a private or civil wrong or injury, causing damage, to a third party resulting from a breach of a legal duty. In such cases the third party has a right of action.

*Recent developments with respect to liability*
No developments are taking place which may significantly alter the above answers.

**Insurance**

*Voluntary professional indemnity insurance*
Indemnity insurance for the legal profession is voluntary in Italy. The professional indemnity insurance cover is taken out by almost all of the legal profession.

*Insurance facilities*
Available for insurance are policies issued by commercial insurers. Generally Italian lawyers enter commercial insurance contracts with domestic insurers, but it is also possible to take out insurance with foreign companies.

*Level of cover*
The level of cover varies according to the size of the law firm and the area of the legal activity covered.

The insurance can be taken out in the form of an aggregate for all claims within a policy period and/or a maximum for each claim within the agreed limit.

The loss, destruction and damage to money, precious metals, bearer bonds, the auditing of the balance sheets of the joint stock companies listed at the stock exchange, the offices of director or of auditor in companies or institutions (which nevertheless can be insured otherwise) are normally excluded.

*Deductibles*
Normally the deductibles payable by the insured lawyers themselves are in the range of ten per cent of the insured amount. There are no deductibles for personal injuries to third parties (including the clients) in the premises where the lawyer carries out his activity.

*Recent developments with respect to insurance*
At the time of writing this book there are no new trends or potential developments in the area of insurance which may significantly alter the framework summarised above.

## JAMAICA

### The civil liability of legal advisers

*Basis of liability*

The general duty of a lawyer in Jamaica is to act on his client's behalf in all kinds of legal matters, and to give legal advice in accordance with the agreement with his client. The standard of care and skill expected of him is that of a reasonably competent and diligent lawyer. Essentially, these principles are based on the underlying theme that the lawyer, as a professional, will perform his duties with reasonable skill and care.

There are two branches which define the liability of lawyers. The first is judicial precedent. As Jamaican law is founded upon English Common Law, judgments emanating from the English Courts are of binding authority in Jamaica. Judicial decisions are, however, not to be seen as comprehensive or exhaustive but as a framework within which the liability of lawyers is set.

The second branch is statute law. This can be further divided into two distinct sections: potential lawsuits and disciplinary action. In Jamaica, under the Legal Profession Act, a Disciplinary Committee has jurisdiction to hear complaints of professional misconduct (including any default) by aggrieved persons against any lawyer. This committee comprises members or former members of the General Legal Council, persons who hold or have held high judicial office, attorneys who were members of a former disciplinary body and attorneys who have been in practice not less than ten years. The Legal Profession Act provides statutory-based relief for any person who claims professional misconduct (including any default) or breach of duty committed by any lawyer. Out of the two branches, the emphasis is placed on case law precedents.

There is no restriction on the relief available to aggrieved clients. Two forms of relief are generally available: compensation and disciplinary action carried out by Jamaica's General Legal Council.

There is no financial limit to the level of compensation a client may recover. Under the Jamaican Legal Profession Act, a lawyer may be required to pay such sum as is deemed reasonable in compensating an aggrieved client, without any limits placed on such sum. Additionally, proceedings may be brought separately against the attorney for breach of contract, duty or fiduciary responsibility.

The second form of relief is again governed by the provisions of the Legal Profession Act and includes disciplinary action. Under the Act the disciplinary committee has the power to make any such order as to:

- the striking off from the Roll of the name of the offending attorney, suspending him from practice, or imposing on him such fine as they think proper;
- the payment by any party of costs or of such sum as they may consider a reasonable contribution towards costs;

- the payment by the attorney of any such sum by way of restitution as they may consider reasonable.

*Restrictions on liability*

There are certain restrictions on the circumstances in which lawyers, other than advocates, may be held liable to their clients. For example, there is a limit on the time period within which a person may bring proceedings, the length of which depends on whether the action is tortious or contractual.

Further, if a lawyer sought and accepted counsel's advice on specialist matters, this tends to immunize the lawyer from suit because, as a general rule, it can hardly be said that he acted unreasonably, unless an exceptional set of circumstances exists.

Turning to the situation where lawyers appear as advocates, the former blanket immunity which advocates once enjoyed in the past has been somewhat eroded. This is largely due to the current position in English case law in this area which is of binding authority in Jamaica.

Nowadays, the 'special immunity' of advocates only extends to work performed in court, or to work which was intimately entwined with that performance.

As with other professions, lawyers can, by agreement with their clients, limit their liability for particular matters as well as generally by way of standard conditions. However, the very nature of the lawyer-client relationship suggests that any agreement will be construed against the legal adviser who occupies the position of having special training, expertise and experience in legal matters. There is no statute of a professional body in Jamaica which curtails the level to which lawyers may limit their liability in respect of work done on a client's behalf. The financial restrictions which can be agreed will depend upon the size and complexity of the issues involved. However, the fact is that in Jamaica such arrangements are not common.

The limitation period for bringing an action against an attorney depends on the nature of the claim being brought. If the claim involves fraud, there is no time limit within which to bring an action. This is the only area in which no limitation period for actions against lawyers (and others) exists. In Jamaica, the limitation period for bringing a claim in contract or tort is six years starting from the date when knowledge of the breach is apprehended.

*Liability to non-clients*

Part of the liability of lawyers to third parties depends upon the ordinary Law of Agency, usually in both contract and tort, the position will be clear whether he is acting as agent or principal. If the lawyer acts without authority, he will render himself liable to be sued for breach of warranty of authority. A lawyer may also be liable in circumstances where a beneficiary loses out because he has been negligent in drawing up a will for his client.

*Recent developments with respect to liability*
Over the last twenty-five to thirty years, the principle of a 'special relationship' between lawyer and client has taken root. It is clear that the scope of liability in negligence relating not only to lawyers but to other professions is still in a developmental stage (as can be seen from recent decisions in English law).

Nowadays a higher standard of care is required of a lawyer than was the case thirty years ago. This higher standard of care owed to clients has led to the increasing use of liability insurance by lawyers and law firms.

**Insurance**

*Voluntary professional indemnity insurance*
Indemnity insurance for the legal profession is not compulsory in Jamaica, but it is recommended as a safeguard in relation to actions brought against a lawyer or law firm.

There is no information available to indicate what proportion of the legal profession takes out professional indemnity insurance.

*Insurance facilities*
Professional indemnity insurance is privately arranged through commercial insurers — both inside and outside Jamaica.

*Level of cover*
There are no statistics available to indicate the level of cover generally obtained by the legal profession.

It is left up to the lawyer of law firm's discretion as to whether, what type, and how much professional indemnity insurance is taken up.

*Deductibles*
There are no statistics available on the range of deductibles payable by the insured lawyers.

*Recent developments with respect to insurance*
At the time of writing this book there are no new trends or potential developments in the area of insurance which may significantly alter the framework summarised above.

## JAPAN

### The civil liability of legal advisers

*Basis of liability*
There is no special statute or legal doctrine governing the liability of lawyers. Malpractice is covered by tort or breach of contract. These principles are usually defined by court decisions.

The Bar Association has the authority to discipline those who act in violation of ethical standards. The severest cases are dealt with in the courts. Relief is restricted to compensation only. The Bar Association may suspend the licenses of the lawyers for a specified period of time. There is no financial limit.

*Restrictions on liability*
Lawyers may limit their liability by contract but this is considered highly unusual. It is likely that if an attorney suggests that such a contract be entered into, the client will assume that he is lacking the proper legal advice that one must have before agreeing to such a contract. There are no restrictions.

The Statute of Limitations dictates that in a tort action a claimant must commence proceedings within three years of becoming aware that his loss was attributable to the act complained of. There is a long-stop limit of twenty years after which time no action can be brought against a lawyer irrespective of the date of knowledge of the claimant.

*Liability to non-clients*
Except for tort actions (including criminal actions), there are no circumstances in which a lawyer is liable to third parties.

*Recent developments with respect to liability*
There is no legal framework but recent trends indicate that clients are beginning to take action against lawyers.

### Insurance

*Voluntary professional indemnity insurance*
Indemnity insurance for the legal profession is voluntary in Japan. It is estimated that less than ten per cent of the legal profession takes out professional indemnity insurance.

*Insurance facilities*
Policies are issued by commercial insurers, usually from insurers in Japan.

*Level of cover*
The level of cover generally taken up by the legal profession is estimated to be USD2.3 million per case and USD6.9 million in total insurance for a term of two years.

*Deductibles*
There are no statistics available on the range of deductibles payable by the insured lawyers. There is no requirement for the insured lawyers to pay any part of the claim themselves.

*Recent developments with respect to insurance*
At the time of writing this book there are no new trends or potential developments in the area of professional indemnity insurance.

## KENYA

### The civil liability of legal advisers

*Basis of liability*
The Advocates Act of Kenya does not contain any provisions dealing with the issue of civil liability. The Act clearly recognises that an advocate may be liable to his client for negligence but provides no guidance as to the definition and the standard of a lawyer's duty of care or as to the nature of that liability. It has therefore fallen on the courts to define the principles applicable to the civil liability of advocates and a significant volume of common law has developed on the point.

On the whole the Kenyan courts have drawn from and affirmed the position taken by the English courts and it is true to say that, with the exception of the very few matters on which it has been difficult to reconcile the differences between the legal professions of the two jurisdictions, Kenyan Law in this area is identical to the English common law.

Furthermore, the civil liability of advocates is a matter in which parliament has not yet intervened with legislation, nor any professional body or institution with rules or schemes or other such mechanisms of regulating or guiding the operation of the common law.

In respect of advice given, but possibly not advocacy, the guiding principles of an advocate's liability are the same as those applied by the English courts. This is the case if the action against the advocate is based on the duty of care owed to the client in tort, or that which is an implied term of the contract between advocate and client. The duty owed by an advocate to his client is that he will exercise a reasonable degree of care and skill. The standard of care is that of a reasonably competent and diligent advocate.

The liability of lawyers is a matter decided solely by the courts. There is a Complaints Commission which has the duty to investigate complaints made regarding the conduct of advocates and where such conduct discloses a disciplinary offence, to refer the matter to the Disciplinary Committee. Where there is substance in a complaint but the circumstances of the case do not disclose a disciplinary offence, the duty of the Commission is to advise the complainant to refer the matter to the courts for appropriate redress.

All the remedies available in tort and contract are available to the client plaintiff. However, there is no reported case where the courts have made any order other than that to pay compensation. The Complaints Commission has the power to award to the complainant "reimbursement of expenses" where the complainant has suffered loss or damage by reason of the advocate's conduct, but that conduct does not amount to a disciplinary offence. To this end, the Commission may issue a warrant for the levy of the amount of the award on the property of the advocate concerned, and the amount may be recovered by distress and sale under warrant. The Commission will award an amount which it considers to be just and proper in the circumstances of the case, but the amount may not exceed approximately USD225,000.

There are no financial limits on the compensation which lawyers may be ordered to pay. Damages are assessed, in the usual manner, on the basis of the client plaintiff's loss, applying the principles of the common law to the assessment of damages.

*Restrictions on liability*

It is unclear whether advocates are immune from suit in relation to the conduct of litigation. The uncertainty arises from the fact that Kenya's legal profession is fused, and as such, some of the main arguments which have featured in the English courts for this immunity are inapplicable, in particular that of the English barrister's contractual incapacity to sue for fees. Although there are no Kenyan decided cases restricting the circumstances in which an advocate may be held liable to his client at present, there is a strong argument for immunity in litigation which may yet be approved by the Kenyan courts in case the negligent act allegedly relates to things done or not done during appearances in court as opposed to matters preliminary to hearings or trials.

Any agreement which purports to limit an advocate's liability to his or her client is thought to be void by virtue of the Advocates Act, which states:

> Nothing in this Act shall give validity to any agreement relieving any advocate from responsibility for professional negligence or any other responsibility to which he would otherwise be subject as an advocate.

However, this section is open to interpretation. It could be argued that the section allows such agreements to be valid at common law or under a provision of some other Act and clears up uncertainty which only arises from the Advocates Act. This lends itself to the belief that any provision therein provides validity to such an agreement. Unfortunately there are no court decisions to assist in the clarification of this matter. It can only be stated that there is no Act of Parliament which specifically lends validity to such agreements.

In respect of claims in negligence, the time limit is three years for tortious actions, and three and six years for actions for breach of contract. In respect of disciplinary proceedings there is no limitation period.

*Liability to non-clients*

It is clear that an advocate may be liable to non-clients in respect of advice given where the appropriate circumstances exist. An advocate may also be liable in defamation to a non-client. Absolute privilege in this respect only applies for defamatory words uttered in judicial or *quasi-judicial* proceedings. In all other legal matters such as correspondence and negotiation, only qualified privilege attaches and as such, if a non-client can prove malice or bad faith on the advocate's part, an action in defamation against that advocate would stand.

*Recent developments with respect to liability*

No significant changes to or developments in the present framework are expected in the foreseeable future.

**Insurance**

*Voluntary professional indemnity insurance*

Indemnity insurance for the legal profession is voluntary in Kenya. Only a small proportion of the legal profession takes out professional indemnity insurance.

*Insurance facilities*

Available for insurance are policies issued by commercial insurers. Due to the provisions of the Kenyan Insurance Act, all insurance must be placed with a licensed Kenyan insurer. Reinsurance for those firms which carry a high level of cover would generally be obtained from overseas reinsurers.

*Level of cover*

There are no statistics available to indicate the level of cover generally obtained by the legal profession. The level of cover can be as high as USD5 million, but most practices would carry a significantly lower level of cover.

For a firm with a level of cover of USD5 million, the professional indemnity insurance premium can represent approximately eight per cent of the annual expenses of the practice.

*Deductibles*
The range of deductibles payable by the insured lawyers, like any other term of the insurance contract, is negotiable and therefore varies according to the different policies.

*Recent developments with respect to insurance*
The Law Society of Kenya has been working on the introduction of a compulsory indemnity insurance scheme as well as a compensation fund over the past three years. The schemes have now been agreed upon in principle, and the drafting of the enabling amendments to the Advocates Act and the relevant Rules has reached an advanced stage.

It is hoped that the mechanisms of new schemes will be fully in place by the end of 1995. Both will be modelled closely on the English Solicitors Law Society Schemes. However, the professional indemnity scheme will be along the lines of the older scheme contained in the 1986 Rules of the Law Society, rather than the 1987 scheme.

## KOREA

### The civil liability of legal advisers

*Basis of liability*
The main guiding principle of a lawyer's liability to a client is based on a duty of good care. This is set out in the Korean Civil Code which requires an agent mandatary to manage the affairs entrusted to him with the care of a good manager in accordance with his instructions.

The standard of duty of good care is decided according to the degree of skill and care to be expected of a competent lawyer.

The principles are defined both by statutes under the Korean Civil Code and by court decisions. The general principle of duty of care is also provided for in the Korean Civil Code, and the standard of duty of care has been developed by court decisions.

The liability of lawyers is decided by court decisions. Aside from the liability of a lawyer against the client, the relevant local Bar Associations may decide to suspend the licence of a lawyer involved or it may decide to take other disciplinary actions. The local Bar Associations may also act as a mediator between a lawyer and the client regarding a dispute. However, the findings of the local Bar Associations in such cases only amount to recommendations and therefore, the Associations do not have the power to enforce their findings.

*Restrictions on liability*

The relief available is restricted to compensation and there are no limits on the compensation which lawyers may be ordered to pay. There are no restrictions as to the circumstances in which lawyers may be held liable to their clients.

Lawyers may limit their liability with clients by way of standard conditions. The standard conditions are not specific but general, such as a rule of good faith, prohibition on abuse of rights, good customs and social order.

Financial restrictions can be agreed upon under the Korean Civil Code which permits parties to an agreement to determine in advance the amount of damages payable in the event of the non-performance of an obligation. However, agreements limiting lawyers' liability are rarely made in Korea.

There are no rules which prevent lawyers from restricting their liability to their clients.

A claim by a client based upon a contract between the lawyer and the client will expire if it is not exercised for ten years. A claim by the client based upon a tort will expire if not brought within the following time periods, whichever comes first:

- three years from the date when the client became aware of the damage and of the identity of the tort-feasor (lawyer); or
- ten years from the time when the tort was committed.

*Liability to non-clients*

Generally lawyers are not liable to a non-client. Contractual liability does not arise because there is no contract between the lawyer and the non-client. But tort liability may, theoretically, arise if a direct causation can be found between the lawyer's tortious act and the resulting damages to the non-client. This rarely occurs.

*Recent developments with respect to liability*

There are no trends or developments taking place which may significantly alter the framework summarized above.

**Insurance**

*Professional indemnity insurance*

There is no professional indemnity insurance available for the legal profession in Korea.

## LATVIA

### The civil liability of legal advisers

*Basis of liability*

If a sworn advocate breaches his duty to his client and causes a loss, the client may claim against the advocate for losses attributable to the breach.

The Latvian law of the Advocature 1993 states that in addition to a claim being made by the client, the Board of the Latvian Sworn Advocates may bring disciplinary proceedings against the advocate at the request of the court, Public Prosecutor, an aggrieved client or on its own initiative. Disciplinary proceedings shall be commenced if, in the Board's opinion, the allegations relate to:

- a breach of the advocate's duty to his client;
- a breach of the statutes of the collegium board of the Latvian Sworn Advocates; or
- the instructions regulating the activities of sworn advocates or the professional ethics of sworn advocates.

In conforming with the "Fixed Rate Payment for the Judicial Help of the Sworn Advocate", if the advocate fails to carry out his professional duties honestly and as a result causes losses to his client, the Board of the Sworn Advocates has the right to ask the advocate to repay the whole or part of his fees to his client. In addition, the advocate in those circumstances may also be asked to pay off his client's losses insofar as those losses may be recoverable by his client under the law of Latvia.

*Restrictions on liability*

Sworn advocates may, in their written retainers, set out the extent of their potential liability to their clients and may put restrictions on their liabilities. However, it is rare for advocates to actually include such provisions in their retainers. Ultimately, in cases where claims are made against an advocate, it is usually the court which decides the extent of that advocate's liability in any particular case.

Time limits for claims are set out in the Civil Law of the Republic of Latvia.

*Liability to non-clients*

Under the law of the Advocature of the Republic of Latvia, advocates cannot be held liable for oral or written statements made by them when honestly fulfilling their professional duties. However, liability to non-clients in other ways is possible.

*Recent developments with respect to liability*

There are currently no trends or changes which could significantly alter the legislation of the Republic of Latvia insofar as it applies to sworn advocates.

### Insurance

*Voluntary professional indemnity insurance*
Indemnity insurance for advocates is voluntary in Latvia. The Law of the Advocature in the Republic of Latvia states that professional indemnity insurance is possible for sworn advocates and assistants to sworn advocates.

The professional indemnity insurance of sworn advocates is not widely spread and it is estimated that only a few sworn advocates make use of it.

A sworn advocate has to inform his client if he is not insured for professional indemnity.

*Insurance facilities*
Available for insurance are policies issued by commercial insurers in Latvia.

The Board of the Sworn Advocates of Latvia has not certified the policies of any commercial insurers, because indemnity insurance is voluntary for sworn advocates.

*Level of cover*
There are no statistics available to indicate the level of cover obtained by advocates.

*Deductibles*
There are no statistics available on the range of deductibles payable by the insured advocates.

*Recent developments with respect to insurance*
It is expected that in the future, when the insurance system develops further in Latvia, advocates will use their rights more widely by insuring their professional activity.

## LIECHTENSTEIN

### The civil liability of legal advisers

*Basis of liability*
A lawyer is liable for negligence in advising clients and in conducting matters on their behalf. Liability is strict and the principles are defined by statute. The liability of lawyers is a matter decided by the courts and no other professional body has jurisdiction. Where a lawyer is in breach of his professional duties, he may also be subject to disciplinary proceedings. The *Obergericht* (Court of second instance) exercises a disciplinary jurisdiction over lawyers.

The relief available is restricted to compensation. If, however, the damage has been caused maliciously or as a result of gross negligence, the aggrieved party may seek full satisfaction (*volle Genugtuung*), which requires the lawyer to compensate his client for his anticipated profit. There are no financial limits on the compensation which lawyers may be ordered to pay.

*Restrictions on liability*

In general, a lawyer who has negligently or intentionally caused damage to his client will be held liable to the client for the damage caused. There is no immunity when appearing as an advocate. The client must, however, prove that the damage has occurred and that it has been caused by the lawyer's negligence, in breach of duty to his client. If there has been contributory negligence on the part of the client, this may reduce the liability of the lawyer.

The question of whether or not a lawyer may limit, or even exclude entirely, his liability has never been fully clarified by the Liechtenstein courts. It may be assumed, based on guiding principles, that, where a lawyer has acted for his client free of charge, he may limit or exclude his liability to that client in all cases, except in respect of damage caused intentionally. If a lawyer does receive remuneration, he will be entitled to limit or exclude his liability in respect of negligence, but not in respect of gross negligence. A lawyer's liability may be limited by way of standard conditions, but it is advisable for the limitation of liability to be recorded by way of a written agreement. Such agreements are rare.

If an exclusion or limitation of liability is contrary to public policy, it will be invalid (as in the case of intentional damage).

The time limit for making a claim or instituting proceedings against a lawyer is three years from the date on which the damage and the identity of the person causing the damage become known or should have been known to the claimant. There is a time limit of thirty years when the damaged person does not know the damager or about the damage.

*Liability to non-clients*

In general, a lawyer will not be liable for damage caused to non-clients. Where, however, a lawyer's negligent advice causes damage to a non-client, and provided the conditions necessary to be found liable are satisfied, the lawyer may be liable to that person. Such claims are the exception rather than the rule.

*Recent developments with respect to liability*

There are no trends appearing and no developments taking place which may significantly alter the framework summarised above.

## Insurance

*Compulsory professional indemnity insurance*

Indemnity insurance for the legal profession is compulsory in Liechtenstein, as required by law.

*Insurance facilities*
The policy has to be issued by a commercial insurer from within the country. All major Swiss insurers have offices in Liechtenstein.

*Level of cover*
The minimum level of cover is regulated by law and is USD831,000 for each claim. Often the level of cover is more than USD831,000 (up to USD8.3 million or more).

The minimum insurance cover for patent attorneys is USD1.6 million.

The insurance premium for indemnity insurance is higher than USD8,300. It is estimated that one to three per cent of the annual expenses are insurance premiums.

*Deductibles*
The range of deductibles payable by the insured lawyers themselves — before a claim becomes large enough to involve a payment by insurers — differs from law firm to law firm. The larger the law firm, the higher the amount the lawyer pays himself. We are of the opinion that claims less than USD10,000 are paid by lawyers themselves.

*Recent developments with respect to insurance*
There are no recent developments or trends in the area of insurance.

## LUXEMBOURG

### The civil liability of legal advisers

*Basis of liability*
A distinction has to be made whether the lawyer is advising his client or whether he is acting in purely procedural matters. In the first case, the lawyer just has an obligation to use all means available to achieve the best possible result. These principles are based on the general liability principles of agency contracts. The lawyer's liability may be established only by proving a fault committed by the lawyer which has as a consequence caused loss.

In the second case the lawyer has an obligation to achieve the result that he has been asked to achieve, which means that he will be liable if he commits a fault in executing purely procedural actions. For example, if a lawyer has been instructed to introduce a court action, and if he has missed the date to do so, he will be liable, if the client can prove that the error of the lawyer has caused him a prejudice. If the lawyer has failed to introduce the action in time, his client may claim damages for losing a chance of winning the case before the court.

The lawyer may not be held liable for inadequate pleadings, for taking a view of the law that is not accepted by the court, especially if the legal point is controversial, or for the result obtained by his pleadings. Even here there could be liability for committing a gross error. However, the lawyer may be liable for wrong procedure, for errors committed in the correct application of the law, for the introduction of appeals, or for the service of judgements. The lawyer may be liable even when committing minor faults.

The guiding principles of lawyers' liability are based on general contractual principles, determined by law and court decisions. The liability of lawyers is a matter decided by the courts, according to the principles of liability in general. The relief available to the client is restricted to compensation. It has to be noted that if the lawyer is liable for missing a time limit in procedural matters, the client will only receive compensation for the loss a chance to win the case, as the final result of the court action could never proved.

There are no financial limits to compensation, except for the situation where the lawyer has restricted his liability in the contract binding him to his client.

The lawyer may be held liable for his client's entire loss, if the prejudice has been caused exclusively by his fault.

*Restrictions on liability*
As well as the restrictions mentioned above, lawyers have immunity from any action for slander in respect of arguments before the court that might be helpful to their clients.

According to the general principles regulating agency agreements and the principles of contractual liberty, lawyers may limit their liability by special clauses inserted in the contracts concluded with their clients. However, even if the lawyer's liability has been limited, the client can always turn against the lawyer, if he has committed a gross error or fault which has caused damage to the client.

The lawyer and his client may agree on any kind of financial restriction by a written agreement accepted by both the client and the lawyer. Lawyers are very rarely bound by a written contract to their client. As a consequence, they very rarely restrict their liability towards their clients, except by introducing certain reserves into their legal opinions.

The time limits for making claims or instituting proceedings against lawyers is thirty years, which is the general time limit.

*Liability to non-clients*
Lawyers can be liable to non-clients whenever a fault committed by the lawyer has caused a prejudice to a third person. The liability towards non-clients is based on the common principles of delictual and *quasi-delictual* responsibility as defined in the Civil Code.

*Recent developments with respect to liability*
No significant alteration of these liability principles is presently foreseen.

## Insurance

*Compulsory professional indemnity insurance*
Indemnity insurance for the legal profession was made compulsory in Luxembourg in 1994 by the Luxembourg Bar.

*Insurance facilities*
The Luxembourg Bar has decided to contract with one single insurance company — a collective insurance policy — for all the members of the Luxembourg Bar.

The insurance policy subscribed to by the Luxembourg Bar is issued by a Belgian insurance company, and is similar to the collective professional indemnity insurance contracted by Belgian Bars.

*Level of cover*
The minimum level of cover is approximately USD500,000 per claim. The collective insurance policy offers the option of taking out excess cover up to USD3 million per claim.

The premium for professional indemnity insurance represents probably less than one per cent of the annual expenses of a law practice in Luxembourg.

*Deductibles*
The deductible payable by the insured lawyer himself of the first claim is twenty-five per cent of the loss, with a minimum of USD305 and a maximum of USD3,050.

However, if the damage is caused by the violation of a time limit for introducing an action before the court, the minimum deductible is USD1,500, while the maximum varies as follows:

- USD3,800 for the first claim;
- USD5,700 for the second claim;
- USD7,600 for the third and further claims.

As the insurance policy is a collective policy for the entire Bar, the bonus-malus varies according to the number of claims from the entire Bar, while the annual premium will increase or decrease in relation to the number of claims made by all insured lawyers.

*Recent developments with respect to insurance*
As compulsory insurance has only been introduced recently, we are not expecting further developments at this time. However, after the Bar has gained some experience with this type of insurance, perhaps some adaptations to the conditions of insurance will be necessary.

## MALAWI

### The civil liability of legal advisers

*Basis of liability*

The guiding principles of lawyers' liability to their clients for advice given and conduct of matters are those applicable in the Tort of Negligence. If a lawyer, in the performance of his duties to his client fails to meet the standard of skill and care to be expected of a competent lawyer, as a result of which the client suffers damage (most likely, economic damage) then the lawyer is liable to his client.

There is no strict liability. It is for the client to establish that his lawyer has performed below the standard of a competent lawyer, and that, as a result he has suffered some loss. There is no statute in place, defining the principles of lawyers' liability to their clients. There have, however, been abundant authorities decided by the courts in Malawi in which such liability has been established along the lines set out in the first paragraph.

The Legal Education and Legal Practitioners Act, of the Laws of Malawi, establishes a Disciplinary Committee within the Malawi Law Society. The committee deals with matters of misconduct by legal practitioners. The whole Act is concerned with matters of misconduct (including theft of the client's money or property), but does not deal with legal practitioners' negligence in handling an action in court or in giving advice.

If we are to move in the direction of providing for such a situation, it would be the Disciplinary Committee of the Malawi Law Society that would have jurisdiction over its members, of course without usurping the inherent jurisdiction of the High Court.

*Restrictions on liability*

The awards in this type of case that have so far been made are compensatory, but if the counsel for the applicant can make a strong case for any other orders, there is no reason why the court would not grant any other relief which it deems fit.

There are no financial limits imposed on the compensation that can be awarded. The courts will look at the loss and damage which the client has suffered and will compensate him accordingly. The financial means of the legal practitioner is not the court's concern. Its concern is restitution, in money terms.

There is no special immunity in any particular circumstances, but the courts have held the view that counsel will not be held liable for every error, as no attorney is bound to know all the law. The test is whether the lawyer appearing as an advocate exercised a reasonable degree of care, skill and the knowledge of a reasonably competent lawyer.

The relationship between lawyer and client is a contractual one, as such it should be possible for a lawyer by agreement with his client to limit his liability. The court would, however, retain its jurisdiction to test the reasonableness of such exemption or limitation clauses. The court would look at the bargaining powers of the parties. This situation has, however, not arisen, but it is likely that a Malawi court would be slow to approve such agreement or conditions since it might still take the view that they would cause a decline in professional standards.

The Legal Education and Legal Practitioners Act is silent on preventing lawyers from restricting their liability to clients. The practice has, however, been that a lawyer cannot do so, and a lawyer cannot set up a law practice with limited liability. This practice seems to have been copied from the United Kingdom.

By statute, as in any tort action, except for personal injuries and death claims, the period of limitation is six years from the date the damage occurred.

*Liability to non-clients*

A lawyer instructed by a mortgagee in exercise of the mortgagee's rights to auction real property in respect of which premiums have not been paid for a considerable time might describe the property wrongly and be sued by the owner of the property which appears in the advert which is, in fact, not the subject of any mortgage at all. This would be one of the situations where a lawyer would be liable to non-clients.

*Recent developments with respect to liability*

We are likely to move towards legislation in this area which could, *inter alia*, deal with the following matters:

- no lawyer shall limit or restrict his liability to a client whether by agreement or otherwise, since to do so would reduce the level of professional skill, care and attention;
- no financial ceiling shall be placed on a lawyer's liability;
- the lawyer shall be liable to his client not just for misappropriation, but for negligent handling of his client's matter in whatever capacity the lawyer is acting.

This trend has been observed from seminars held by the Malawi Law Society, where the need for compulsory professional indemnity insurance to be taken out either by the respective law practices or by the Malawi Law Society on behalf of its members has been appreciated, so that not only clients are protected, but the integrity of the profession of the law is preserved.

## Insurance

*Voluntary professional indemnity insurance*

Professional indemnity insurance for the legal profession is voluntary in Malawi, though in practice it is virtually compulsory if a lawyer practises in the field of Banking and Finance. Lending institutions put indemnity insurance as a condition before giving the lawyer any work. The New Building Society, for example, will not give work to any firm without such cover.

As the mortgage business is very profitable, a large part of the legal profession takes out indemnity insurance. It is estimated that approximately seventy-five per cent of the legal profession is insured.

*Insurance facilities*
The only insurance cover available is issued by local commercial insurers and specifically arranged by the firms themselves.

*Level of cover*
As cover is arranged by each firm individually, the level of cover depends upon the volume and nature of business, the size of its staff and number of partners. The level of cover, however, is likely to be determined by the institutions that insist on such cover. The cover is an aggregate of all claims in a particular insurance year.

*Deductibles*
The range of deductibles payable by the insured lawyers is negotiable. It ranges from one to ten per cent or more.

The higher the deductible, the less the insurance premium. Many lawyers actually believe that the need to invoke the indemnity policy will not arise, and as a result they raise their deductibles with a view to paying less premiums.

*Recent developments with respect to insurance*
At recent meetings of the Malawi Law Society, the need for compulsory professional indemnity insurance to be taken out either by the respective law practices, or by the Malawi Law Society on behalf of its members, has been acknowledged, in order to ensure that not only the clients are protected, but that the integrity of the profession of the law is also preserved.

On November 4, 1994, the Malawi Law Society requested the Association of Law Societies of the Republic of South Africa to provide it with background information to facilitate the establishment of professional indemnity insurance to be taken out by the Society on behalf of all its members.

## MALTA

### The civil liability of legal advisers

*Basis of liability*
The guiding principles in assessing whether a lawyer is liable towards his client in respect of advice given and conduct of matters are the following:

- the degree of diligence to be exercised is that of a *bonus paterfamilias*, ("a good head of the family": a concept going back to Roman law) i.e. whether he used that degree of skill and care which a competent lawyer would have used in his stead; and

- a lawyer is not responsible for any mistake made by him which has not been made intentionally, fraudulently or through gross ignorance or gross negligence.

These guiding principles are based on the fundamental principles of law contained in the Civil Code and are defined by court decisions. The juridical nature of the relationship between the lawyer and his client has been described by the courts as having similar characteristics to mandate and to the contract of works (*locatio operis*), but as being identical to neither. This relationship is *sui generis* because, although the client seems to appoint the lawyer as far as his case is concerned as his *sui generis* mandatary, this relationship differs from that contemplated under the institute of mandate, where, the mandatary must act within the limits of his mandate and cannot exceed such mandate. On the other hand, the lawyer appearing for his client in a civil or commercial suit, should act according to the provisions of the law, according to doctrine and according to his conscience, and cannot be considered as dependent on his client in the way he carries out this activity. This is because the advocate is at the same time a public functionary in front of the court and is regulated and disciplined by certain special rules.

Unlike a remunerated mandatary, an advocate is not bound to exercise a higher degree of skill and care than that of a *bonus paterfamilias* and is not responsible for *culpa lievis*.

Court judgments are not binding as precedent in Malta, although they are considered as authoritative and reference is made to them in submissions to the court.

These principles have been largely reproduced in the draft "Code of Ethics and Conduct for Lawyers". It states:

- An advocate must properly administer, using the diligence of a bonus paterfamilias, any matter or thing entrusted to him in his professional capacity and must not make use thereof or derive any benefit therefrom in any manner other than as expressly or impliedly directed or allowed by the person who shall have entrusted such matter or thing to him; and must give due account thereof when so requested.
- An advocate must not act or continue to act in circumstances where the client cannot be represented with competence or diligence.
- An advocate who has accepted instructions on behalf of a client is bound to carry out those instructions with diligence and must exercise reasonable care and skill.

The liability of lawyers for advice given or the conduct of matters in a particular case falls within the jurisdiction of the civil court. The remedy available is damages payable to the injured client.

When the conduct of an advocate or legal procurator is tantamount to misconduct, the advocate or legal procurator is subject to proceedings in terms of the Commission for the Administration of Justice Act 1994. "Misconduct" in relation to advocates or legal procurators is:

> any breach of a code or codes of ethics relative to the profession of advocate or legal procurator, as the case may be.

Allegations of misconduct are a matter for the Commission for the Administration of Justice and the Committee for Advocates and Legal Procurators, which may investigate complaints and carry out its own enquiries. It can impose penalties ranging from an admonition up to a request for the permanent suspension of such advocate or legal procurator by the President of Malta.

There are no financial limits on the damages payable to the injured client in the event the lawyer is liable. Damages, however, must be proven and would consist of the actual loss suffered and consequential loss of earnings arising from the negligent act or omission. Advocates and legal procurators found guilty of misconduct by the Committee of Advocates and Legal Procurators may be condemned by the Committee to pay a pecuniary penalty, recoverable as a civil debt by the Secretary of the Commission, not exceeding ten per cent of the annual salary of the Attorney General.

*Restrictions on liability*

There are no restrictions as to the circumstances in which lawyers may be held liable to their clients. Agreements by which lawyers limit their liability towards their clients are, as far as we are aware, unheard of in Malta. The matter is not regulated by legislation nor has it been considered in court decisions. The matter must be considered in the light of the general principles of the law of contract contained in the Civil Code, in particular that the parties are free to make any agreement that they wish unless it is prohibited by law or contrary to morality or to public policy. Court decisions (mainly dealing with commercial agreements) have in a number of cases accepted and applied limitation of liability clauses. On the other hand, there are several court decisions (again mainly dealing with commercial agreements) which have declared exclusion of liability clauses invalid on the ground that they are contrary to morals or public policy. Consequently if the limitation of liability agreement is tantamount to effectively excluding liability, it may be declared invalid.

Claims or proceedings by clients against lawyers, on the basis of the general rule of prescription applicable to actions for damages arising out of contract, are barred by the lapse of five years from the date on which such claim is exercisable against the lawyer.

*Liability to non-clients*

Lawyers can be liable to non-clients on the basis of the fundamental principle of the law of delict that every person is liable for the damage which occurs through his fault.

There must be a relationship of causality between the negligent act and the damage caused; if the act which gave rise to damage to the third party arose from a mere counsel from the advocate but not from legal advice, then according to the Roman Law principle, there is no liability unless there has been fraud or bad faith.

According to Obligations to others — Relations with third parties, the Draft Code of Ethics states:

> Advocates must not act, whether in their professional capacity or otherwise, towards anyone in any way which is fraudulent, deceitful or otherwise contrary to their position as advocates. Nor must advocates use their position as advocates to take unfair advantage either for themselves or another person.

Actions for damages by non-clients against lawyers (which do not arise out of contract) are barred by the lapse of two years unless such actions arise from a criminal offence in which case the rules of prescription relating to criminal actions are applicable Prescription can be suspended or interrupted.

*Recent developments with respect to liability*
The Chamber of Advocates, the lawyers' professional body, is in the process of drafting a new Code of Ethics. This is the draft "Code of Ethics and Conduct for Lawyers" referred to above.

**Insurance**

*Voluntary professional indemnity insurance*
Indemnity insurance for the legal profession voluntary is in Malta. There is no data available to indicate what proportion of the legal profession takes out professional indemnity insurance. The proportion, however, is certainly very low.

*Insurance facilities*
Available insurance facilities are policies issued by commercial insurers. Commercial insurance is generally obtained from foreign insurers via Maltese insurance agents.

*Level of cover*
The average cover taken up by a single practitioner is approximately USD120,000 for each claim. For a law firm, the level of cover is approximately USD750,000 for each claim.

*Deductibles*
Generally, there are no deductibles payable by the insured lawyers themselves. In rare cases, however, the range of deductibles may be between approximately USD750 to USD1,500 for a single practitioner, and approximately USD30,000 for a law firm.

*Recent developments with respect to insurance*
The boom in economic and financial activity and the corresponding introduction of a considerable amount of legislation, particularly in the financial services sector over the past few years, is creating an increasing awareness amongst lawyers of the need for insurance cover.

It is likely that the next few years will see an increase in the proportion of lawyers taking out professional indemnity insurance cover.

## MEXICO

### The civil liability of legal advisers

*Basis of liability*
Under Mexican law there are no specific provisions regarding lawyers' professional liability. Graduates are bound to use all their scientific knowledge and technical resources to render services to their clients in accordance to the nature of the business. They will be liable for negligence, lack of expertise or fraud and must indemnify their clients for any damage or loss of profit. The principle of strict liability applies and is defined by statute. The liability of lawyers is a matter decided by the courts.

Although the relief available to a client who has damaged by a lawyer is limited to the payment of damages, such lawyer may be temporarily suspended or permanently prevented from practising. The compensation which lawyers may be ordered to pay is limited to the amount of damages caused.

*Restrictions on liability*
Civil liability may be regulated by agreement between the parties. In litigation, lawyers are not liable with respect to court resolutions, provided the lawyer did comply with his duties as such. It is not possible for a lawyer to absolve himself from responsibility if the negative result of the case is not attributable to his actions. However, liquidated damages or penalty clauses can be agreed upon. These types of agreements are extremely rare in Mexico.

A person wishing to sue a lawyer must do so within ten years from the date such person had knowledge of the unlawful action or omission of his lawyer.

*Liability to non-clients*
In general terms lawyers are not liable to non-clients in respect of any advice given. Likewise, lawyers are not liable to non-clients when acting on behalf of a client, provided they have been granted powers by the client for such purposes and have acted according to law and good custom.

*Recent developments with respect to liability*
At the time of writing this book there are no developments to speak of.

**Insurance**

*Professional indemnity insurance*
In Mexico, there is no compulsory professional indemnity insurance for the legal profession. Interested attorneys could contract such insurance.

## NETHERLANDS

### The civil liability of legal advisers

*Basis of liability*
A lawyer's professional liability arises from either the contractual relationship between the lawyer and his client or the law (tort committed by the lawyer against his client or third parties).

Default in the performance of a contractual obligation and/or breach of the duty of care (tort) are tested by the criterion of the "average prudent and skilled professional". The standard is "the reasonably skilled and reasonably acting professional". This does not mean "the perfect lawyer" but one who performs his task properly.

Case law shows that ever stricter requirements are imposed on the quality of work done by lawyers (and other members of the liberal professions).

The standard of "the reasonably skilled and reasonably acting professional" implies a subjective element (care for the client, his interests and wishes) and an objective element (professional skill in general).

The act or omission for which the lawyer is being held liable is assessed taking into account the following factors:

- skills (generalist as compared to specialist; much or little experience);
- independence (client's interest versus own responsibility);
- compliance with the duties to investigate, to inform and to warn;
- rules of the profession (Code of Professional Responsibility, Disciplinary Rules).

A lawyer's liability based on the contractual relationship or on tort is decided according to the degree of skill and care to be expected from a competent lawyer. The principles of lawyers' liability are basically defined by statute. The "average prudent and skilled professional" criterion has been developed by case law and became statutory at the introduction of the New Dutch Civil Code.

*Restrictions on liability*
The relief available in the Netherlands is restricted to compensation of losses and damages. Punitive damages cannot be claimed. In principle, there are no financial

limits on the compensation which lawyers may be ordered to pay. If the amount of compensation claimed exceeds the cover of the compulsory professional indemnity insurance (minimum cover: USD570,000 per event twice a year, or USD1.14 million a year), the particular lawyer's financial capacity will be taken into account. The power of the courts to moderate follows from the Civil Code. It should be understood that in the Netherlands only the *advocatuur* (i.e. the legal profession organized within the Dutch Bar) has to comply with the professional rules and regulations of their profession. The organized profession (the *advocaten*) has the exclusive right to represent the client in civil and penal court proceedings. Anyone with a law degree (a lawyer) and even non-lawyers may render legal advice.

Both *advocaten* and lawyers may limit the risk of personal liability by means of an "exoneration clause" in a written contract with their clients. The Dutch Bar, however, adapted its Directive on Compulsory Liability Insurance in 1991:

- requiring every *advocaat* to have the minimum insurance coverage; and
- allowing the *advocaat* to exonerate himself from personal liability for risks above the compulsory insurance coverage.

For the rest, *advocaten* do not have any specific privileges, like a right of immunity, in cases of a possible personal liability claim. As explained above, an "exoneration clause" should be agreed upon, in writing or by imposing standard conditions (after enabling the client not to accept these).

An obvious disadvantage of a contractual restrictions on liability is that it cannot be invoked as against third parties. As a result it could therefore be successfully circumvented. Another disadvantage is that the courts may overrule the whole or part of such an exoneration clause under the Civil Code. Also as regards private (i.e. non-corporate) clients, an exoneration clause would be one of the conditions on the "grey list", which are presumed by the courts to be unreasonably burdensome.

Although lawyers are allowed to limit their liability by means of an exoneration clause, in practice this rarely happens.

*Liability to non-clients*

Where third parties suffer damages or losses caused by a lawyer's error or negligence, they may under all circumstances sue the lawyer in tort.

*Recent developments with respect to liability*

Since assertive clients' readiness to file compensation claims and the number of successful claims are on the increase, the legal profession has raised the question whether unrestricted liability for the profession is still reasonable. There now seems to be a broad consensus that limitation of liability should no longer be deemed to be in conflict with the honour and dignity of the profession.

At this moment the Executive Board of the Dutch Bar is studying various methods to introduce an acceptable system which would protect the individual lawyer against the risks of very large damage claims.

A standard regulation is possible for agreements within a particular profession or branch of industry but only for agreements of certain categories to be determined by an Order in Council (administrative order). To date no such order has been made. A standard regulation must be adopted (and, as the case may be, amended or revoked) by a commission especially appointed for that purpose by the Minister of Justice. To date such commission has not been appointed. A standard regulation must subsequently be approved by the Crown.

Limitation of liability under the Civil Code creates the possibility of limitation of liability by Administrative Order in areas where one cannot obtain adequate insurance coverage on reasonable terms. This possibility is a reaction towards the increase of strict liability under new legislation, coupled with the opinion that such strict liability is acceptable only when it is possible to take out insurance for it. So far, however, the Government is not keen on applying the above principle. Indeed, the legislator's intention was that it should be used sparingly. Yet the legal profession increasingly takes the view that this Section is the most obvious means for designing a both socially acceptable and practically manageable formula by which the liability of lawyers (and other professionals) in the Netherlands can be limited.

## Insurance

*Compulsory professional indemnity insurance*

Indemnity insurance is compulsory for members of the Dutch Bar Association (*advocaten*) and public notaries in the Netherlands, due to requirements of the professional bodies.

For other legal advisors, such as those tax lawyers who are not a member of the Dutch Bar Association, professional indemnity insurance is not compulsory.

*Insurance facilities*

Each member of the Bar is personally responsible for arranging cover that complies with the minimum requirements of the Directive on Professional Liability.

Available for insurance are policies issued by commercial insurers. Commercial insurance with a level of cover under USD14.3 million is generally obtained from insurers within the country. The excess — if any — is often obtained from abroad.

*Level of cover*

The compulsory level of cover for each law firm is USD570,000 for each claim, and the insurance must cover at least an aggregate of USD1.1 million per year.

The level of cover taken up ranges from the compulsory cover of USD570,000 to USD57 million, and varies per practice. As a general indication, small firms tend to take out cover ranging between USD570,000 and USD2.8 million, middle-sized firms take out cover from USD11 million and up, and only the largest law firms take out cover for USD57 million.

This cover mentioned is a maximum for each event, but generally the aggregate per year is limited and the cover can be divided in layers.

For Dutch public notaries, it is compulsory to arrange for cover for the first USD570,000. For the next USD5.1 million, the liability is covered under a collective insurance scheme arranged for by the professional body. Further cover is optional.

The insurance premium varies according to the level of cover obtained. It is estimated that the proportion of the annual expenses of a law firm represented by the premium ranges between one and two per cent.

*Deductibles*

Deductibles payable by the insured lawyers themselves are negotiable. The maximum deductible allowed by the Directive on Professional Liability for a sole practitioner or law firm with two *advocaten*, is USD14,300 per claim.

For larger law firms, the deductibles may not be higher than an amount that equals as many times USD5,700 as the number of insured *advocaten*, with a maximum USD114,000 in total.

*Recent developments with respect to insurance*

Recently, the insurance premiums were increased by approximately fifteen per cent. We fear that the cost of insurance will increase continuously and substantially in the future.

## NEW ZEALAND

### The civil liability of legal advisers

*Basis of liability*

The professional liability of lawyers to their clients may arise under contract, in tort, in equity, or by statute. Some forms of liability are strict and others depend on the degree of skill and care exercised.

The professional liability of a lawyer can be analyzed under four headings:

- the obligation to exercise reasonable skill and care
- fiduciary obligations owed to clients
- obligations owed pursuant to undertakings
- obligations imposed by specific statutes.

The duties in contract, tort and equity tend to overlap. The source of the duty is less important than the nature of the obligation.

In most cases the contract of retainer is oral, or a combination of part oral instructions and part written material. As with all contracts, a contract of retainer will be a combination of express and implied terms. In most cases, the only express terms in the contract will relate to the actual job entrusted to the lawyer. Even these may not be clearly defined. The retainer is not a general retainer in respect of anything that might concern the client's affairs. It is specific and limited to the particular job. Although the contract of retainer is analyzed in the same way as any other contract, it is a contract for professional services and this fact cannot be ignored (see Consumer Guarantees Act 1993 below). In addition, the lawyer is an officer of High Court whose practice is governed by a code of ethics (Rules of Practice). These ethical obligations may give rise to circumstances in which a contract of retainer may or should be terminated by the lawyer.

Sometimes the lawyer will have conflicting obligations to his client and the court. As an officer of the court concerned in the administration of justice, he has an overriding duty to the court, to the standards of his profession, and to the public, which may lead to a conflict of his client's wishes with what the client thinks are his personal interests. The lawyer cannot be held liable for a breach of contract if it conflicts with his overriding duty to the court.

*The obligation to exercise reasonable skill and care.* An obligation is owed to the client, by virtue of an implied term in the contract of retainer (which will apply in the absence of any express term imposing a different standard), that the lawyer will exercise a reasonable degree of skill and care in performing the instruction undertaken. The obligation may also be owed to persons who are not clients in tort (see below).

The standard of skill and care expected of a lawyer is that which would be exercised by the reasonably competent and careful lawyer in the particular circumstances. The circumstances can, however, vary greatly and, as the cause of action is breach of contract for improper performance of the implied undertaking, the exact nature of the duty depends upon what it can be fairly be said the lawyer has been employed to do. The usual test of whether the particular actions or omissions complained fall short of the required standard of reasonable skill and care is whether the conduct is in accordance with the generally accepted practice of the profession. This is normally established by evidence of other experienced practitioners as to the usual practice (not merely their own practice). The court may nevertheless hold that a particular action, even though it accords with the general practice of the profession, is inadequate.

A lawyer's obligation to exercise reasonable skill and care is now embodied in statute in the form of the Consumer Guarantees Act 1993 (CGA). Members of the legal profession come within the definition of "supplier" in section 2 of the CGA which includes a person who in trade supplies services to a consumer. The CGA expressly includes "professions" in the definition of services, but maintains the existing rule of law conferring immunity from suit on a barrister or solicitor for work done "in the course of or in connection with proceedings before any Court or Tribunal".

Whether a particular service is subject to the CGA depends on whether the service is of a kind ordinarily acquired for personal, domestic or household use as defined in the CGA. Services supplied for resupply in trade or consumed in the course of production are excluded. Arguably this exclusion extends to a barrister's opinion to a solicitor who in turn incorporates the advice into a report to a client. However, it is also arguable that, in providing an opinion through a solicitor, a barrister may be using the solicitor as an agent in trade or supplying the advice to the consumer client by virtue of a contract of service with the solicitor. It is as yet unclear whether a barrister's services of this type attract the statutory liability.

The test for determining who is a "consumer" of legal services focuses on the purpose for which the service is ordinarily acquired rather than the purpose to which the actual client would put it. However, in case of legal services which would ordinarily be domestic (such as a house conveyance) but which the client intends for business use, the lawyer may contract out of the provisions of the CGA. The agreement to contract out must be in writing.

The CGA imposes similar duties to those imposed by the common law in the form of statutory guarantees. At a minimum, a lawyer must:

- be competent in the relevant area of the law;
- understand and record the client's desired purpose and result;
- carry out any instructions in a proper and timely manner; and
- give appropriate warnings as to likely results.

If a lawyer breaches any of the guarantees provided in the CGA, and the failure is able to be remedied by the lawyer, he must be given the opportunity to remedy it. The remedy must be provided within a reasonable time. If, by reason of neglect, failure or delay, the failure is not remedied, the client may have the failure remedied elsewhere and recover reasonable costs or may cancel the contract.

If the failure cannot be remedied or is of a substantial character the client may:

- cancel the contract; or
- obtain damages for reduction in the value of the product below the charge paid or payable for the service; and
- in all cases, the consumer may claim damages for loss or damage to the consumer which was reasonably foreseeable as liable to result from the failure.

*Fiduciary obligations owed to clients.* A lawyer has a fiduciary duty to his or her client to act with the utmost good faith. A fiduciary duty is an equitable duty embracing the duty to act with absolute fairness and openness. Breaches of fiduciary obligation can arise from:

- a conflict of interest between clients;
- a conflict of interest between client and solicitor; and
- knowing participation in a breach of trust by a person under a fiduciary obligation.

As a fiduciary, a lawyer must avoid a conflict between his duty to a client and any personal interest he may hold. Evidence of such a conflict of interest will make him prima facie liable for any loss that his client may incur. For example, if a lawyer advises a client to invest in a company in which he personally has a shareholding, without disclosing his interest, he will have to account to his client for any losses the client may incur if the company fails, even though he may not have caused that loss. The ability of one firm of lawyers to act for two clients in dispute is also limited by fiduciary obligations. It had been thought possible to do so through the use of a "Chinese wall", ie an arrangement separating some partners and fee earners in the firm from others. However, such arrangements do not meet the obligations owed by lawyers to their clients to use all their knowledge and abilities to benefit each client's particular affairs. The exception is where both clients consent to such an arrangement and to the inherent limitation on the duty.

In a recent decision of the Privy Council (*Mouat v Clark Boyce* [1993]) their Lordships overturned a decision of the New Zealand Court of Appeal which would have had the effect of extending the fiduciary obligations owed by lawyers. The Court of Appeal had imposed a duty on solicitors to refuse to act when they believed the transaction was not in the client's interest, even though the client had rejected that advice.

*Obligations owed pursuant to undertakings.* In respect of undertakings, every lawyer has a professional duty to honour an undertaking, whether written or oral, given in the course of a legal proceeding or the course of his practice. This rule applies whether the undertaking is given by the lawyer personally or by a partner or employee in the course of the practice. If a lawyer breaches an undertaking, the New Zealand Law Society is able to discipline him in terms of the breach only. Insofar as civil liability arising from the breach of the undertaking is concerned, an undertaking may be enforced on normal contractual principles. In addition to this, the High Court has a summary punitive jurisdiction over lawyers as officers of the court and enforcement by this method is the most effective as a lawyer will not be able to raise the usual contractual defences. The principles are reasonably well established. The court can require that a lawyer who has defaulted on a personal undertaking to a third party with respect to his client's affairs pay:

- damages for the loss suffered by the third party in consequence; and/or
- the third party's costs on a solicitor and client basis.

If such payment is ordered the solicitor normally has the right of indemnity against his client.

In order for an undertaking to be enforced in this manner, it must be a personal undertaking given by the lawyer in his professional capacity. It is not sufficient if the undertaking is merely given on behalf of the client or if it is given by a lawyer in some capacity other than as a lawyer. Before such an undertaking can be enforced it must be clear in its terms and, in construing the meaning of such an undertaking, it will generally be assumed that the undertaking was intended to facilitate the successful completion of an essentially commercial dealing. It should not normally be construed in any technical or legalistic fashion but rather by reference to the evident substance and intention.

*Obligations imposed by specific statutes.* The Fair Trading Act 1986 has, in very recent times, given rise to a number of decisions imposing, or potentially imposing, liability on lawyers for actions which can be categorised as misleading or deceptive. Such cases represent a significant additional potential source of liability for practitioners. Section 9 of the Fair Trading Act 1986 provides that no person shall, in trade, engage in conduct that is misleading or deceptive or is likely to mislead or deceive. It is clear from the authorities that lawyers carrying out their professional duties are acting "in trade" and that an intention to mislead or deceive is not required for liability.

Both the Commerce Act 1986 and the Fair Trading Act 1986 contain provisions whereby parties aiding or abetting a breach of either Act can be subject to remedy. In most cases the provision of legal advice will not result in liability on the part of the lawyer under those sections, but it remains a possibility. There have been no reported cases finding liability of this sort in New Zealand, but there are a small number in Australia under the corresponding legislation (Trade Practices Act 1974).

Civil liability to clients in New Zealand is solely decided by the courts. However, the relevant District and New Zealand Law Societies have jurisdiction in disciplinary proceedings under the Law Practitioners Act 1982 in respect of ethical obligations.

*Restrictions on liability*

Relief in tort and contract is restricted to compensation, although in certain cases damages may contain a punitive component which increases the damages payable to the plaintiff beyond mere compensation for loss. The jurisdiction of the New Zealand courts to award punitive or exemplary damages is less restricted than that assumed by the courts of England, although the breach must be contumelious and deserving of punishment beyond compensatory damages. Relief for breaches of fiduciary duty and under the Fair Trading Act 1986 may include mandatory or other orders which benefit the client. However, it would be unusual for the New Zealand courts to impose a mandatory order in respect of the performance of professional services. Compensation is payable for a breach of fiduciary duty, but the basis of calculation is different from that of damages, being based on equitable principles.

There are no specific financial limits but the compensation is limited by the principles of causation and remoteness under the common law. Recently the New Zealand courts have tended to view the assessment of damages in claims for professional negligence against solicitors as, in the end, a question of fact. Reasonable foresight or contemplation, while important considerations, are not the only considerations. Other factors including directness, "naturalness" as distinct from freak combinations of foreseeable circumstances, the magnitude of the claim and the degree of the defendant's culpability are also relevant.

Until comparatively recently, general damages for distress and inconvenience for claims in contract were not recoverable. There have, however, been a number of recent cases where such awards have been made, in both contract and tort. Generally the amounts have been relatively modest.

The Contributory Negligence Act 1947 applies principally to tortious claims. Nevertheless, the Court of Appeal has signalled that a contribution can be sought from a plaintiff who is alleging breach of the implied contractual term of reasonable care and skill. It now seems clear that the Act can be applied even where the claim is in contract.

Immunity from suit in negligence is provided under the common law for advocates in respect of the performance of advocacy services. As the profession in New Zealand is "fused", the immunity is not restricted solely to barristers and extends to those practising as barristers and solicitors when performing advocacy services. The protection covers not only the conduct of the case in court but extends to work so intimately connected with the conduct of the cause and court that it can be fairly said to be a preliminary decision affecting the way the cause is to be conducted when it comes to a hearing.

It is not usual for lawyers to limit their liability by contract and their ability to do so is restricted by the Rules of Practice imposed by the New Zealand Law Society, their fiduciary duties to their clients and certain statutory provisions. The Rules of Practice require lawyers to accept legal responsibility for their actions and, subject to the provisions of the Rules, to meet any liability arising out of any act, error or omission in the course of their professional duties or business. Lawyers may not exclude by contract their liability to a client except as provided by the Rules, which outline the minimum requirements for a contractual limitation of liability. The central requirement is the maintenance of professional indemnity cover for civil liability to a minimum of approximately USD1.2 million per claim. If such cover is in place, a practitioner may contractually exclude liability in excess of that minimum amount per claim, provided that the client is fully advised of the position and the limitation is fair and conscionable in all the circumstances. Only risks which are substantial or unusual should be the object of a contractual exclusion of liability and it is not regarded as appropriate to exclude liability in everyday transactions. The rule is subject to the general fiduciary obligations of practitioners (which may limit their ability to exclude liability) and certain statutory liabilities (Fair Trading Act, CGA) cannot be excluded by contract.

The foregoing restrictions do no affect the ability of lawyers to qualify their advice on a particular matter. It is often appropriate to do so if the law is uncertain or complex or where there is the possibility of unknown or material facts. It is rare for lawyers to restrict their liability by contract as provided for in the Rules of Practice.

Time limits are imposed by statute. The general time limit for claims in contract and tort is six years from the date that the cause of action arose. However, section 28 of the Limitation Act 1950 provides, inter alia, that in the case of an action based upon the fraud of the defendant or his agent, the period of limitation shall not begin to run until the plaintiff has discovered the fraud, or could with reasonable diligence have discovered it. In addition, the Court of Appeal has held more generally that, if damage forms part of the cause of action, the cause of action does not arise until the damage is reasonably discoverable. An action commenced under the Fair Trading Act 1986 has a three year limitation period from the date the matter giving rise to the contravention arose.

Limitation in respect of claims in equity arises both by the equitable doctrine of laches and by a statutory discretion of the court (conferred by the Limitation Act 1950) to apply the statutory six year limitation period by analogy.

*Liability to non-clients*

Lawyers can be liable to non-clients arising out of the performance of their professional duties. In respect of breaches of fiduciary obligation, a lawyer can be liable as a trustee to a non-client, including liability as a constructive trustee for knowing receipt of money which is the subject of a breach of trust or for knowingly assisting another in a breach of the latter's trust. Breaches of undertakings to non-clients may be the subject of the summary jurisdiction of the High Court. Liability under the Fair Trading Act 1986 and Commerce Act 1986 is not restricted to clients and can extend to non-clients.

The duty in negligence of care to clients has already been discussed above. Lawyers may also be liable in negligence to non-clients when they act in a way that creates a duty of care to that person. There are several cases where such a duty has been upheld. For example, a solicitor has been held to owe a duty of care to a beneficiary under a will which he had negligently drafted. Where a claim was brought by a husband, a party to a matrimonial property agreement, against the solicitor for his wife, alleging that the solicitor had failed to advise the wife properly in relation to the agreement resulting in the wife being entitled to avoid the agreement, the Court of Appeal held that the wife's solicitor could in those circumstances be liable to the husband.

*Recent developments with respect to liability*

The approach taken by the New Zealand Court of Appeal in the development of the law of negligence has gradually extended the liability of lawyers to their clients. A similar expansion of liability for breach of fiduciary duties has been recently checked by the decision of the Privy Council in *Mouat v Clark Boyce*.

## Insurance

*Voluntary professional indemnity insurance*

Indemnity insurance for the legal profession is voluntary in New Zealand. An estimated ninety to ninety-five per cent of the legal profession takes out professional indemnity insurance cover.

*Insurance facilities*

Insurance is currently available through policies issued by commercial insurers.

Insurance is usually obtained abroad for larger firms and internally for smaller firms and sole practitioners. Lloyds of London and the FAI/Justitia Mutual Association are the dominant sources of professional indemnity insurance cover for New Zealand solicitors.

Some practitioners in New Zealand practice solely as barristers. One insurer — C E Heath Insurance — offers a policy on favourable terms to those practising as such and a substantial proportion of those so practising are insured under that policy.

*Level of cover*
The average level of cover is approximately USD3 million per claim. Usually a maximum for each claim is imposed by the insurer as well as the aggregate total liability being limited for the period of the policy.

Approximately three to five per cent of the annual expenses of a practice are represented by professional indemnity insurance premium.

*Deductibles*
The range of deductibles payable by insured lawyers is between USD31,000 and USD150,000, depending on the size of the law firm.

*Recent developments with respect to insurance*
The New Zealand Law Society is currently undertaking a review of professional indemnity insurance for the legal profession in New Zealand.

It is possible that there will be significant developments in the near future through a proposed compulsory insurance scheme. The New Zealand Law Society has proposed that USD150,000 cover be taken by the profession as a minimum based on prescribed minimum criteria.

Compulsory insurance cover in New Zealand, if it proceeds, is expected to be arranged by approved insurance policies and regulated by requirements set down by the New Zealand Law Society.

## NIGERIA

### The civil liability of legal advisers

*Basis of liability*
In Nigeria the guiding principles of lawyers' liability to clients in respect of advice given and the conduct of matters are governed by the common law and the statute. These principles are founded on the special nature of the relationship between a lawyer and his client, and the duties arising therefrom. Accordingly, a breach of any of these duties could render a lawyer liable for damages or otherwise.

A lawyer has a duty to exercise reasonable care and skill to be expected of a normally competent and careful lawyer.

A lawyer has a duty to disclose any conflicting interest, and is obliged not to accept any brief or instruction which may give rise to a conflict of interest. A lawyer stands in a fiduciary capacity to his client, accordingly he is required to act with a high degree of good faith and for the benefit of his client.

These principles have been defined by both statute and by common law, that is court decisions. The applicable statute in Nigeria is the Legal Practitioners Act 1990.

The liability of lawyers is a matter solely determined by the courts. No professional body has jurisdiction to determine a lawyer's liability to his client. However, by virtue of the provisions of the Legal Practitioners Act a Legal Practitioners Disciplinary Committee established by that Act may consider and determine any case where it is alleged that a lawyer has 'misbehaved' in his capacity as a legal practitioner. The penalties for misbehaviour amounting to unprofessional conduct include striking off the name of the lawyer from the roll or a suspension from practice.

There is no express restriction either in statutory legislation or by virtue of court decisions which limits the relief obtainable by a client against his lawyer solely to compensation. The reliefs obtainable by a client would depend on the facts giving rise to the client's claims and the nature of the cause of action. If the breach complained of is a continuing one, mandatory or other orders can be obtained to suit the circumstances.

The law provides no financial limits on the amount of compensation which a lawyer may be found liable to pay to his client.

*Restrictions on liability*

There are restrictions provided by the Legal Practitioners Act as to circumstances in which lawyers may not be held liable to their clients. They are:

- where a lawyer gives his services without reward either by way of fees, disbursements or otherwise;
- where a lawyer is conducting proceedings in the face of any court, tribunal or other body as an advocate;

Under the Legal Practitioners Act any provision in a contract which purports to exclude or limit a lawyer's liability for negligence in the exercise of his professional capacity will be void. There are no other restrictions on the lawyer's ability to limit his liability. Accordingly, provided the liability sought to be limited does not derive from a cause of action based on negligence, a lawyer will be permitted to do so, subject to his client's consent. There are no other express statutory provisions or directives of a professional body which stipulate on the issue of a lawyer's ability to limit his liability.

There are no specific laws stipulating time limits within which claims may be instituted against lawyers specifically. The periods of limitation stipulated in the limitation laws for the various causes of action would apply. Actions founded in simple contract, *quasi-contract* and tort must be commenced before the expiration of six years from the date on which the cause of action accrued. Also, claims founded on fraud must be brought within six years of the discovery of the said fraud.

*Liability to non-clients*
Lawyers can incur liability to non-clients in various circumstances, for instance:

- where a lawyer acting on behalf of a client as principal enters into contractual relations without disclosing the fact that he acts as such, he will be found to be personally liable for breaches arising therefrom;
- where a third party to whom a duty of care is owed, suffers loss due to the fact that he has placed reliance on statements made by a lawyer which were found to be carelessly made, where the third party stands in such proximate relationship to the lawyer that he ought to have been in the lawyer's contemplation as a person likely to be affected by the lawyer's negligent conduct.

*Recent developments with respect to liability*
There are no trends or developments which may significantly alter the framework above. Due to the low literacy rate in Nigeria, there is a low level of awareness amongst Nigerians as to obligations and duties of lawyers to their clients. Accordingly, very few claims are presented against lawyers, save in cases where the lawyer is alleged to have misappropriated money or property.

**Insurance**

*Voluntary professional indemnity insurance*
Indemnity insurance for the legal profession is voluntary in Nigeria.

To our knowledge, no lawyers have taken out indemnity insurance. Lawyers in Nigeria have little or no knowledge about the existence of such a policy, largely because there are very few incidents of clients suing their lawyer.

*Insurance facilities*
Available for insurance are policies issued by commercial insurers.

*Level of cover*
There are no statistics on the level of insurance cover obtained by the legal profession, as no lawyers have taken out professional indemnity insurance.

*Deductibles*
The range of deductibles payable by the insured lawyer is negotiable.

*Recent developments with respect to insurance*
There are no current developments taking place which would significantly alter the position as set out above.

## NORWAY

### The civil liability of legal advisers

*Basis of liability*

Under Norwegian law there is a distinction between the liability of "lawyers" and that of "legal advisers", since these two terms are not necessarily interchangeable. The term "lawyer" (or "attorney" or "advocate") is reserved for persons who (i) have a law degree; and (ii) are admitted to the Norwegian Bar. Law graduates may, however, give legal assistance without having been authorised as advocates. This chapter will focus on lawyers who are permitted to practice as advocates.

The guiding principles of lawyers' liability to their clients in respect of advice given and the conduct of matters are as follows:

- the lawyer must have acted at least negligently (simple negligence is in principle sufficient);
- the client must have suffered a loss;
- there must be a causal connection between the lawyer's act or omission and the client's loss.

Lawyers have a professional liability. The question, therefore, is whether the lawyer has met the obligations and expectations that would reasonably be imposed upon a lawyer in a similar situation. Lawyers' liability is thus decided according to the degree of skill and care to be expected of a competent lawyer.

The principles of lawyers' liability are defined partly by statute and partly by case law. With respect to lawyers who are employed by others, liability is defined by statute. Section 2-1 of the Torts Act of 1969 imposes liability where "the demands that reasonably may be made in respect of the employee's activity or service have been neglected". As regards lawyers in private practice (i.e. lawyers who are not employed by others), liability is defined by case law. The distinction between acceptable conduct on the part of a lawyer and that which does not meet the standard required will, however, be the same regardless of whether he is a private practitioner or an employee. The liability of lawyers is, under Norwegian law, solely decided by the courts.

*Restrictions on liability*

The relief available to those seeking redress is restricted to compensation. There are, however, no financial limits on the compensation which lawyers may be ordered to pay, provided that the conditions set out above necessary to found liability are satisfied.

Apart from the criteria referred to above, there are no restrictions as to the circumstances in which lawyers may be held liable to their clients. Lawyers may not, for example, invoke immunity when appearing as advocates. Lawyers may, in principle, enter into agreements with their clients whereby they limit or exclude their liability for a particular matter. Whether or not such a disclaimer of liability would be upheld by the court will depend on the nature of the work covered by the disclaimer. If the work involves questions which the lawyer would not normally be responsible for, such as advice concerning arguable legal questions or strictly commercial advice, a disclaimer would generally be acceptable, provided that the advice given is not deliberately incorrect.

On the other hand, a disclaimer will not normally be upheld if it relates to clear or simple points of law or matters of a straightforward nature. Nevertheless, even if a disclaimer is related to an undisputed legal issue etc. (and therefore would not normally be acceptable), it might, under certain circumstances, be permitted. This would be the case, for example, where the client, despite a lawyer's explicit warnings, still wishes to pursue a certain risk. In such circumstances, the lawyer is unlikely to be held responsible in the event that his client suffers a loss in pursuing the risk.

In general, it is acceptable for lawyers — as other advisers do — to provide for a financial limit to their liability. The restriction must, however, be reasonable. To our knowledge, agreements restricting lawyers' liability are practically non-existent in Norway.

Pursuant to section 36 of the Norwegian Agreements Act, an agreement may be set aside, in part or in its entirety, to the extent that it would be unreasonable or contrary to sound business practice to apply it. This provision is general and therefore applies to agreements in which lawyers seek to restrict their liability to their clients. Ultimately, the validity of a disclaimer is a matter for the courts to determine in each individual case.

The general provision of the Norwegian Act relating to the Limitation Period of Claims provides that claims for damages are subject to a limitation period of three years from the date upon which the injured party acquired, or should have acquired, knowledge of the damage and the identity of the person responsible.

The limitation period will, however, expire, at the latest, ten years from the date upon which the damage occurred or twenty years after the basis for the liability has ended. This provision will apply to claims against lawyers. The ten year limit will have effect where the injured party did not acquire, and should not have acquired, knowledge of the damage and the identity of the person responsible until more than seven years after the damage occurred. The twenty year limit will have effect where the damage occurs only after a long period of time. It is currently proposed that the ten year limit be cancelled. If this proposal is put into effect only the three year and twenty year limitation periods will remain.

It is unlikely, however, with respect to lawyers' liability, that the ten and twenty year limitation periods will be relevant, as a client with a claim against his lawyer will normally have acquired, or at least should have acquired, the necessary knowledge within the three year limit. Accordingly, the three year limit will, as a general rule, apply in the context of lawyers' liability.

*Liability to non-clients*

Lawyers may be liable to the following categories of non-clients:

- the general public;
- the other party; and
- a third party.

A lawyer may, pursuant to section 202 of the Norwegian Act relating to the Courts of Justice, become liable to the general public if he has initiated a legal action when it is clear that there are no grounds to do so. In such circumstances, he may be ordered to compensate the general public for the costs incurred in bringing the action. This provision is, however, very rarely applied.

A lawyer may also become liable to the other party in a transaction or in litigation. Although such cases are limited, there are a few cases in which the courts have held lawyers liable to the other party. In one case, for example, a lawyer was held liable for receiving interest and instalments on behalf of his client mortgagee without ensuring that the mortgage was reduced accordingly, so that the debtor faced a loss.

Under rare circumstances a lawyer may also become liable to a third party. Since a lawyer's first and foremost liability relates to his client, liability towards non-clients is a rare occurrence.

*Recent developments with respect to liability*

In Norway over the last few years we have experienced an increasing focus on civil liability for consulting professions such as auditors, engineers, real estate brokers and lawyers. Consequently, there has been an increase in the number of claims against lawyers. For the most part, such claims are settled amicably and only a very limited number of claims are determined by the courts. We do not believe it likely, however, that this recent development will significantly affect the framework set out above.

## Insurance

*Compulsory professional indemnity insurance*

Indemnity insurance for the lawyers (*advokater*) conducting legal practice on their own behalf has been compulsory in Norway since January 1, 1993. This surety is required by statute.

Lawyers employed by the state or municipality, who only conduct work on behalf of their employers, are not obliged to take out an insurance cover.

*Insurance facilities*

Facilities available for insurance are policies issued by commercial insurers and a voluntary collective scheme introduced by the Norwegian Bar Association.

The voluntary collective scheme introduced by the Norwegian Bar Association is as a main rule available for members only. Approximately seventy-five to eighty per cent of the members participate in this voluntary collective scheme.

Commercial insurance is generally obtained from insurers within the country. Prior to the European Economic Area (EEA) Agreement only Norwegian insurers were accepted as insurers. Due to the EEA Agreement insurance companies within EEA-states may also act as insurers.

*Level of cover*

The minimum compulsory level of cover is approximately USD734,100, the cover being an aggregate for all claims within a policy period. The insurer may, however, limit liability per assignment per injury by agreement, but not below USD293,700.

Lawyers who employ associates are obliged to take out excess insurance cover of at least USD440,500.

Lawyers working in the field of debt collection, must have an insurance cover equal to at least 1/40 of the lawyer's accounts receivable at the end of the previous fiscal year, and at least double the amount of collected, not paid out amounts and other funds deposited with the advocate during his work as debt collector at the end of the fiscal year.

In certain cases the Supervisory Council for Legal Practices can decide that a higher insurance cover is required.

As a main rule, legal work in Norway is performed by *advokater* only. However, according to the Norwegian Act relating to the courts of justice, non-lawyers with a law degree may give legal advice outside court proceedings. State authorized accountants may give legal advice in tax law. Furthermore, district sheriffs may give limited legal advice. The Ministry of Justice can decide that non-lawyers educated in certain legal fields may give legal advice in those fields. These non-lawyers are also obliged to take out professional indemnity insurance for the performance of legal work. The level of cover is at least USD440,500. If the legal work is conducted on behalf of a law firm, the level of cover is increased to USD734,100.

*Deductibles*

Under the Norwegian Bar Association's voluntary collective scheme, the deductible payable by the insured lawyer himself before a claim becomes large enough to involve a payment by insurers is approximately USD7,340 for the first claim.

For the second, third and fourth claim within a three year period the insured lawyer's own risk is increased to respectively USD11,000, USD14,700 and USD22,000.

*Recent developments with respect to insurance*

As the Norwegian statutes and government regulations regarding compulsory insurance cover came into force on January 1, 1993, this recent implementation would indicate that comprehensive changes are unlikely in the near future.

At present, we are unable to discern any significant trend of change which might affect the position as set out in our answers.

There is, however, an increasing focus on liability for damages both in general and in respect to legal practice. The general level of damages seems to be increasing. These factors may in the future alter the level of cover.

Over the last couple of years insurance cover by means of surety has been implemented in various areas (for example for persons working with debt collection and real estate agents). There is no reason to believe that other forms of insurance coverage will replace surety in the near future.

## PANAMA

### The civil liability of legal advisers

*Basis of liability*

The liability of lawyers to their clients in respect of advice given and the conduct of matters is dependent on the degree of skill and care to be expected of a competent lawyer. The principles that guide lawyers as to their responsibilities to their clients are defined mostly in the Panamanian Civil Code. The relationship between a client and a lawyer is akin to an agency contract. In agency contracts, the agent has to act with due care and as a prudent man.

In addition the "Code of Ethics and Professional Liabilities of Lawyers" establishes other responsibilities that lawyers have to their clients. The Code sets out the general ethical principles to be followed by lawyers, including that of performing their duties with integrity, punctuality, precision and within a lawful practice. The law regulates the Legal Profession in the Republic of Panama. It states, among other things, that the National Bar Association (*Colegio Nacional de Abogados*) will create an "Honor Tribunal" which will investigate all violations to Legal Ethics reported by an interested party.

By violations to Legal Ethics, the law means the infringement of all the rules contained in the "Code of Ethics and Professional Liabilities of Lawyers" and other laws relating to this issue.

Criminal courts are competent to hear any criminal infringement of a professional in the legal practice. Civil courts are competent to hear any civil claim, such as negligence, in the practice of the profession. Also, in the case of infringement of legal ethics, the law states that the Supreme Court of Justice will notify all cases regarding legal ethics to the "Honor Tribunal" which will have the power to declare the following disciplinary sanctions for members (members not mandatory):

- private admonition;
- public admonition;
- suspension from the legal profession for a period no less than a month and not more than a year for first time offenders; and

- exclusion from the legal profession for a minimum period of two years for second offenders.

The interested party may receive monetary compensation, if the case is tried in civil courts. Mandatory or other orders can be imposed by the court trying the case. These orders may consist of any action or restraint on the part of the lawyer or at his expense. For example, the Civil Code of Panama establishes the possibility of a judge ordering the publication of an extract of the verdict when the honour or reputation of the injured party has been affected.

There are no financial limits on the compensation which lawyers may be ordered to pay regarding material damages. In the case of moral damages, the amount of compensation will be determined by each judge considering factors such as the degree of liability, the financial situation of both the lawyer and the victim, and other circumstances determined in each case.

*Restrictions on liability*
There are no restrictions on the circumstances in which lawyers may be held liable to their clients. It is rare for lawyers to limit their liability. Although it is possible, but not common, to limit liability by way of contract, by requiring a client to sign a waiver for a particular matter, this will be ineffective in cases of gross negligence.

The limitation period for instituting civil claims against lawyers in cases of negligence or fault is one year from the date that the injured party learned of the injury against him.

The limitation period for instituting criminal claims against lawyers for their practice depends on the punishment applicable to the particular crime.

If the crime is punishable by fifteen years or more in prison, the limitation period is twenty years from the date the crime was committed. If the crime is punishable by six to fifteen years in prison, the limitation period is twelve years from the date the crime was committed. If the crime is punishable by six months to six years in prison, the limitation period is six years from the date the crime was committed. If the crime is punishable only by a fine, the limitation period is three years from the date the crime was committed.

*Liability to non-clients*
Lawyers cannot be held liable to non-clients.

*Recent developments with respect to liability*
There are no developments which may significantly alter the framework set out above.

## Insurance

*Voluntary professional indemnity insurance*
Indemnity insurance for the legal profession is voluntary in Panama. To the best of our knowledge, no law firm in Panama has taken out indemnity insurance to this date. It is not customary for lawyers to have or seek this type of insurance. Most lawsuits against lawyers are settled outside the courts, and do not even make it to trial.

*Insurance facilities*
At this moment no insurance company offers professional indemnity insurance for the legal profession in Panama.

Generally speaking, commercial insurance has to be obtained from insurers within the jurisdiction. The insurance policies must be approved by the Insurance Superintendency (*Superintendencia de Seguros*), which is a governmental body, in charge of regulating insurance operations.

*Level of cover*
As indemnity insurance is not available, we have no comment about the level of cover.

*Deductibles*
See above under "level of cover".

*Recent developments with respect to insurance*
Professional indemnity insurance is not available in Panama for any profession.

Medical groups are in great demand of malpractice insurance because of recent lawsuits in these area. Medical malpractice insurance is expected to be the first type of malpractice insurance to be introduced in Panama in the near future, followed by other types of professional liability insurance.

So far only a small percentage of firms have really tried in vain to obtain insurance. Developments in the area of insurance for the legal profession seem very slow.

Because of the way the Panamanian market is structured, at this moment the only alternative is the possibility of a foreign reinsurance company wanting to sell this professional indemnity insurance in Panama, in which case a Panamanian insurance company could do the "fronting" or take all steps to make the insurance legal and issue an acceptable policy locally. The full risk would remain with the reinsurers. In this case, the Panamanian insurance company would only receive a fee for the use of its name.

## PAPUA NEW GUINEA

### The civil liability of legal advisers

*Basis of liability*

Lawyers in Papua New Guinea may be held liable to their clients in any of the following circumstances:

- failing to act in accordance with the standards of skill and care which apply to the whole profession;
- failing to act with strict openness and fairness with a client;
- failing to act in accordance with any special terms of a retainer;
- acting in litigation without authority;
- entering a contract as agent for a client without authority;
- failing to perform an undertaking given personally to the court;
- improperly incurring costs in litigation or wasting costs by undue delay or default;
- making profit or receiving any benefit other than the lawyer's professional remuneration from the transaction which the client has retained him to carry through;
- disclosing confidential information which has come to the lawyer's knowledge in acting for the client.

A lawyer may also be liable for acts of his agents and may be liable in some circumstances regardless of whether acting for reward or gratuitously and regardless of whether the lawyer has a practising certificate in force at the time.

The principles are defined by the underlying law of Papua New Guinea which comprises the principles and rules of common law and equity in England as they existed immediately prior to the date of independence (September 16, 1975) except to the extent that:

- they are inconsistent with statute;
- they are inapplicable or inappropriate to the circumstances of Papua New Guinea from time to time; or
- they are inconsistent with custom.

In developing the underlying law, the local courts often have regard to persuasive post-independence cases in England and elsewhere.

The liability of lawyers is a matter decided either by the courts, or by the Lawyers' Statutory Committee — a professional body established under the Lawyers Act 1986.

In addition to compensation, the following orders can be imposed in appropriate circumstances:

- orders denying the lawyer's right to recover part or all of his costs from the client;
- restitutionary damages, an account of profits and other equitable remedies;
- injunctions;

- orders to perform an undertaking;
- orders to deliver up papers;
- orders that the lawyer perform work for such persons within such time and for such fees, if any, as the Lawyers' Statutory Committee determines;
- orders that the lawyer waives any lien he possesses.

*Restrictions on liability*

A lawyer's duty to the court (e.g. not to mislead the court) is paramount and so may limit the duty owed to the client. Lawyers acting as advocates are immune from liability in some limited circumstances but are generally liable for the consequences of such things as ignorance or non-observance of the rules of practice, want of care in preparing an action for trial and failure to attend with witnesses. A lawyer is not liable for merely acting upon a client's instructions in the reasonable belief that they were correct or if the lawyer has fully explained the position to the client and is nevertheless instructed to proceed, or merely because the lawyer has committed an error of judgment, whether on matters of discretion or of law, for example, on points of new occurrence or of doubtful construction. The Lawyers Act 1986 renders void any provision in an agreement between a lawyer and his client that the lawyer is not liable for negligence or that he is relieved from any responsibility to which he would otherwise be subject as a lawyer.

The general limitation period applicable in Papua New Guinea under the Frauds and Limitations Act 1988 is six years.

*Liability to non-clients*

A lawyer is liable to third parties for acts done in the lawyer's capacity as agent for the client where the lawyer acts without authority, rendering the lawyer liable for breach of warranty of authority. A lawyer may be liable to third parties in tort in circumstances where the lawyer is instructed by his client to carry out a transaction that will confer a benefit on an identified third party. The lawyer may owe a duty of care to the third party if he can reasonably foresee that the third party is likely to be injured by his acts or omissions.

A lawyer may be liable as a constructive trustee when deliberately acting with trust property, when using his fiduciary position to obtain a private gain or assisting with knowledge in a fraudulent design on the part of trustees.

*Recent developments with respect to liability*

Since Papua New Guinea obtained independence in 1975, there has only been one reported case where the courts have dealt with the question of liability of lawyers. That case largely adopted the English and Australian common law positions. It is reasonably likely that recent trends in England, Australia and elsewhere could be highly persuasive in further cases which come before the courts in Papua New Guinea.

## Insurance

*Compulsory professional indemnity insurance*
Indemnity insurance for the legal profession is compulsory in Papua New Guinea. Compulsory cover is required by reason of section 43 of the Lawyers Act 1986.

*Insurance facilities*
Lawyers in Papua New Guinea have the following options available in arranging their professional indemnity insurance:

- insurance under a policy issued by a commercial insurer which has been arranged by the Papua New Guinea Law Society. It provides the minimum level of compulsory cover, but some lawyers have a higher level of cover under the policy. The majority of lawyers are insured under this policy;
- insurance arranged independently by a lawyer but approved by the Law Society, with minimum cover of at least the compulsory limit;
- insurance beyond the minimum cover required by the Law Society, which is either included as part of the policy arranged by the Law Society or is arranged independently. No approval is required by the Law Society in respect of such additional insurance.

All commercial insurance is obtained from overseas.

*Level of cover*
The minimum obligatory cover is USD375,000. That cover is an aggregate for all claims within the twelve month policy period. As to cover beyond the minimum, the insurance is either effected through the policy arranged by the Law Society or through other policies arranged by the lawyers independently.

The additional levels of cover provided under the policy arranged by the Law Society are respectively USD560,000, USD750,000, USD1.5 million and USD3.75 million. The cover is for an aggregate of all claims within a twelve month policy period.

There are no statistics available to indicate what level of excess cover is taken up by the profession.

*Deductibles*
In respect of the insurance arranged by the Law Society, the deductibles are USD750 per partner for each and every claim, with a maximum of USD3,750 per partnership for each and every claim involving more than one partner.

For sole practitioners the deductible is USD750 in respect of each and every claim.

*Recent developments with respect to insurance*
There are no new trends or developments in the area of professional indemnity insurance for the legal profession at this time.

## PARAGUAY

### The civil liability of legal advisers

*Basis of liability*
The liability of lawyers is dependent on the degree and skill expected of a competent lawyer which has been defined by court decisions. The liability of lawyers is a matter solely decided by the courts. The professional association of lawyers does not have disciplinary faculties nor jurisdiction to determine a lawyer's liability.

The relief available to the client is limited to monetary compensation as determined by the courts and there are no financial limits on the compensation that lawyers may be ordered to pay. Negligence on the part of lawyers will be compensated on the basis of the damage caused and eventual loss of profits.

*Restrictions on liability*
Lawyers may limit their responsibility by agreement with the client for a particular matter. However, it is likely that the courts would invalidate a provision of a general nature.

*Liability to non-clients*
Lawyers can be liable for negligence in the performance of their duty as a professional and a representative of the client before the courts. However, lawyers cannot be liable towards those with whom they do not have a contractual relationship.

*Recent developments with respect to liability*
There have been no claims against lawyers for professional liability to this date. However, in the last two years there have been several law suits against medical doctors for malpractice. It is likely, therefore, that it will only be a matter of time before actions are initiated against lawyers.

### Insurance

*Professional indemnity insurance*
There is currently no professional indemnity insurance available for the legal profession in Paraguay.

We expect that in the next three to five years, international clients of large law firms will demand liability insurance. For small firms or sole practitioners, the need for insurance will arise when malpractice cases are initiated against other professions, including lawyers.

## PERU

### The civil liability of legal advisers

*Basis of liability*

According to the Civil Code of Peru all persons aged eighteen or more years have full capacity to exercise their civil rights, unless they come within a specific exclusion and are not persons of full capacity. All persons of full capacity to exercise their rights are responsible for their conduct.

The Professional Ethic code of the Lima Bar Association states that a lawyer must act prudently, honestly and in good faith. Consequently, a lawyer must not make deceitful, false, incorrect or malicious allegations or conduct himself in a manner contrary to the administration of justice.

The Organic Law of the Judicial Power establishes that a lawyer must represent his client with loyalty, probity, decorum and in good faith. The lawyer must respect the confidentiality of his clients' affairs and follow the rules of the Professional Ethnic Code.

A lawyer is expected to act with the degree of ability and care of a competent lawyer. Professional liability is not generally very developed in Peru.

If the lawyer has committed a delict, is guilty of corrupting or misleading the court or has breached client confidentiality, the Criminal Court of Justice has power to penalise the lawyer and prevent him from exercising his profession for a prescribed period. In very serious cases, the Court may order the cancellation of the lawyer's professional title, and send him to prison.

A civil court may order a lawyer to indemnify his client, the amount of the payment depending upon the severity of the misconduct. If the misconduct relates only to a breach of the rules of the Bar Association the lawyer may receive a private or public warning and be suspended from practice for a period of up to six months.

In summary, a lawyer may be suspended by the Court of Justice or by the pertinent Bar Association if he has committed a contempt of court or insulted the other lawyers. If a lawyer acts in good faith for the purpose of the defence of his client he will not however be subject to sanction. If a client sues for malpractice, which rarely occurs in Peru, the matter is ordinarily resolved by the client instructing another lawyer after reimbursing his initial lawyer for his fees, in full or part, and expenses.

There are no statutory limits upon the decision of a civil judge. These limits are fixed by the judge with regard to the degree of responsibility of the lawyer, the importance of the matter adjudged and the likelihood of payment from the lawyer. The lawyer can appeal to a Superior Court of Justice against the decision of the judge.

*Restrictions on liability*

In Peru, a lawyer appearing as advocate on behalf of a client is not immune from suit. Agreements to restrict liability of a lawyer to his client are rare, as is malpractice itself. At any rate, such agreements would be of dubious enforceability in Peru, especially in cases where a lawyer is guilty of international wilful misconduct.

Where a lawyer is guilty of deceit or gross negligence, a prior agreement to exclude or limit this lawyer's liability to his client will be null and void. The statutory period of limitation in which a client must commence legal proceedings against his lawyer is ten years from the date on which damage occurred. For actions in tort the period is two years from the date of damage.

Finally, in the case of complaints that must be heard by the appropriate Bar Association, the regulations say that there is a limitation period of three years after the occurrence.

*Liability to non-clients*

If a lawyer, in carrying out his obligations to his client, causes a non-client to suffer damage by reason of the lawyer's negligence or intentional misconduct, then the lawyer will be liable in tort to the non-client. The level of compensation payable by the lawyer in such cases is determined judicially.

*Recent developments with respect to liability*

In the last decade the Peruvian legislation has implemented the following changes:

- the Code of Civil Procedure (1912) has been substituted by a new Code of Civil Process (1993);
- the Penal Code (1924) has been replaced by a new Penal Code (1991);
- in 1995 a Commission has been installed in the Legislative Power with the task of amending the Civil Code of 1984;
- the Commerce Code of 1902 governs contracts of insurance. In 1993 a Legislative Decree was issued, approving a new General Law of Banking, Financial and Insurance Institutions, which mainly concerned the control by the Government of such institutions but which also laid down some rules on insurance matters.

In 1965, the Peruvian Government considered it convenient to modify certain sections of the Civil Code of 1936 and designed a commission to work on this matter. After successive governments and commissions the new Civil Code of 1984 was produced.

It is not expected that there will be substantial changes in the Civil Process and Penal Codes in the near future.

## Insurance

*Voluntary professional indemnity insurance*
Indemnity insurance for the legal profession is voluntary in Peru and it is very rare to take out this insurance.

*Insurance facilities*
There is no specific insurance available to cover professional indemnity for the legal profession. If a lawyer should desire to take out such insurance, the terms would be negotiated with the insurance company.

*Level of cover*
Statistics are not available to indicate the level of cover obtained by the legal profession.

*Deductibles*
Statistics are not available on the range of deductibles payable by the insured lawyers.

*Recent developments with respect to insurance*
There are no new trends or potential developments in the area of insurance which may significantly alter the framework summarised above.

# PHILIPPINES

## The civil liability of legal advisers

*Basis of liability*
In order for a lawyer to be liable to his client, it is essential that the lawyer-client relationship be established, that there is want of reasonable care and diligence and that injury was suffered by the client which was the proximate result. A lawyer has no power to act as counsel or legal representative for a person without being retained, nor may he appear in court for a party without being retained unless by leave of court. There must be a contract of retainer, express or implied, between him and the party he purports to represent or that party's representative.

Under the Civil Code, what is required of the lawyer in the performance of his duties is to exert that degree of vigilance and attention expected of a good father of a family (the *pater familias*).

The liability of a lawyer to his client is dependent on the skill and care commonly possessed by the members of the legal profession. This will have to be determined by the particular facts of the case.

A lawyer owes fidelity to the cause of his client but not at the expense of truth and the administration of justice. This is so because a lawyer is first and foremost an officer of the court. Accordingly, a lawyer may perform acts which may be contrary to the instructions of his client but are consistent with his duties as a member of the Bar, and not be liable therefor.

A lawyer is not liable for mere error in judgment. If lawyers of ordinary skill and ability might differ as to the answer to the question, then it cannot be said that there was lack of ordinary diligence on the part of the lawyer in conducting the suit. Lawyers cannot be made answerable for mistaken judgment upon a doubtful question of law. Nor can they, after due diligence, be held liable for losing the litigation. Moreover, where a judgment becomes final through the fault of a lawyer, that fact alone is not a sufficient ground for the losing party to recover damages from his lawyer since the action for damages rests on the unsubstantiated and arbitrary supposition of the injustice of the decision which became final through the negligence of the lawyer.

Although a contractual relationship exists between the lawyer and his client, this will not bar a malpractice suit based on a *quasi-delict*.

The Code of Professional Responsibility, promulgated by the Supreme Court 1988, lays down the basic principles underlying a lawyer's liability to clients for advice and conduct of matters. The rules provide:

- a lawyer shall serve his client with competence and diligence;
- a lawyer shall not undertake a legal service which he knows or should know that he is not qualified to render. However, he may render such service if, with the consent of his client, he can obtain as collaborating counsel a lawyer who is competent on the matter;
- a lawyer shall not handle any legal matter without adequate preparation;
- a lawyer shall not neglect a legal matter entrusted to him, and his negligence in connection therewith shall render him liable;
- a lawyer shall keep the client informed of the status of his case and shall respond within a reasonable time to the client's request for information.

A client who is prejudiced by the negligence or misconduct of his lawyer can recover damages against him. The financial limit on compensation which a lawyer may be ordered to pay will depend on the damages suffered, and proved during the trial, by the client.

Under the Revised Penal Code, a lawyer who, for any malicious breach of professional duty or inexcusable negligence or ignorance, prejudices his client or reveals any of his client's secrets learned by him in his professional capacity, may be held criminally liable. Four acts are punishable:

- malicious breach of professional duty;
- inexcusable negligence or ignorance;
- revelation of secrets learned in his professional capacity; and
- undertaking the defence of the opposite party in a case without the consent of the first client whose defence has already been undertaken.

Prejudice to the client is essential when there is malicious breach of professional duty or inexcusable negligence or ignorance. Prejudice is not essential in the case of revelation of secrets or in the representation of conflicting interests.

Offences under the Penal Code are punishable by a term of imprisonment of between six months and one day to two years and four months, or a fine, or both, in addition to the proper administrative action.

The authority to decide whether or not a lawyer is liable to a client is exclusively with the courts. The determination of liability for damages is purely a judicial process which may not be delegated to any other body, not even to the Integrated Bar of the Philippines. In fact, an administrative complaint against a lawyer need not be referred to the Integrated Bar of the Philippines. Similarly, the authority to determine the criminal liability of a lawyer is exclusively vested with the courts.

Apart from compensation and criminal liability, under the Philippine Revised Rules of Court proceedings for the disbarment, suspension, or discipline of lawyers may be taken by the Supreme Court, of its own motion, or by the Integrated Bar of the Philippines upon the verified complaint of any person.

*Restrictions on liability*

No standard condition, statute or directive of a professional body specifically governs the limit of liability of lawyers. Generally, a lawyer-client relationship is a matter of agreement and thus is governed by the general rules on contracts. Accordingly, the lawyer and his client may agree to limit the lawyer's liability so long as such agreement is consistent with law, morals, good customs, public order or public policy.

Such stipulations will be void if they purport to exclude liability for gross negligence. Although as a general rule stipulations excluding liability for negligence are valid, the court has a discretion and the stipulation will not be upheld if there are strong reasons not to do so, for example where there is no equality of bargaining power between the lawyer and client.

The professional service contract, including the agreed limitation on liability, will be construed in favour of the client and against the lawyer.

Lawyers do not as a matter of practice limit their potential liability to their clients in their proposals for professional engagement.

An action against a lawyer based on a written contract prescribes within ten years from the time the right of action accrues. If based on an oral contract the prescription is six years. If the action is based on *quasi-delict*, it prescribes within four years from accrual of the cause of action.

*Liability to non-clients*

In certain situations, a lawyer may be held liable to third parties in pursuing his client's interest. One such situation is the use of intemperate and abusive language in court or in the pleadings. If found to be immaterial to the case, the lawyer may be liable for libel and ordered to pay damages to the aggrieved party.

*Recent developments with respect to liability*
In 1987, one year before the Code of Professional Responsibility came into force, the Supreme Court decreed that "an attorney is bound to protect his client's interest to the best of his ability and with the utmost diligence". In two more recent cases, however, the court has reverted to the standard of due diligence. In these cases it was held that a lawyer was required to exercise a "reasonable degree of diligence and competence" or "ordinary diligence or that reasonable degree of care and skill having reference to the character of the business he undertakes to do".

## Insurance

*Voluntary professional indemnity insurance*
Indemnity insurance for the legal profession is voluntary in the Philippines. It is uncommon for the legal profession to take professional indemnity insurance.

*Insurance facilities*
Generally speaking, policies issued by commercial insurers and approved by the Insurance Commission are available for insurance.

There are no insurance policies available specifically for the legal profession.

*Level of cover*
We are not aware of any lawyer taking out professional indemnity insurance to this date. Therefore there are no statistics available to indicate what level of cover might be obtained.

The cover taken up by certain professionals, for example medical doctors, is for an aggregate for all claims within a policy period.

*Deductibles*
There are no statistics available on the range of deductibles payable by the insured lawyers.

*Recent developments with respect to insurance*
The Integrated Bar of the Philippines has recently examined the possibility of compulsory professional indemnity insurance for the legal profession.

At this time, the legal profession is not in favour of compulsory indemnity insurance. It is expected that compulsory insurance will lead to additional costs. Furthermore, it is felt that making insurance compulsory may lead to a flood of claims against lawyers. From the consumer's point of view, it is believed that the available legal remedies and sanctions provide adequate protection.

## PORTUGAL

### The civil liability of legal advisers

*Basis of liability*

The Portuguese Civil Code provides that advice, recommendations or information given do not by themselves create legal liability, even when there has been negligence. However, legal liability exists whenever, *inter alia*, the person or entity who has given such advice, recommendations or information has a legal or contractual duty to provide them and has failed to do so in a proper way acting negligently or wilfully or when the conduct is legally punishable.

The position is therefore that under the general law, a lawyer or a law firm who has professionally engaged with the client through a mandate or a service agreement to provide advice, recommendations or information is subject to the legal regime mentioned above.

The By-laws of the Portuguese Bar Association and the Code of Professional Conduct of Lawyers, set out the following major duties to the client, which were summarised as follows:

- study and deal with the matter he has undertaken using, for such purpose, all recourses of his experience, knowledge and care;
- give to the client his conscientious opinion about the merits of the question as well as provide, whenever requested by the client, information about its progress;
- hold in strict confidence all information acquired in the course of the professional relationship concerning the business and affairs of his client;
- refuse to accept instructions or provide services in a matter on which he has already intervened in a different capacity or in a matter on which he represents or has represented the other party;
- not accept *quota litis* i.e. a participation, as remuneration for his services, in the results of litigation, transaction or business in general of his client;
- observe all relevant duties regarding the preservation and safekeeping of the property of the client entrusted to him;
- advise a just composition whenever such is the appropriate remedy;
- not to withdraw his services, except for good cause;
- follow the normally expected standards of conduct of the profession in his relationship with the client.

The lawyer's liability (as in any other profession) is established in accordance with the Civil Code and exists if the lawyer:

- has committed an unlawful act or omission (i.e. conduct in a manner contrary to his legal professional duties);
- has proceeded negligently or wilfully against the interests of the client (there is no liability for indirect action);
- acts in a way which results in damages caused to his client;

- and there is a causative link between such unlawful, negligent or wilful conduct and the resultant damage.

The amount of indemnity is, *prima facie*, assessed according to the extent and seriousness of the negligence or wilful conduct as well as the degree of professional experience and knowledge which that particular lawyer possesses. Portuguese law does not acknowledge the existence of specialised lawyers in a specific branch of law and therefore the degree of skill is not a factor which is taken into account in assessing the amount of indemnity.

The principles mentioned above are defined by statute. The Portuguese Bar Association (*Ordem dos Advogados*) holds exclusive jurisdiction to impose disciplinary sanctions on lawyers infringing their duties. However, only the courts have power to ascertain matters of civil liability and determine the level of indemnity due to the client. The courts have no jurisdiction to determine disciplinary matters. In applying disciplinary rules, the Bar Association may also observe the Declaration of Perugia, dated September 16, 1977, which was adopted by the Consultative Committee of the Bars and Law Societies of the European Community, of which the Portuguese Bar is a member, as well as the Code of Conduct of the same Committee adopted in Strasburg on October 28, 1988. Although the instruments of the Consultative Committee of the Bars and Law Societies of the European Community's instruments are valid within the Bars as a result of their participation as members of the Committee, they are not international treaties and are thus not enforceable by the courts.

Relief for breach of legal duties available from the courts is, in principle, restricted to compensation. However, the Bar Association, in fixing disciplinary sanctions, may apply the following:

- warning;
- censure;
- fine (up to a certain limit);
- suspension (up to six months period);
- suspension (for a period higher than six months up to two years);
- suspension (for a period higher than two years up to ten years);
- suspension (for a period higher than ten years up to fifteen years).

Along with any of the sanctions above, the Bar may impose the obligation of restitution of money, documents or objects as well as the loss of the lawyer's right to fees.

In fixing the sanction, the Bar will take into consideration the degree of negligence or wilful conduct, the extent of damage and all other relevant circumstances of the case. There are no financial limits on the compensation which lawyers may be ordered to pay. As a general rule the amount of the indemnity is determined according to the Civil Code and will be the sum needed to put the situation back to one where no damaging act or omission has been performed.

*Restrictions on liability*

The Civil Code, in governing the general duties of the attorney in a contract of mandate, states that the attorney is obliged to practice the acts contained in the mandate following the instructions of his client (the principal). A substantial part of the lawyer's activity is performed within the limits of a mandate entered into with his client. However, this is a special mandate as the lawyer, besides having a technical function which cannot be subject to technical instructions of the client, also enjoys intellectual and functional independence. He cannot practice acts or perform in general his activity against the ethical rules of the profession and against his professional conscience. Therefore, the lawyer cannot be found liable for not having followed the instructions of the client which are against that legal framework described above concerning the independence of the lawyer. This is the major, if not the unique, restriction to the circumstances in which a lawyer may be held liable to the client. There is no statute dealing specifically with a lawyer's ability to limit or restrict liability for his negligence. Under Portuguese law if a party agrees in advance to waive its rights of indemnity against the other party, in the event of that other party failing to perform its contractual duties, then this agreement is null and void.

Some legal commentators have held that that provision should be construed restrictively in the sense that a limitation or exclusion agreement or clause is lawful whenever the infringement is not serious. On the other hand, if a lawyer is guilty of serious negligence or wilful misconduct an agreement to restrict or exclude his liability will be void. If such doctrine is accepted, then lawyers may agree with their clients, case by case or in general, on the limitation or exclusion of liability.

The Supreme Court has held that the Civil Code operates only to restrain parties from agreeing to waive the right to indemnify and not to prevent them agreeing to limit the quantum of liability. This is not concerned with limitations on the actual obligations of the parties to contact in normal circumstances, or with waiving the right of indemnification after the breach has occurred. Finally, under the Civil Code, any party to a contract (therefore, including a lawyer) is entitled to limit or exclude his liability, through a prior agreement, as regards actions or omissions of his legal representatives or agents (e.g. employees).

It is not usual practice for a lawyer to seek to exclude or limit his liability to his client by agreement.

The Civil Code governs the limitation rules for actions brought by a third party or a client against a lawyer. The time bar for liability in contract is twenty years, for liability in tort three years and for disciplinary action — exercised by the Bar Association — three years.

If there is civil liability arising out of the same situation that has created criminal liability, the limitation periods of criminal law (fifteen, ten and five years — depending on the seriousness of the crime) are applied to the extent they are longer than the limitation periods for civil liability.

*Liability to non-clients*
The questions of lawyers' liability to a non-client seldom arises in practice because the lawyer is acting upon the instructions and in the interests of his client. A lawyer may, however, be liable in tort if he harms a third party in a conflict of interest situation. Also, a lawyer is liable whenever he violates a law protecting public interest or the specific right of a third party.

*Recent developments with respect to liability*
There are no trends or recent developments in the field of lawyer's liability.

**Insurance**

*Voluntary professional indemnity insurance*
Indemnity insurance for the legal profession is voluntary in Portugal. The professional indemnity insurance cover is taken out by approximately twenty-five per cent of the lawyers in Portugal.

*Insurance facilities*
Facilities available for insurance are an indirect voluntary collective scheme introduced by the Social Security for Lawyers Institution — which is related to the Portuguese Bar Association — and a direct voluntary scheme between individual lawyers or law firms and an insurance company.

The insurance is generally obtained from insurers within the country.

*Level of cover*
The maximum level of cover for the indirect voluntary collective scheme is USD200,000 per claim per year. The maximum level of cover for insurance taken out through the direct voluntary scheme is also for a maximum cover of USD200,000 per claim per year.

The amount of USD200,000 is the average amount covered per individual lawyer. The average level of cover for law firms is USD500,000. The maximum level of cover is USD1 million.

The insurance premium for the indirect voluntary collective scheme and the direct voluntary scheme is respectively USD3,000 and USD4,200 per year.

*Deductibles*
The first ten per cent of a claim is payable by the insured lawyers themselves.

*Recent developments with respect to insurance*
At the time of writing this book there are no new trends or potential developments in the area of insurance which may significantly alter the framework summarised above.

## PUERTO RICO

### The civil liability of legal advisers

*Basis of liability*
The professional standards and duties of a lawyer are based on the principle of a duty of diligence. For a lawyer to be liable to his client for malpractice the following three conditions must be met:

- there must be an attorney — client relationship;
- the client must show that the attorney violated the duty of diligence; and
- there must be a causal link between the attorney's violation of the duty of diligence and the loss suffered by the client.

The standard of care is based upon "a reasonable attorney standard" and the principle is defined in the Civil Code of Puerto Rico. This imposes a duty on all persons not to cause harm to others.

The courts have the sole responsibility for adjudicating on matters concerning lawyers and it is the Supreme Court which imposes penalties where a lawyer has been found guilty of malpractice. If a client feels particularly strongly about an issue, he may wish to file an ethics complaint against the attorney involved with the Supreme Court. The Supreme Court has within its jurisdiction the power to impose sanctions on the attorney if it believes the attorney to have been guilty of malpractice or to have violated the Code of Ethics.

*Restrictions on liability*
The client's remedy in a malpractice suit will be based on monetary compensation only and the amount awarded will be limited to the actual loss he has suffered. It is not within the court's powers to impose punitive damages.

A lawyer owes a duty of diligence in all areas of his practice and will therefore not be subject to immunity when he is advising as a lawyer or advocate. Any attempt by contract or otherwise to limit or exclude his liability will be declared void in accordance with of the Code of Ethics.

If an attorney chooses to settle a malpractice action out of court he is limited to settling the claim for compensation only and may not prevent the client filing an ethics complaint against him.

The limitation period for a malpractice action is one year from the date on which the client became aware of the attorney's malpractice.

*Liability to non-clients*
Lawyers cannot be liable to non-clients because the existence of an attorney-client relationship is a necessary condition in a malpractice action.

*Recent developments with respect to liability*
At present there are no developments taking place which would alter the above.

**Insurance**

*Voluntary professional indemnity insurance*
Indemnity insurance for the legal profession is voluntary in Puerto Rico. Less than five per cent of all Puerto Rico lawyers take out professional indemnity insurance.

*Insurance facilities*
Available for insurance are policies issued by commercial insurers. Insurance can be obtained both from insurers within the country and from abroad.

*Level of cover*
The level of cover generally obtained by the legal profession ranges from USD100,000 to USD300,000. For large firms the level of cover can be as high as USD15 million. This cover is generally an aggregate for all claims.

In small firms, the insurance premium is a very small proportion of the annual expenses of the practice. For a large firm, the cost of insurance cover may be 1,9 per cent of the annual expenses.

*Deductibles*
Sole practitioners will usually have a USD2,000 to USD3,000 deductible payable by the insured lawyer. For a large firm with a level of cover of USD15 million, the deductible can be as high as USD250,000.

*Recent developments with respect to insurance*
Recent developments in the Congress of the United States may affect professional indemnity insurance in Puerto Rico.

## RUSSIAN FEDERATION

### The civil liability of legal advisers

*Basis of liability*
There is no special or unified body of law in the Russian Federation governing the liability of legal advisers in the course of professional activity. Indeed this whole area of law is rather undeveloped. In the absence of any special rules or principles specifically applicable to legal advisers, liability is based on general civil law principles under the Russian Federation Civil Code (the "Civil Code") pursuant to which a provider of services may be held liable for harm caused by his non-performance or inadequate performance.

The general standard for liability for negligence is whether the service provider exercised the degree of care and attention appropriate to the matter at hand and customary in the business or profession, and whether he took all reasonable measures to fulfil adequately his obligations to the customer/client. If the services are deemed to be commercial in nature liability for non-performance or inadequate performance may only be avoided if they result from force majeure circumstances, unless otherwise provided by law or agreement between the parties. Since legal services are currently deemed to be commercial in nature, this latter standard would apply. A lawyer who is also an employee of an enterprise or organisation may bear limited liability under labour law principles for material damage caused by his negligence or wilful acts in performing his employment responsibilities.

In addition, various cities and other jurisdictions in the Russian Federation have a Collegium of Advocates (for example the Moscow Collegium of Advocates). Each particular Collegium has its own internal rules pursuant to which it may discipline and even expel a member. It is not clear whether violation of such rules would automatically serve as the basis for a civil claim.

Although summaries of court practice and cases are published and analyzed frequently, official court decisions are not generally published and it is not known whether there are any court decisions relating to the civil or labour liability of lawyers. Only a court would have jurisdiction to hear a claim for damages asserted against a legal adviser (either the People's Court or the Arbitration Court). No professional body exists which would have jurisdiction over such claims.

There are no court decisions requiring payment of compensation or imposing specific performance on a lawyer relating to his legal practice. Nevertheless, both of these remedies are in principle available as a matter of general civil law in the event of a finding of liability. There are no statutory financial ceilings on the amount of compensation which a court could award against a lawyer in the event that liability were found. Compensation for harm would be decided by the court on a case by case basis, based on the actual material harm and, potentially, moral damages caused by the non-performance or inadequate performance of the lawyer, if such damages were caused by a lawyer whose client is an individual.

*Restrictions on liability*

There are no special immunity provisions or general restrictions as to the circumstances in which a lawyer may be held liable to his client under Russian law. Under the Civil Code, an agreement with an individual client which seeks to limit liability would be invalid if (i) damage measures were established by law and (ii) if the agreement were concluded prior to the rendering of the services out of which the liability arises. It would appear to be possible in principle, therefore, to limit damages *vis-à-vis* a corporate client, unless future legislative acts provide for mandatory damage measures. An agreement pursuant to which a party seeks to limit its liability arising out of intentional violation of the law will be null and void and prior agreements which seek to reduce or eliminate liability for intentionally caused harm will also be null and void.

The Civil Code does not impose any financial restrictions, other than the general limitations discussed above on the circumstances under which agreements on limitation of liability may be used. The use of such agreements in the Russian Federation is extremely rare.

There is a general three-year limitation period, commencing from the moment when the injured party learned or should have learned about the violation of his rights.

*Liability to non-clients*

The only circumstances in which a lawyer could generally be found liable to a non-client would be if he committed a criminal infraction in the course of carrying out (or failing to carry out) his obligations to his clients, damaged an individual's or legal entity's business reputation by circulating faulty information or independently committed a tort.

*Recent developments with respect to liability*

On April 15, 1995, the Russian Federation Government issued Decree No. 344 approving Regulations "On the Licensing of Activity for the Provision of Paid Legal Services" (the "Regulations"). The Regulations establish a mandatory licensing requirement for the rendering of paid legal services on the territory of the Russian Federation. Previously, the practice of law was essentially unregulated in the Russian Federation.

Under the Regulations, the Russian Federation Ministry of Justice and corresponding organs of political subdivisions are authorized to issue licenses for the practice of law. Such licenses may be issued to individuals, without the formation of a legal entity (individual practitioners) and to legal entities, including foreign legal entities, irrespective of their legal form. Individual practitioners may be licensed to advise on questions of Russian law only if they hold a degree from a Russian legal educational institution, and may advise on the law of a foreign state only if they hold a degree from a foreign educational institution. Application procedures under the Regulations are still in the process of being implemented at the time of writing this book.

The Regulations state that persons rendering paid legal services without a license or in violation of the terms of a license shall bear liability as provided by Russian legislation. The Regulations themselves, however, do not establish any specific penalties or sanctions for the unlicensed practice of law or standards of liability for malpractice.

More generally, there have been recent developments in law regarding the circumstances under which plaintiffs can claim moral damages. There are no statutory limits or clearly defined measures for calculating such damages. Historically, damage awards in the Russian Federation for material harm and, where permitted, for moral damages have been very low by Western standards.

### Insurance

*Voluntary professional indemnity insurance*
The possibility of obtaining professional indemnity insurance for members of the Collegium of Advocates is recognized under Russian insurance law, but such insurance is not mandatory.

Due to the absence of a history of private legal practice, limited claims in practice filed against lawyers and a very recently established insurance industry in the Russian Federation, only a small percentage of the legal profession takes out professional indemnity insurance.

*Insurance facilities*
To our knowledge, no local insurance companies are currently providing professional liability insurance for lawyers. In general, Western law firms obtain such coverage in their home jurisdictions and do not seek to insure locally in the Russian Federation.

As most policies are obtained from abroad and, by definition, from different jurisdictions, it is not possible to identify common forms of policies.

*Level of cover*
Statistics are not available to indicate the level of cover generally obtained by the legal profession.

*Deductibles*
Statistics are not available on the range of deductibles payable by the insured lawyers.

*Recent developments with respect to insurance*
The private insurance industry has only recently developed in the Russian Federation, and there is little established practice of obtaining professional liability insurance in the Russian Federation. Russian commercial law firms are also a relatively new phenomenon. The abovementioned draft laws on the legal profession that have circulated in Moscow over the last couple of years may well lead to developments in the field of professional indemnity insurance as well.

## SCOTLAND

### The civil liability of legal advisers

*Basis of liability*
A solicitor's duty to his client is contractual although liability may also arise in delict. Unless otherwise agreed the common law standard of care will apply which

requires a solicitor to exercise such skill and care and have such knowledge as could be expected of a reasonably competent solicitor. Except in cases of fraud where a higher standard obtains, the burden of proof is the "preponderance of probability" whether a claim arises in contract or in delict. In addition, the profession imposes its own standards of conduct. Solicitors are expected to act in the best interests of their clients, subject to preserving their independence and observing the law, professional practice rules and the principles of good professional conduct. Until very recently the principles of professional conduct for Scottish solicitors were largely unwritten but have to an extent been codified now in the Code of Conduct (Scotland) Rules 1992, made by the Council of the Law Society of Scotland under the Solicitors (Scotland) Act 1980.

The principles of liability are defined chiefly by court decision. However, solicitors are also subject to practice rules (covering various subjects) and to guidelines relative to inadequate professional services, produced by the Law Society of Scotland.

The disciplinary procedures of the Law Society are not designed to provide damages for an injured client. Lawyers' liability, however, may be decided either by the courts or by the Council of the Law Society of Scotland or the Scottish Solicitors Discipline Tribunal. Liability for inadequate professional services, for example, may be established by the Council under the Solicitors (Scotland) Act 1988 or the Discipline Tribunal which has concurrent jurisdiction with the Law Society as well as appellate jurisdiction. Proceedings to obtain compensation under the Solicitors (Scotland) Act 1980 may not be founded on proceedings to establish negligence although both remedies may be pursued.

Under common law a client will ordinarily have a claim for damages only. In regard to inadequate professional services, the Law Society may order a solicitor to waive or reduce fees for particular services, to do the legal work again without charge or pay another solicitor to do the work and may also order limited compensation. Clients may also benefit from the Guarantee Fund, created by the Solicitors (Scotland) Act 1949 which will meet claims made against solicitors arising from dishonesty, and the Master Policy for professional indemnity insurance held by the Law Society of Scotland may meet other types of claims. In the case of grants from the Guarantee Fund, the Council has discretion and may refuse to make a payment if it believes that negligence on the part of the applicant has contributed to the loss.

Where inadequate professional services are alleged in a complaint to the Council, compensation is restricted to a sum not exceeding approximately USD1,500. If the client has suffered a loss in excess of that, clearly a civil action for professional negligence will be a more satisfactory remedy. The Guarantee Fund, on the other hand, has no upper limit.

*Restrictions on liability*
Usually a solicitor is protected when acting on the advice of Counsel (a barrister) although this protection is not absolute. A solicitor may enjoy the same immunity as a barrister when he is acting as the advocate in court or performing pre-trial work closely associated with the conduct of a case in court.

Solicitors may limit their liability by contract but will be subject to the restrictions of the Unfair Contract Terms Act; thus terms which are unreasonable will be unenforceable.

Solicitors are subject to the general law and most claims will be subject to the five year limitation period. There is no time bar for complaints to the Council of the Law Society of Scotland.

*Liability to non-clients*
Recent case law suggests that solicitors can be liable to third parties where the facts warrant. For example, potential beneficiaries under a will may have a claim against a solicitor if, because of his negligence, the will is invalid or, because of unreasonable delay, a will has not been prepared before the testator's death.

*Recent developments with respect to liability*
There are no recent trends or developments that would significantly alter the position set out above.

**Insurance**

*Compulsory professional indemnity insurance*
Professional indemnity insurance is compulsory in Scotland.

*Insurance facilities*
There is one master insurance policy which is held by the Law Society of Scotland. Commercial insurance is obtained from insurers within the United Kingdom and primarily from within Scotland.

The cost of compulsory cover is estimated to be three per cent of the annual expenses of a practice.

*Level of cover*
The compulsory cover is approximately USD1.5 million for each and every claim. Larger practices tend to purchase top-up insurance based on a calculation of risk.

*Deductibles*
The deductible/excess is based on the number of principals in a firm with an assumed maximum of ten principals. The excess is approximately USD3,000 per principal (or USD6,000 per principal at a reduced premium).

*Recent developments with respect to insurance*

There are no recent trends or developments that would make a significant difference to the position set out above.

## SINGAPORE

### The civil liability of legal advisers

*Basis of liability*

English common law and equity are highly persuasive and often followed in Singapore though they are not strictly binding. It must be noted at the outset that there is a fusion of the legal profession in Singapore. As such, no distinction is made between solicitors and advocates (barristers). Liability is not strict. A lawyer's civil liability to his client is founded in equity and common law.

In equity, the relationship between the lawyer and his client is viewed with utmost strictness as it is recognised as a fiduciary relationship. This arises from the reliance of the client upon the lawyer as a source of advice, guidance and confidence. As such the lawyer is to act with utmost fairness and openness towards the client. The lawyer will be liable to compensate the client where his failure to fulfil this obligation leads to loss by his client. Thus where a lawyer advises a client on a certain business transaction, the lawyer may be liable to account for profits earned in the transaction if the lawyer is also an interested party in the transaction but had failed to disclose this fact to the client.

At common law, the lawyer's retainer imposes on him the obligation to exercise reasonable skill and care. Failure to fulfil this obligation may lead to liability in contract, whether the lawyer is retained in return for a fee or gratuitously. In deciding whether the lawyer has fulfilled this obligation, the court applies the standard of skill and care to be expected of a competent lawyer. By reason of his contract of retainer, the lawyer may also be liable in the Tort of Negligence. The lawyer owes the client a duty to act with reasonable skill and care. Thus in determining whether he is liable, the following factors are taken into consideration:

- whether he has conducted himself in such a way as to breach that duty of care. In determining whether there has been a breach, the question of whether the lawyer has exercised the requisite degree of skill and care is relevant;
- whether the breach has caused the client to suffer loss. This second condition is qualified by the scope of the lawyer's duty. Where a lawyer is under a duty to protect only against a specific loss he will not be liable for an unrelated consequential loss suffered by the client.

A lawyer may be liable for negligent conduct of both contentious and non-contentious matters. In contentious matters, a lawyer is liable in negligence where he has mismanaged or carelessly prepared an action for trial or failed to observe the rules of practice. In non-contentious matters, a lawyer is liable in negligence where he fails to carry out his instructions according to the usual method prescribed by statute, rule or custom.

A lawyer may also be liable to a third party in negligence if the lawyer breaches a duty of care owed to that party who suffers a resultant loss. It has been held in some cases that financial loss, as well as direct loss, is recoverable where there is sufficient proximity between the negligent act and the resulting financial loss. To a large extent the principles defining a lawyer's civil liability are determined by court decisions based on equity, common law and public policy, taking into consideration prevailing circumstances and needs of the society.

The Lawyers' Rules promulgated by the Law Society from time to time may be used as a guide to determine whether the lawyer has exercised the necessary degree of skill and care. For example, a lawyer who, in breach of the Solicitors' Accounts Rules, transfers money from his client's account to another party without proper instructions is liable for the loss occasioned by his client if the money is irrecoverable. The civil liability of lawyers is determined solely by the courts. The Law Society as a professional body only has the power to promulgate rules for regulating the professional practice, etiquette, conduct and discipline pursuant to the Legal Profession Act, and to institute disciplinary proceedings against any lawyers who fail to comply with its rules. It does not adjudicate upon matters of civil liability.

Where damage has already occurred, the relief is usually compensatory in nature. However, where the act proposed to be done will necessarily lead to a loss, the court may grant an injunction. This is so in circumstances where the act threatened to be done may amount to a breach of confidentiality; for example a lawyer, having acted for a client in one matter, intends to act for the opposite party in the same matter, or in another, which would involve a breach of confidentiality arising out of the first or original retainer. The general rule is to prevent the lawyer from being placed in a position which conflicts with his duty to his client. This duty seems to continue even after termination of the retainer if there is a threatened breach of confidentiality.

*Restrictions on liability*

Where the lawyer has been negligent in handling his client's affairs, he is liable to his client for the loss occasioned. It is difficult to see how he can escape liability under any set of circumstances.

Where a lawyer acts upon his client's instructions, or with the reasonable belief that his actions are correct, or, having explained the situation to his client, is instructed to proceed then the lawyer is not liable to his client for the loss occasioned provided he has not been negligent. The final example seems to give authority to the proposition that a lawyer may enter into an agreement with his client to restrict or totally absolve himself from liability. However, it is said that for such agreement to be effective, a full disclosure of the prevailing circumstances of the case must be made known to the client. The lawyer cannot, having entered into such an agreement, then handle the case in a haphazard manner as this would be contrary to public interest.

In England, barristers and solicitor-advocates are accorded the special privilege of immunity from actions for negligence in the conduct and management of litigation. In Singapore, given the fusion of the profession, the immunity is accorded to all lawyers alike. This immunity extends to all pre-trial work which is so intimately connected with the conduct of the cases in court as to amount to preliminary decisions affecting the way that the court hearing is conducted. The basis for such immunity is public policy. Further, immunity from suit extends to advice on pleas in criminal proceedings. A litigant, having exhausted all avenues, should not be allowed effectively to reopen his trial by proceeding in negligence against his lawyer.

However, it should be noted that, notwithstanding the above, a lawyer is liable where the conduct of the litigation amounts to a blatant negligence. Examples of blatant negligence include obvious breaches of rules and conventions such as failing to serve a writ of summons on time.

A lawyer is protected from defamation actions in respect of words written or spoken by him in the course of judicial hearing, however improper or even malicious his behaviour may have been. Such words are privileged on the grounds of public policy. This privilege covers everything that is done from the inception of the proceedings onwards and extends to all pleadings and other documents brought into existence for the purpose of the proceedings.

Presently there is no statute in Singapore which limits or bars liability from arising out of the negligence of a lawyer in the course of acting for his clients. It is also unlikely that lawyers will seek to introduce standard conditions into their contract of retainers to exclude civil liability. Firstly, such standard conditions would have a hard time passing the test of "reasonableness" of the Unfair Contract Terms Act, 1977. Secondly, even if such terms are valid, lawyers would face a large loss of clientele, not to mention an immeasurable amount of face and goodwill for trying to impose such standard terms on their clients.

The Law Society has not promulgated any rules restricting the liability of a lawyer. Such a move is most unlikely in view of the inclination of the Law Society to introduce more rules to govern and restrict the conduct of lawyers.

The time limit for instituting claims against lawyers is regulated by the Limitation Act. Thus, actions founded in contract and tort may not be brought after the expiration of six years from the date on which the cause of action accrues. A cause of action accrues when the plaintiff is able to plead every fact which would be necessary for the plaintiff to prove, if traversed, in order to support his right to judgment. This has been amended by the Limitation (Amendment) Act 1992 by the inclusion of a knowledge element to mitigate the harshness which would otherwise be caused to a plaintiff in circumstances where the plaintiff, through no fault of his own, lacked the requisite knowledge to bring a claim. A plaintiff now has three years after obtaining the knowledge prescribed by the Amendment Act in which to commence an action even if the "old" limitation period has expired. However, there is a long stop period of fifteen years from the date of breach within which the requisite knowledge must be obtained.

Three subsections in the Amendment are devoted to the explanation of the nature and source of the knowledge which the plaintiff must have before the limitation period starts to run.

A lawyer's contractual duties to his client may in some instances be continuing duties. As such, the limitation period runs from the date when the obligation becomes impossible to perform or when the client elects to treat the continued non performance as repudiation of the contract.

There remains the issue of computation of the limitation period. The Act does not expressly provide whether or not the date on which the cause of action accrues is to be included in calculating the limitation period.

*Liability to non-clients*

A lawyer is liable to a non-client where it is foreseeable that damage would be suffered as a result of the lawyer's negligence, and that there is a close and direct relationship with the non-client, and that it would be fair, just and reasonable in the circumstances of the case to impose liability on the lawyer.

In one particular case a lawyer was liable in negligence to a non client where the latter had unwittingly executed a mortgage. The lawyer allowed his client to take the mortgage away to obtain the plaintiff's signature and then signed the mortgage as a witness even though he had not been present. Despite the absence of a contract between the lawyer and the non client it was held that the lawyer owed a duty of care to the plaintiff as his action had fallen below the required standard of care.

*Recent developments with respect to liability*

There are no recent developments which significantly alter the framework as summarized above.

**Insurance**

*Compulsory professional indemnity insurance*

Professional indemnity insurance was made compulsory and implemented on April 1, 1991 by the Law Society of Singapore. The Law Society is empowered by the Legal Profession Act to make such rules.

*Insurance facilities*

At present, there is one collective insurance scheme — issued by commercial insurers together with a lead insurer — approved and implemented by the Law Society. This so-called New Scheme became effective on April 1, 1994.

Excess insurance can be obtained from commercial insurers. The insurance broker that offers the approved collective scheme also offers excess insurance cover.

*Level of cover*
Under the New Scheme, the level of cover is USD720,000 for each and every claim.

It is estimated that lawyers spend no more than five per cent of their annual expenses on professional indemnity insurance. However, the exact figure depends on the number of lawyers practising in the firm, the size of the staff and other expenses.

*Deductibles*
Each firm is subject to a deductible proportionate to the premium payable based on the number of lawyers practising in the same firm. The range of deductibles is given in a Rating Schedule contained in the Insurance Policy. The smaller firms, i.e. firms with less than forty lawyers, are free to choose between three deductible levels. Where the deductible is low, the premium payable is higher and vice versa. For example, for a firm of eight lawyers the range of deductibles payable by the insured lawyers themselves is between approximately USD14,500 and USD32,500.

*Recent developments with respect to insurance*
In 1994, the level of cover was doubled from USD360,000 to USD720,000. Given the high number of claims made in recent years, a large proportion of which are claims arising out of conveyancing matters, it is doubtful that the present level of indemnity cover will remain sufficient for long, given the ever increasing property prices in Singapore. It is expected that the level of cover be increased in the near future.

## SOUTH AFRICA

### The civil liability of legal advisers

*Basis of liability*
South Africa has a divided bar. Advocates (barristers) enjoy the sole right of appearance in the superior courts whilst attorneys (solicitors) may appear only in the regional and magistrates courts.

The law and practice relative to the civil liability of lawyers has hitherto been concentrated largely upon those practising at the side bar (i.e. attorneys). The bulk of Roman-Dutch law suggests that an advocate's liability will be limited to loss arising from fraud or deliberate misconduct. There are, however, clear indications that the historic distinction between advocates and attorneys will not prevail and that claims arising from negligence will be entertained against both advocates and attorneys.

The nature, extent and limitation of civil liability is not defined or curtailed by statute. Common law principles are applied to determine the extent to which a lawyer is liable. Liability could arise as a result of the breach of a contractual duty or delictually, through failure to exercise care, skill and diligence.

*Restrictions on liability*

If liability is found to exist, relief is in the form of damages which are not limited by statute or common law. The courts enjoy absolute discretion in making awards of damages. In determining damage, the courts will attempt to restore the successful claimant in the *status quo ante*. A court would consider issuing a mandatory order in appropriate circumstances.

An advocate who appears in court for a client currently enjoys immunity from claims for damages on the basis that potential liability should not attach to a lawyer who takes decisions or acts in accordance with his own judgement on the spur of the moment, whilst on his feet. That immunity is likely to be extended to attorneys as well, if the issue is ever canvassed in a South African Court.

Lawyers may introduce a limitation clause in a contract with a client to restrict his liability for damage, provided that he does not seek to exclude liability arising from the breach of the duty to exercise care, skill and diligence, which would not be upheld by the courts. Although the courts have not ruled on the issue, it is anticipated that lawyers will not be allowed to escape liability by relying on a limitation clause in a contract with a client where public policy would demand that they be held liable. There are, however, no restrictions, statutory or otherwise, which prevent lawyers from inserting limitation clauses in contracts with clients and the effect thereof will only be known when it is ultimately tested in court.

The Prescription Act 68 of 1969 provides for the time periods which govern limitation of actions. The normal prescriptive period is three years and prescription runs from the time the damage is discovered or ought to have been discovered.

*Liability to non-clients*

The right to sue is limited to the parties to the contract. A non-client may establish the right of action based on delict provided a duty of care on the part of the lawyer can be proved.

The best example of potential liability to non-clients is that of the lawyer who fails to exercise skill, diligence or care in drawing or executing a will for a client, resulting in damage to a potential beneficiary under the will. Case law indicates that a lawyer will be liable in delict at the suit of the beneficiaries under a will if the will is declared invalid because of the lawyer's lack of care. The lawyer owes a similar duty to a *diligens paterfamilias* who, in particular circumstances, is compelled to foresee the possibility of harm being caused and who would take steps to guard against such occurrence.

*Recent developments with respect to liability*

As explained earlier, a divided bar is in operation in South Africa. In 1993 with the advent of a new constitution, the Constitutional Court was established and although rights of appearance are still limited to advocates in terms of the rules of the Constitutional Court, attorneys have already been given permission to appear in that court and it is anticipated that in the foreseeable future attorneys will be granted the right of audience in all courts.

In addition to this development, the South African Law Commission, the statutory body entrusted with the task of advising government on the need of amending and introducing new statutory provisions, was advised to investigate the need for the introduction of a statutory cap on damages and a limitation on time for bringing actions under the Prescription Act. The Commission's decision recommended the retention of the existing legal rules governing professional liability. This decision was not welcomed by the profession and pressure is being brought on the Commission to reverse its stance.

## Insurance

*Compulsory professional indemnity insurance*

All attorneys admitted to practice in South Africa are compelled to have a Fidelity Fund Certificate issued by the Attorneys Fidelity Fund. The Attorneys Fidelity Fund operates a scheme — the Attorneys Insurance Indemnity Fund — under which all practising attorneys who are in possession of Fidelity Fund Certificates are automatically indemnified against professional liability up to certain levels of cover, at no cost to the attorneys.

*Insurance facilities*

Professional Indemnity Insurance for attorneys is provided automatically by the Attorneys Insurance Indemnity Fund, a scheme which affords indemnity to each and every practising attorney in South Africa.

The professional indemnity insurance cover is arranged through one "master" insurance policy. Insurers are the Attorneys Insurance Indemnity Fund, a registered non-profit company wholly owned by the Attorneys Fidelity Fund, together with a further commercial co-insurer backed by various reinsurance programmes.

Insurance in excess of the levels of insurance cover available under the aforesaid Scheme is purchased from commercial insurers both within the country and from Lloyd's of London.

*Level of cover*

In 1994 the professional indemnity scheme offered cover for a limit ranging from USD280,000 per year to USD560,000 per year, depending on the number of principals in each practice. This cover is an aggregate for all claims in a policy period. The levels of cover and provisions relating to deductibles are determined annually.

An estimated fifteen per cent of all practices purchase cover in excess of the Scheme, up to a maximum cover of USD280 million. Local commercial insurers can provide cover up to USD140 million per year. Should a firm require cover in excess of USD140 million per year, same is purchased from Lloyd's of London.

Insurance premium for professional indemnity insurance generally constitutes the second or third highest expense in an attorney's firm, and surveys have shown that an amount ranging between one per cent to 2,5 per cent of gross fees earned represent the premium for professional indemnity insurance.

*Deductibles*

Under the Scheme operated by the Attorneys Indemnity Insurance Fund, the deductible payable by attorneys ranged from USD1,680 to USD10,080 in 1994, depending on the number of partners in the practice. In 1995, it is anticipated that the deductibles will rise to amounts ranging between USD2,100 and USD25,200 per practice per claim.

Due to the aggregate limit of indemnity, once cover offered by the Attorneys Indemnity Insurance Fund is exhausted, and should the attorney have purchased additional cover through the commercial market, such commercial insurers will levy a further deductible, which is usually pegged at a minimum of USD14,000 per claim, and a maximum of USD50,400 per claim.

*Recent developments with respect to insurance*

The Attorneys Indemnity Insurance Scheme has been in existence since the early 1970's, and the level of cover has increased from USD5,600 per practice to USD280,000 and USD560,000 per practice per year in 1994.

Prior to 1994, insurance cover could be purchased on an each and every claim basis. This, however, is no longer possible as insurers and reinsurers are no longer prepared to offer each and every claim limits, due mainly to the claims experience and to their reinsurance treaties.

Risk Management has become a very important aspect to the Attorneys Insurance Indemnity Fund and the Attorneys Fidelity Fund, and various risk management programmes have been implemented. It is hoped that such programmes will minimise the professional indemnity risk of lawyers. As the premium payable is becoming prohibitive, it is also foreseeable that individual attorneys and practices may have to contribute financially to the automatic cover provided by the Attorneys Fidelity Fund.

## SPAIN

### The civil liability of legal advisers

*Basis of liability*

The services of lawyers are characterised as qualified *contratos de arrendamiento de servicios* or "provision of services" contracts (Decision of the Supreme Tribunal,

February 4, 1992). The Civil Code dedicates one very general provision to such services which states that where the lease of works or services is concerned one of the parties undertakes to perform work or render a service to the other for a certain price. Draft legislation regulating the "services contract" in more detail is being considered in parliament. The professional services contract, therefore, is based upon the general principle of freedom to contract which is the cornerstone of Spanish contract law with certain limitations arising out of a few rules in our law.

Under a services contract the party rendering the services undertakes to render them to the extent of his knowledge and ability but not necessarily to achieve a particular result, goal or objective. Hence, a lawyer will not commit to "win" the lawsuit, but to pursue it in court in the best interest of his client. The lawyer is bound however, by a duty of utmost care and diligence under the General Statute of the Spanish Advocacy as approved by the Royal Decree 1994. A lawyer is not obliged to achieve a successful result, but he is obligated to pursue the action with utmost care and diligence. Utmost care and diligence are difficult to define but in my view involve reliability, dedication, skill and competence on the part of the lawyer. Further, the lawyer's defence of his client is subject to the adequate technical, ethical and moral requirements for providing legal assistance in each matter. In my opinion this is the application of the principle of *lex artis ad hoc* to the legal profession as developed in case law, which mainly concerns the medical profession.

Lawyers are also under a duty to act in good faith and with probity especially in litigation (the Judiciary Power Organic Act 6/1985 July 1) and to keep their client's affairs confidential.

Lawyers are subject when practising law to civil, criminal and disciplinary liability. Civil liability to the client could arise because of a contractual relationship between the lawyer and the client (which would not necessarily exclude an action in tort). Liability would not be strict. It would arise from fault or negligence, malice, and also delay in performance of the contract with the client and any other contravention of the contract.

Normally professional negligence or malice on the part of a lawyer must be proved, whether a lawyer is found to be negligent will depend upon whether he has failed to reach the standard of diligence required in carrying out work for his client which is not fixed but will depend upon the circumstances of the particular case. Whenever the required standard is not provided for in the agreement, the debtor should behave as a good father would. Lawyers, however, are specifically required to act with utmost care and diligence; thus, the standard required of a lawyer is higher than that required of an ordinary man.

Liability principles are defined by statute. Court decisions, however, play an important role in interpreting the statute and cannot be ignored when a case arises. Indeed the courts' trend is now to aim at administering effective justice rather than follow formal limitations which are deemed too restrictive or unreasonable. This is particularly true in civil liability cases in which, if it is found that the injured person is entitled to damages, the court will be likely to find either liability under the broad protection of contract law or under tort law as required by the circumstances to protect the plaintiff.

The concept itself of case law has been changing over the years. In theory the decisions of the Supreme Tribunal may just complement our law — not "create" law. Only judicial trends which constitute solid doctrine may be regarded as a precedent.

In practice, however, there is a reason to speak of judicial legislation. The Supreme Tribunal resorts on occasions to the Civil Code as amended in 1974. Article 5.1 provides that legal norms shall be interpreted according to the proper meaning of the words used in the relevant context, the historic and legislative background and the "social reality" of the time when they are applied, taking into account the spirit and purpose of the words. Using this rule, the Court has altered or changed in specific cases certain rules where it found them to be unreasonable or unfair.

The relevant local law society has disciplinary powers which can be used when a lawyer has breached his duties. There is a guide to breaches of professional conduct and penalties for those breaches. The imposition of any penalties must result from a procedure being followed. The decisions of the law society may be challenged in court. According to the General Statute of the Spanish Advocacy, civil liability can only be demanded and found in court. Civil liability will mean that compensation for damage caused can be awarded. In principle nothing would prevent the plaintiff from requesting interlocutory relief in an action for compensation. The likelihood of obtaining such relief would not be substantial unless the plaintiff's case was good.

Compensation to be paid by lawyers is not limited by statute or otherwise but is limited to the amount of damages suffered by the client. It is for the plaintiff to prove the damages suffered.

*Restrictions on liability*

There are no specific restrictions on liability if a lawyer is sued. Generally, liability arising out of gross negligence or fraud cannot be waived. Any such waiver would be null and void. Under the consumers and users legislation absolute limitations of liability are banned and the trend is to prevent such exemptions of liability. The courts do not like attempts to limit liability. However, in theory, parties could reach an agreement to restrict the lawyer's liability which results from something other than gross negligence.

If such an agreement were reached it would have to be done on a matter by matter basis. Standard conditions would be valid if the client specifically signed the agreement and agreed to each limitation. Such limitation is not laid down by statute or the directive of a professional body. Rather, the directives of the law societies make the lawyer fully liable for his action. Equally, statute and the rules of relevant professional bodies do not actually forbid such a limitation of liability by agreement.

The parties can limit the lawyer's financial liability (arising out of negligence rather than gross negligence or fraud) because of the general principle of freedom to contract which is the cornerstone of Spanish contract law (the Civil Code). Such agreements on financial restrictions are rarely, if ever, made.

The time limit for an action in contract, is fifteen years and for an action in tort, one year.

*Liability to non-clients*

Lawyers can be liable to non-clients and such liability would arise out of the infringement of the general duty imposed by the law of not harming or injuring anyone with whom there is no contractual link.

If a lawyer represents an insured under an insurance policy which provides that the insurance company will defend the insured in court, no services contract had been entered into by the insured and the lawyers but the lawyer could have duties to the insured.

*Recent developments with respect to liability*

The press has reported on the Government's aim to liberalise lawyers' fees which today are subject to schedules approved by the law societies. It now seems these efforts have been blocked by the Catalan nationalists.

It is difficult to foresee if the forthcoming changes will have any influence on the matters summarised above.

**Insurance**

*Voluntary professional indemnity insurance*

Professional indemnity insurance is not compulsory yet, but some of the eighty-two Spanish Law Societies do require lawyers practising in their jurisdiction to purchase insurance cover.

It is estimated that, out of the lawyers not insured through the Law Society requirements, approximately ten per cent take out indemnity insurance.

*Insurance facilities*

Several Law Societies offer voluntary collective schemes to their members. Generally the insurance is offered as one "master" insurance policy, contracted with a single commercial insurer.

Apart from the collective schemes, insurance policies issued by commercial insurers are also available, as well as commercial insurance policies approved by the professional body.

The insurance is generally — with some difficulty — obtained from insurers within the country. However, this should not mislead the readers regarding the capacity of the Spanish insurers. Still, a large portion of the risk is not retained but ceded abroad.

*Level of cover*
The minimum level of cover varies per Law Society. The Madrid Bar provides a cover of USD19,230, while the Vizcaya Bar requires its members to take out a minimum cover of USD192,300. The cover is a maximum for each claim per insured, with a total global cap during the policy period to all claims of USD769,230.

It is estimated that the cost of insurance cover is between 0,1 to 0,5 per cent of the annual expenses of a practice.

*Deductibles*
The range of deductibles is between USD769 and USD7,692, with an average deductible of USD3,846.

For certain types of law practice, deductibles may be higher. For example, the Madrid Law Society coverage provides for a USD3,846 deductible where general matters are concerned, and for a USD7,692 deductible for claims relating to tax, labour and real estate matters.

*Recent developments with respect to insurance*
It is expected that insurance premiums will increase in the near future.

A draft General Statute of the Spanish Advocacy is being discussed at the moment. Although it does not propose compulsory insurance so far, it is likely that the Council of State, when reviewing it, will amend the draft Statute and require compulsory insurance.

## SRI LANKA

### The civil liability of legal advisers

*Basis of liability*
The standard of care owed by a lawyer is decided according to the degree of skill and care to be expected of a competent lawyer. Where a lawyer renders a service or gives advice even for no reward, if another person acts upon the service or advice and sustains loss, the person who renders such advice or service is liable to compensate the person who relied upon the same if there was a lack of knowledge, skill or diligence on the part of the lawyer. The duty to be diligent, however, does not prescribe a standard of perfection.

An attorney is not liable to his client for mere errors of judgment. The error must be such that no reasonably well-informed and competent attorney acting with ordinary care and skill could have made. The test is the standard applicable to the ordinary skilled man professing to and exercising special skill.

The civil liability of a lawyer to his client is solely decided by the courts. The relief available is restricted to sufficient compensation or damages to cover the loss, injury or harm suffered by the client. A lawyer who has failed to act diligently or who has been incompetent in the discharge of his duties is liable to disciplinary sanctions which may be imposed by the Supreme Court.

*Restrictions on liability*
It has been laid down that no action can be brought against an attorney in respect of words uttered in the course of any judicial proceeding even if such words were uttered maliciously or without any justification or relevance to the case.

It may be inconvenient to individuals that attorneys should be at liberty to abuse their privilege of free speech subject only to punishment from a presiding judge. But it would be a far greater inconvenience to suitors if attorneys were embarrassed or enfeebled in endeavouring to perform their duty by the fear of subsequent litigation.

The part played by the lawyers in the judicial process not only requires them to act in the best interest of their client; they also have an overriding duty to the courts in the interest of due administration of justice. Therefore, to enable the courts to arrive at a fair decision, an attorney is obliged to call attention to all relevant documents and authorities whether or not they are in favour of the client's cause.

In respect of limitation the terms of the Prescription Ordinance applicable of Sri Lanka would apply. The Ordinance states that claims in respect of loss and damage should be brought within two years from the time when such cause of action has accrued.

*Liability to non-clients*
A lawyer in representing a client has a duty not to use means that have no substantial purpose other than to embarrass, delay or burden a third party, or to use methods of obtaining evidence that violate the legal rights of a third party. A lawyer who has done so may be subject to disciplinary sanctions, but will not incur civil liability. A lawyer in his professional capacity cannot incur civil liability to a third party.

*Recent developments with respect to liability*
A Committee of the Bar Association of Sri Lanka looks into any developments which can be adopted. But so far there are no developments to alter the established framework.

**Insurance**

*Voluntary professional indemnity insurance*
Indemnity insurance for the legal profession is voluntary in Sri Lanka. A very small proportion of the legal profession (estimated as being only one per cent of all lawyers) takes out professional indemnity insurance.

*Insurance facilities*
Available for insurance are policies issued by many local commercial insurers. Commercial insurance is generally obtained from insurers within the country.

Voluntary collective schemes introduced by a professional body are available as well, but no lawyers have taken out this insurance because the premium is very high.

*Level of cover*
Commercial insurance companies in Sri Lanka generally offer cover for any negligent act, error or omission in the conduct of the business undertaken by or on behalf the lawyer in his professional capacity. The insurance can be obtained by an individual or by a firm of lawyers.

The level of cover generally taken up by the legal profession is USD20,000. This figure is an aggregate for all claims within a policy period.

The cost of insurance cover may be 0,5 to one per cent of the annual expenses of a practice.

*Deductibles*
The range of deductibles payable by the insured lawyer himself is between ten and fifteen per cent of a claim.

*Recent developments with respect to insurance*
Professional negligence suits are rare in Sri Lanka. However, in 1994 the District Court of Colombo held that a medical specialist was liable to pay heavy damages to a lawyer whose young daughter died after treatment by the doctor. This case is pending in appeal.

Soon after this judgment the subject of taking out indemnity insurance by professionals including lawyers became much considered by all professionals.

Thereafter voluntary collective covers have attracted the attention of all professionals in Sri Lanka.

## SWEDEN

### The civil liability of legal advisers

*Basis of liability*
Lawyers' professional liability to their clients basically comes from the contractual relationship between the lawyer and the client. However, in practice legal liability is very rarely, if ever, expressly regulated in the agreement. Therefore, it can be said that the lawyers' liability in respect of advice given to clients and conduct of matters for clients is unlimited and based on negligence. Lawyers are in principle liable for

costs and any other financial loss which their clients may suffer as a consequence of the lawyer being negligent in the performance of his or her services.

If a lawyer claims to possess expertise within a certain field of law, clients are entitled to expect a higher standard of skill and care from him or her than from a non-specialist. It is likely that a court, when deciding on the liability issue, would take these matters into consideration.

Lawyers' duties to their clients are defined by statute. The Code of Judicial Procedure (*Rattegangsbalken*) states that a lawyer must carry out the matter he has been entrusted with by his client with honesty and all due speed. He must give it sufficient attention and resources. At all times he must conduct himself as a good lawyer. A lawyer is also obliged to keep the client's money and other assets separate from his own.

What is to be regarded as the conduct of a good lawyer is defined by rules on lawyers' conduct issued by the board of the Swedish Bar Association in 1984. Lawyers are supervised by the Disciplinary Committee. The aim of the ruling of the Disciplinary Committee is to further define and to develop the guiding principles. The rulings are published.

The code of conduct for lawyers in the European Community issued by the Council of the Bars and Laws Societies of the European Community (CCBE) is incorporated in the rules followed by the members of the Swedish Bar. In the Code of Conduct for Lawyers in the European Community professional indemnity insurance is regulated. According to this Code lawyers engaging in crossborder activities have to be insured at all times against claims based on professional negligence to an extent which is reasonable having regard to the nature and extent of the risks which lawyers incur in practice. The liability of lawyers is a matter exclusively decided by the courts but the Board of Swedish Bar Association and the Disciplinary Committee have a great influence and impact on these matters. It is not unusual that a disciplinary remedy is followed by a claim from the client or a third party against the lawyer for damages. The fact that the lawyer has been the subject of a disciplinary remedy might then be held against him in the civil case concerning his liability to pay damages. But if the lawyer rejects a claim for damages, the matter can be decided only by the courts. The Disciplinary Committee cannot adjudicate on whether damages should be awarded or on the level of damages. It can only impose disciplinary punishment such as fines. There are few court decisions concerning lawyers' liability.

*Restrictions on liability*

The remedy available to those seeking redress is restricted to monetary compensation. There are no financial limits on the compensation which lawyers can be ordered to pay. The lawyer's responsibility for losses due to negligence is in principle unlimited. This follows from the general principle under Swedish tort law that a party who has suffered financial loss due to a negligent act (or sometimes omission) is entitled to full compensation for his loss.

A lawyer's liability is not restricted in any way, statutory or otherwise. In principle a limitation of liability agreed between two contracting parties is valid under Swedish law unless damage has been caused wilfully or by a party who is clearly in a weaker position than another party — a limitation of liability on the part of the lawyer might be deemed unreasonable and therefore invalid in accordance with the Contract Act. The prevailing opinion is that lawyers cannot limit their professional legal liability to their clients. Furthermore, a limitation of liability would also raise doubts about ethical issues. A law firm would probably not want to use a general limitation of liability because of its negative reflection on the firm from a marketing and competition point of view. In certain specific areas the risks of being held liable for professional negligence are so insignificant that they can be disregarded. Defence work is one example.

There is no specific time bar for instituting proceedings against lawyers or claiming damages from lawyers. The normal time bar of ten years is applicable.

*Liability to non-clients*

Lawyers can be liable to non-clients in a number of cases. For instance when they are acting as receivers in insolvency matters or when they act for the benefit of third parties.

*Recent developments with respect to liability*

There is a growing awareness among the public about the liability of professionals including lawyers. The number of cases where damages are claimed from lawyers and other consultants is alleged to be increasing. However, no statistics on these cases have been assembled as at the date of going to print.

When business transactions involve larger sums and international aspects, awareness of lawyers' liability is growing, not only among clients but also among lawyers. The exposure to the American system has played a role in this process. I believe many lawyers would like to limit their professional liability insurance as insurance premiums are increasing as a result. However, the lawyer's liability must be limited in a way that is acceptable to the client. The client must be convinced that the limitation is reasonable and fair.

One way to limit liability would be to organise law offices and the legal business of the lawyer as limited companies or partnerships with limited personal liability. However, even if a law firm is organised as a limited company or a partnership with limited personal liability the lawyer in question might still have an unlimited personal liability towards his client. According to Swedish regulations a lawyer can conduct his business within the scope of a limited partnership or company with limited liability but his or her professional personal liability remains unrestricted towards his client. This is unlikely to change as it would be detrimental to the reputation of lawyers if claims by clients were referred to law firms organised as limited companies which are used as a cover behind which the lawyer or lawyers could hide in order to escape personal liability.

Preventative measures are likely to attract more attention in the future. Continued education, good organisation and management control and monitoring will reduce professional risks substantially. Insurance will still be available but at higher premiums and the insurance companies will most likely work together with the professional bodies to improve quality.

Agreements concerning the limitation of lawyers' liability in specific cases and with specific clients might be made in the future. There is no sign of such a development in Sweden but it might very well be that the internationalisation of the profession will bring such a development.

## Insurance

*Compulsory professional indemnity insurance*

Indemnity insurance has been compulsory for all members of the Swedish Bar Association since 1984.

*Insurance facilities*

The compulsory collective liability insurance is contracted by the Swedish Bar Association with a single commercial insurer, and the premium is paid by the lawyers through their contribution to the Bar Association.

Apart from the compulsory collective scheme, insurance policies issued by commercial insurers are also available, as well as commercial insurance policies approved by the professional body. Most lawyers, particularly those active in a high risk field, have additional insurance.

Commercial insurance is generally obtained from insurers within Sweden. Many firms, however, have started to look abroad to obtain the best and most cost effective insurance cover.

A voluntary collective scheme introduced by the professional body concerning illness, accidents, etc. is also available.

*Level of cover*

The compulsory collective liability insurance contracted by the Bar Association provides base cover of USD415,000, which is a maximum per claim, year and insured. The cost of the compulsory collective cover is USD552.

The additional cover taken up by the profession varies. The same insurance company contracted for the compulsory cover offers additional insurance cover of USD1.65 million.

*Deductibles*

For the compulsory cover of USD415,000, the first USD4,935 of a claim is self-insured by the lawyer.

*Recent developments with respect to insurance*
The problems relating to professional liability are starting to be discussed in Sweden, and will be increasingly discussed in the future. The Law Society will need to deal with the issue of limitation of liability of lawyers.

Not long ago, the scope of activity of the normal Swedish lawyer was national. As the work performed by the members of the Swedish Bar is becoming more international, the risk exposure grows. The legal business is becoming more and more specialized and difficult, and it is becoming more dangerous to practice law, particularly in the field of international commercial law.

In addition to this, lawyers have seen a development where the general public has become more aware of the possibility to seek compensation through damages from lawyers, as well as from other consultants. The recession in recent years in Sweden has also contributed to this development.

Insurance premiums are running high, as claims are becoming more common and more costly for the insurance companies.

In order to control premiums before they grow sky-high, the Swedish Bar Association has proposed to establish its own insurance company in the form of a captive. Ethical concerns and other doubts concerning the captive's financial strength and possibility to reinsure its risks recently stopped the launching of this project, at least for the time being.

The Swedish Bar Association has, together with some Swedish insurance companies, started analysing the cause of damages.

Risk managers will be consulted by law firms, in order to assess their risks and to monitor their business. It is our belief that, in commercial law, risk are less significant when the lawyer or law firm assists a client on a regular basis than where a lawyer undertakes a single task. Since clients tend to engage lawyers more often for single transactions than before, the risk increases. Good risk management should include control systems for legal opinions and/or other important documents, for example suggesting that such documents shall always be crosschecked by a lawyer not involved in the matter. Deadlines should be noted in special registers in order to supervise that deadlines are met. The education and training of lawyers should focus on the prevention of risks. The preparation of guidelines for risk managers based on what experience lawyers would suggest from what they have been through should be drafted and implemented.

## SWITZERLAND

### The civil liability of legal advisers

*Basis of liability*
A lawyer's liability in Switzerland is based on negligence. In view of the high level of skill and care expected of a lawyer admitted to the Bar, the requirements with

regard to establishing negligence are not very high. The principles of liability are set out in the statute (Code of Obligations, Contract of Mandate) and numerous court decisions.

Each Canton has a cantonal Bar and most of them have a committee dealing with ethical questions. In addition many Cantons have a commission composed of lawyers and judges, who have a statutory right to decide cases concerning breaches of duty of a lawyer, with the exception of claims for damages, which have to be decided by the ordinary courts.

The Cantonal Commission may impose reprimands, fines or temporary withdrawal of the lawyer's licence. There are no financial limits on compensation, which lawyers may be ordered to pay.

*Restrictions on liability*

There are no restrictions on the circumstances in which lawyers may be held liable by clients. Some cantonal statutes do not allow lawyers to limit their liability towards clients. Cantonal and Federal Laws do not allow lawyers to limit their liability by way of agreements. In particular liability cannot be limited to cases of gross negligence. Liability can also not be limited by lawyers incorporating companies with limited liability.

The limitation period within which time a claim can be brought against a lawyer is five years if a lawyer is sued by a client and one year if a lawyer is sued by a third party.

*Liability to non-clients*

Under the Law of Torts lawyers could be held liable to non-clients. A negligent act or omission, a loss caused to the third party and a causal connection in the legal sense between the act and omission and the loss caused to the third party could give rise to liability on the part of a lawyer.

*Recent developments with respect to liability*

At this stage there are no visible trends or developments taking place which may alter the basis of the lawyers' liability as outlined above.

**Insurance**

*Voluntary professional indemnity insurance*

Indemnity insurance for the legal profession is voluntary in Switzerland. An estimated ninety per cent of the legal profession is insured for professional indemnity.

*Insurance facilities*

Policies are issued by commercial insurers and the insurance is generally obtained from within the country.

*Level of cover*
The level of cover generally ranges between USD770,000 to USD3.8 million. The average cover is estimated to be USD1.5 million, and usually provides a maximum for each claim.

The insurance premium represents approximately two to five per cent of the annual expenses of a practice.

*Deductibles*
The first ten per cent of a claim is usually self-insured by the lawyer, with a maximum of USD38,500 per claim.

*Recent developments with respect to insurance*
The Swiss Bar Association is investigating the possibility of offering a voluntary collective insurance scheme to its members, at a lower premium than the current commercial insurance policies.

## TAIWAN

### The civil liability of legal advisers

*Basis of liability*
Generally speaking, the principles of Taiwanese lawyers' liability to their clients in respect of advice given and the conduct of matters are subject to and codified in the Civil Code, promulgated in 1929, and last amended in 1995. Their liability is decided according to the degree of skill and care to be expected of a competent lawyer. The Civil Code provides that a lawyer is liable to his client for any damage resulting from negligence in the execution of his mandate or from those acts in excess of his authority. However, if work is done on a gratuitous basis. a lawyer is liable only for his gross negligence. A lawyer is bound to manage the matters entrusted to him in accordance with the instructions of his client and to do so with such care as he would exercise in his own affairs. For non-gratuitous work a lawyer must exercise the case of a "good administrator". In addition, the Lawyer Law passed in 1941 and last amended in 1992, stipulates that if a lawyer causes his client to suffer damage because of his negligence he will be held liable to compensate his client for such damage.

The liability of lawyers is solely decided by the courts in Taiwan unless the contract of retainer states otherwise. Nonetheless, the contracting parties may agree to refer disputes to an arbitration by the Commercial Arbitration Association, or an *ad hoc* committee within the Bar Association.

*Restrictions on liability*

The most usual form of relief is compensation. In certain cases, the clients may apply to the court for provisional measure order against their lodgement of security, or a final peremptory prohibitory or mandatory judgment against the lawyer.

Unless otherwise provided in the contract between a lawyer and his client, the level of compensation payable to the client is subject to the provisions of the Civil Code.

Unless otherwise provided by law or by contract, the Civil Code provides that a lawyer or any person liable to compensate an injured party for damage, must cause that injured party to be restored to the condition which existed prior to the occurrence of the damage. In the case of monetary payment, interest is due from the date on which the damage occurred.

If the guilty party fails to perform his above obligation within a reasonable time fixed by the injured party, the latter can claim monetary payment of damages for the injury sustained.

The Civil Code also provides that if the obligation to restore the injured party to his prior condition is impossible to carry out, or if the performance is obviously hindered by great difficulties, payment of monetary damages is due for the injury sustained.

Also, unless otherwise provided by law or by contract, damages are intended to compensate for the injury actually suffered and for any loss of profit. The latter is defined as profits which would otherwise normally be expected, either according to the ordinary course of events, or according to the injured party's projects, preparations or other special circumstances.

The above limits on compensation are imposed by court judges or arbitration in the terms of final and irrevocable judgments and awards.

Subject to the above, lawyers shall be liable to their clients for any loss and/or damages sustained by their clients due to the events attributable to lawyers. Hence, lawyers shall not be liable for any matters that are not attributable to them. Lawyers are relieved from their obligations to perform if performance becomes impossible by reason of a circumstance for which they are not responsible, and if as a result the lawyers are entitled to claim for damages against a third party, the client may demand from the lawyer that the claim for damages against that third party or the requests of compensation should be transferred to the client pursuant to the provisions of the Civil Code.

Lawyers can according to the Civil Code agree with their clients to limit their liability save for liabilities arising from wilful misconduct and gross negligence.

Financial restrictions on liability, which, under Taiwanese law, are different from the limitations of liability referred to in the preceding paragraphs, can be agreed between lawyers and their clients. These, nevertheless, are subject to the court's discretion. Such agreements, however, are rarely made.

The time limit for making claims against lawyers founded in contract is fifteen years from the date when the alleged damages and/or loss occurred; claims against lawyers founded in tort shall become time-barred after the expiration of a two-year period commencing from the date of the alleged tortious act.

*Liability to non-clients*
If a lawyer's act constitutes a tort the Civil Code provides that he will be liable to compensate the injured party for damage caused by his wilful or negligent conduct. The same rule applies when the injury is wilfully in a manner contrary to the rules of good morals. A person who infringes a statutory provision enacted for the protection of others is deemed to have committed a fault. It is therefore possible for a lawyer to be liable to a third party who is a non-client.

*Recent developments with respect to liability*
There have been no recent developments in this area.

**Insurance**

*Voluntary professional indemnity insurance*
Professional indemnity insurance for the legal profession is voluntary in Taiwan and few lawyers have taken out such insurance.

*Insurance facilities*
All insurance policies in Taiwan must be approved by the Ministry of Finance. A commercial policy — approved by the Ministry — is available for insurance against legal malpractice.

Insurance is generally obtained from insurers within the country, and reinsured abroad.

*Level of cover*
The approved insurance policy offers a cover of approximately USD38,000 as a maximum for each claim and USD76,000 as an aggregate for all claims within a policy period — usually one year.

The annual insurance premium is derived from the following formula:
The total annual premium for a maximum for each claim in the amount of USD38,000 and an aggregate for all claims within a policy period — usually one year — in the amount of USD76,000 equals Basic Number 2,000 plus 3,000, multiplied by the number of practising lawyers plus 1,500, multiplied by the number of assistants and high ranking staff plus 500, multiplied by the number of the other staff. ("Assistants and high ranking staff" refers to those employees who are not typists, messengers, or janitors).

*Deductibles*
The deductible payable by the insured lawyers themselves is one per cent of the claim.

*Recent developments with respect to insurance*
At the time of writing this book there are no new trends or potential developments in the area of professional indemnity insurance.

## THAILAND

### The civil liability of legal advisers

*Basis of liability*
In Thailand, there are no clear guiding principles or statutory guidelines on lawyers' liabilities to clients. In general lawyers can be liable to clients for either breach of contract or in tort. Lawyers must keep to a certain standard of practice in handling cases and dealing with clients. However, there are no guidelines as to this professional standard.

The general principles are governed by statute depending on the nature of the liability. For tort or wrongful acts, the Civil and Commercial Code states that

> A person who, wilfully or negligently, unlawfully injures the life, body, health, liberty, property or any right of another person, is said to commit a wrongful act and is bound to make compensation therefor.

For breach of contract, clients may hold lawyers liable for damages caused by their performance or non performance of a contract

> when the debtor fails to perform his obligations in accordance with the true intent and purpose of the same, the creditor may claim compensation for any damages caused thereby.

The courts process all complaints and charges against lawyers, both civil and criminal cases, with recourse to trial and using the appellate process.

Clients may be awarded damages in financial terms or the equitable remedy of specific performance, if requested. In practice, an order for specific performance is rare and the court will usually award clients compensation in financial terms. The amount of compensation varies from case to case depending on the nature of the charges and the amount of the resulting damages. There is no limitation on the amount of compensation the court may grant.

*Restrictions on liability*
According to the Penal Code a lawyer who expresses opinions or makes statements during court proceedings in favour of his case is not liable in defamation.

For other restrictions, there are no clear statutes or guidelines. Lawyers in Thailand rarely enter into an agreement with clients to limit their liability. Lawyers may make any agreement with clients concerning giving advice and conducting cases as long as the agreement is not expressly prohibited by law or is contrary to public order or good morals.

An agreement made in advance exonerating a debtor from his own fraud of gross negligence is void. Therefore, it would appear that a lawyer may by an agreement limit liability for simple negligence or breach of contract. However, the law in this area is unclear and there is no guiding principle in this matter. Any agreement between lawyers and clients limiting lawyers' civil and financial liability for giving advice and handling cases is only valid to the extent that it is not prohibited by law or is contrary to public order and good morals.

It is still an open question in Thailand as to whether lawyers can or cannot enter into an agreement to limit their liability to clients.

The limitation period for wrongful or tortious acts is one year from the date of both the committal of the wrongful act and the date on which the identity of the wrongdoer (i.e. the lawyer) becomes known to the injured party, but not more than the longstop period of ten years from the day when the wrongful act was committed. For breach of contract, the prescription is ten years.

*Liability to non-clients*

A lawyer may be held liable to a non-client where he enters into an agreement with his client to represent that non-client.

When the non-client declares to the lawyer his intention to take the benefit of the performance of the contract between himself and the lawyer he acquires the right to seek performance of the contract against the lawyer provided that the client has agreed to this (and the contract is genuinely for the benefit of the other person).

A non-client may claim compensation from a lawyer where his advice and handling of a client's case causes damage to a non-client in tort or by reason of a wrongful act or breach of contract.

*Recent developments with respect to liability*

Complaints filed with the court take a long time to process because of the number of cases the court handles. Most clients and injured parties consider that the benefit of compensation is outweighed by the time and expense of taking the complaint to court. The court is now aware of this lengthy process and is trying to bring cases to an end in an expeditious manner.

Clients can also file complaints against lawyers with the Law Society of Thailand under the Lawyers Act. Since clients and injured parties are not generally aware of the roles and authority of the Law Society there have been few cases in the past referred to the Law Society. Also it only investigates complaints about lawyers. It does not have the authority to impose obligations or order compensation by lawyers. Its powers are limited to suspension or revocation of practising licenses or putting lawyers on probation. Recently the Law Society of Thailand has been engaged in informing the public of its supervisory rules regarding lawyers. As more complaints have been filed with the Law Society of Thailand it has tended to observe and supervise lawyers more actively.

### Insurance

*Professional indemnity insurance*
There is no professional indemnity insurance available for the legal profession in Thailand.

With the liberalization of the insurance industry, foreign insurance companies may make professional indemnity insurance policy available to lawyers in Thailand in the future.

## TURKS & CAICOS ISLANDS

### The civil liability of legal advisers

*Basis of liability*
The Territory of the Turks and Caicos Islands ("TCI") is a British dependency with its own legislative assembly. The primary source of law in TCI is the local constitution and local statutes. However, where these are silent, recourse is had to English common law (court decisions) on the topic concerned.

The duty of a lawyer to his client is threefold:

- he has a contractual duty arising out of his retainer. Such a contract gives rise to a complex of rights and duties of which the duty to exercise reasonable care and skill is but one;
- a lawyer owes a fiduciary duty to his client. This duty requires the lawyer neither to abuse nor to take any secret advantage of the special situation that has been created by their relationship;
- the lawyer has furthermore a tortious duty to his client. Thus a lawyer can be liable in damages for the negligent conduct of his client's affairs. In this regard, the standard of care and skill which can be demanded is that of a reasonably competent and diligent lawyer.

The principles referred to are defined by court decisions. The liability of lawyers is a matter of common law.

*Restrictions on liability*
The primary relief available will be compensation. However, injunctive relief may be available in cases in which monetary compensation would be an inadequate remedy for the injured party. Compensation awarded will be limited to the damage sustained. The injured party has a duty to mitigate its loss so far as is reasonable.

Lawyers enjoy an absolute immunity from any form of civil action being brought against them in respect of anything they say or do in court during the course of a trial. The immunity extends only to work which is performed in court or else to work which is intimately connected with that performance. Lawyers may by agreement with their clients limit their liability both in particular matters and generally by way of conditions in their contract with their client. However, such exclusion clauses must be clearly incorporated as a term of the contract and the client must clearly be notified of them. Moreover, an exclusion clause will be construed by the courts strictly against the party which introduced it (the lawyer). Therefore, all such clauses have to be carefully drafted following the common law rules regarding such clauses.

The parties can negotiate terms limiting the lawyer's liability to a certain financial level. Such agreements are, in the writer's experience, made only rarely in this jurisdiction.

Only lawyers admitted to practice as attorneys of the Supreme Court of the Turks & Caicos Islands may charge fees for the drafting of documents or the provision of legal advice. As a body corporate cannot be admitted to practice, lawyers in TCI cannot incorporate to limit their own liability. There is no law which prevents lawyers restricting their liability to their clients.

There is no Statute of Limitations relating to actions arising out of breach of contract, breach of fiduciary duty or negligence in TCI. Therefore there is no statutory time period for the institution of proceedings against lawyers. However a plaintiff who negligently or unreasonably delays in asserting or enforcing his claim may be denied relief under the equitable doctrine of laches.

*Liability to non-clients*

Under English common law a professional man who gives guidance to others owes a duty of care, not only to the client who employs him, but also to another who he knows is relying on his skill to save him from harm. A solicitor has been held to owe such a duty in a situation where a third party relies on his advice. This also applies in TCI.

*Recent developments with respect to liability*

At the time of writing this book there have been no recent developments.

## Insurance

*Voluntary professional indemnity insurance*

Indemnity insurance for the legal profession is voluntary in the Turks and Caicos Islands. Approximately thirty-five per cent of the legal profession takes out professional indemnity insurance cover.

*Insurance facilities*

Available for insurance are policies issued by foreign commercial insurers, typically from London.

*Level of cover*

The maximum level of cover per claim ranges between USD500,000 and USD1 million. The maximum level of cover for an aggregate of all claims in a year ranges between USD2.5 million and USD5 million.

It is estimated that the cost of insurance cover may be as much as three per cent of the annual expenses of a practice.

*Deductibles*

The range of deductibles payable by the insured lawyers is between USD5,000 and USD25,000.

*Recent developments with respect to insurance*

The legal profession has grown considerably in recent years, due to a substantial increase in local development (primarily tourism related) and the expansion of the local offshore finance industry. This has led to a growth of concern amongst the legal profession regarding exposure to claims by clients.

As a result, the interest in professional indemnity insurance coverage is growing. It is likely that, within the next five years, the percentage of the legal profession covered for professional indemnity will grow to sixty to seventy per cent.

A major concern is the cost of such coverage which, in our experience, is substantially in excess of that which applies in mainland jurisdictions, with the possible exception of the United States.

## UNITED STATES

### The civil liability of legal advisers

*Basis of liability*

Lawyer liability in the United States is a matter of state law. Thus, there are fifty different jurisdictions, some of which have unique rules. The following is a review of the general principles used in virtually all states but it is a general review, not state specific.

The most common actions brought by clients against their attorneys are for (a) negligence, (b) breach of a fiduciary duty, (c) breach of contract, and (d) fraud. The standard of care for lawyers typically requires that they have knowledge of the law and apply that knowledge with the skill and care of a prudent lawyer in similar circumstances.

If there is one basic, guiding principle of a lawyer's liability, it is that he should act with "ordinary skill and knowledge." Courts, when they instruct juries, define this standard as "knowledge and skill" superior to that of an ordinary person and comparable to that of other lawyers. This is an example of such an instruction:

> In performing professional services for a client, a lawyer has the duty to have that degree of learning and skill ordinarily possessed by reputable lawyer, practising in the same or a similar locality and under similar circumstances.
> It is a further duty to usc the care and skill ordinarily used in like cases by reputable members of the same profession practising in the same or a similar locality under similar circumstances, and to use reasonable diligence and best judgment in the exercise of professional skill and in the application of learning, in an effort to accomplish the purpose for which the professional was employed.

A distinction must be made at the outset between lawyer liability and lawyer discipline. Courts determine the liability of a lawyer for malpractice. State Bar Associations and the Supreme Courts of each of the fifty states often discipline lawyers for ethical misconduct. When various state Bar Associations discipline lawyers for ethical violations, it takes three forms: (1) disbarment and prohibition from practising, (2) fines, and (3) suspensions.

Courts created and apply the standard of care. The standard varies from state to state, from case to case. The various definitions of the standard of care are found in the published decisions of each state's courts.

The liability of a lawyer to a client for negligence is almost always a matter for the courts to determine. Courts award monetary damages to clients harmed by a lawyer's malpractice.

The objective of most legal malpractice suits is to recover damages. Under American jurisprudence, numerous legal theories define the amount: loss of benefit to client, direct monetary damage suffered, consequential damages to the client, legal fees paid to the defendant attorney, punitive damages, etc.

Consequential damages for attorney malpractice can include injury to reputation, emotional and mental pain, and the expenses of mitigating loss. Courts have broad discretion to fashion orders that will remedy whatever a client's loss may be. There is apparently no limit to the damages a lawyer may face in a liability suit, except the damage the lawyer himself creates.

*Restrictions on liability*

A lawyer cannot limit liability by agreement with a client. Some statutory restrictions will prevent lawyers from limiting their liability to a client. In California, for example, a lawyer cannot contract with a client prospectively to limit his liability for professional liability, or settle a claim for malpractice unless the client is informed in writing that the client may seek advice of an independent lawyer.

The appropriate statute of limitations for legal malpractice can depend upon the theory and nature of the suit and the language of the statute applicable to the action, as well as the various rules of the jurisdiction. For that reason, it is difficult to generalize. But if a generalization can be made, then most periods vary between one and six years, but some are as long as ten.

*Liability to non-clients*

Traditionally, attorneys' malpractice exposure is limited to their clients. Beginning in the 1970s, however, non-clients increasingly began suing lawyers, particularly in negligence. Today, thirteen per cent of all claims against lawyers in the United States are made by non-clients. This figure is spiralling upward.

Most non-client claims come in family law disputes, banking cases, wills and estates matters, and property cases. In the United States, the statutes of limitations is one of the most effective defences by lawyers to malpractice actions and virtually the only effective affirmative defence.

*Recent developments with respect to liability*

Up until 1970, lawsuits against lawyers were almost unheard of. By 1980, the number had quadrupled from just ten years earlier. This staggering pace continues. Currently, lawyers are sued each year nineteen per cent more times than in the previous one. In fact, in the last ten years, more lawsuits have been filed against lawyers than in all of U.S. judicial history.

Why the explosion? Here are a few reasons:

- consumer consciousness. The public is better educated on its rights and less intimidated by lawyers;
- by the mid-1970's, the medical malpractice "crisis" created public awareness of professional liability; and
- lawyers are more willing to sue lawyers and to testify against them.

Forty per cent of all lawsuits are caused by an attorney failing to act. These include the failure to sue within the statute of limitations, failure to file discovery, and creating a lien against real property after the time limit expired. Claims can be broken down as follows:

- twenty-five per cent of suits are filed against personal injury lawyers;
- twenty-three per cent against real estate lawyers;
- ten per cent against bankruptcy lawyers;
- eight per cent against family law lawyers;
- seven per cent against trust and probate lawyers.

## Insurance

*Voluntary professional indemnity insurance*

Professional indemnity insurance for the legal profession is voluntary in forty-nine of the fifty states.

The lone exception is Oregon, in which a State Statute authorizes the Board of Governors of the Oregon State Bar to require all lawyers to carry malpractice insurance. Oregon adopted compulsory insurance for two reasons: first to protect the public; and second to provide stable coverage for lawyers.

*Insurance facilities*
Several facilities are available for insurance:
*Commercial insurance*: commercial insurers issue most malpractice insurance for lawyers in the United States. Lloyd's of London was the first to insure lawyers for malpractice — years before large domestic property and casualty insurance.

Most State Bars create an approved list of insurers that includes one company or organization that the bar sponsors. The State Bar will then recommend that sponsored company to all lawyers that call them with insurance questions. In return for the referral, the sponsored underwriter will pay the State Bar a fee. The State Bar of California, for example, receives approximately USD1 million a year from its sponsee.

Some State Bar Associations have established collective schemes whereby the Bar Association acting as a separate corporate entity will offer insurance to lawyers within their judicial district. Almost eighty per cent of the State Bars provide professional liability insurance.
*Mutuals*: additionally, because insurance is not compulsory, large law firms self-insure. Many two-or-three-hundred lawyer firms will join a mutual insurance company and put their premiums into one fund. This fund will pay any claims, usually with a very high deductible: USD100,000 to USD500,000. Professionals from the insurance business will manage the mutual.
*Client Security Funds*: finally, almost every state has enacted legislation to relieve the pecuniary losses to clients caused by dishonest lawyers. The money for the security fund comes from yearly membership dues collected by each state's licensing agency — the State Bar or Supreme Courts.
*Oregon*: the Oregon State Bar operates a fund into which all attorneys pay a yearly fee.

*Level of cover*
The level of cover generally taken up by the profession ranges from USD100,000 to USD5 million per claim, and USD300,000 to USD10 million for all claims in a policy period.

In Oregon, every member of private practice must purchase insurance from the State Bar. The limit on the policy is USD300,000 per claim for every claim made against a firm. Therefore, a firm's aggregate is USD300,000.00 x the total number of lawyers in a firm.

In addition, the lawyers at their option may purchase additional coverage from either the State Bar or a private carrier.

*Deductibles*
The lowest deductible is approximately USD2,500. The maximum is usually between USD100,000 and USD250,000, but some large firms will pay up to USD500,000.

*Recent developments with respect to insurance*
Some states such as California may introduce legislation requiring lawyers to carry insurance. Another development is the increasing use of mediation and arbitration to settle disputes.

## URUGUAY

### The civil liability of legal advisers

*Basis of liability*
Lawyers' liability to their clients in respect of advice given and the conduct of matters is not strictly set out in legal provisions. Therefore, the general principles on contractual liability apply to the standards of diligence required from a "competent lawyer".

Legal provisions on Judicature and Organization of the Courts enact that

> Lawyers are responsible to their clients for any loss or damage that may be legally attributed thereto.

The obligation of a lawyer does not guarantee of a successful result, but rather to devote the means in order to attain said result.

As a consequence of this, lawyers must act with the diligence that would be employed by a "good family man", as is expressed by the Uruguayan Civil Code. In the particular case of lawyers, it would be correct to establish that their diligence, and consequently their liability, is measured according to the degree of skill and care to be expected of a competent lawyer.

This solution has been unanimously sustained both by the doctrine and the jurisprudence in the country. A lawyer can never guarantee the results of a trial, since said results depend on several factors, not only on the lawyer's activities. Some authors have suggested that lawyers who go beyond this principle and undertake the obligation to obtain a result act in a way contrary to ethics.

These principles have been defined in a general way by authors and by court decisions, as well as by the legal provision mentioned above. Regarding court decisions on lawyers' activities, most of them relate to wrongful attitudes adopted in relation to the Judges or to the counterparties. The cases involving liability to clients are quite limited, and include situations of gross negligence and repeated omissions in the conduct of matters.

Although the Uruguayan Bar Association has published some works on this matter, these are not mandatory for lawyers, and neither is the membership to this Association. Consequently, the only decisive jurisdiction on the matter is the one exercised by the courts and the decisions on this particular point are quite limited.

*Restrictions on liability*

The most common relief is compensation, although we do not discard the application of other solutions. However, to date, there are no precedents establishing other kinds of relief. Generally speaking, and in compliance with the general provisions existing on civil liability (tort and otherwise), there are no limits in principle as to the amount of the compensation. The damages caused will need to be proved by the claimant, and the amount will finally be determined by the court. To date, there have been no significant cases on these matters.

The lawyer may not be held liable when he has carried out his activities under the conditions standard to competent professionals. Furthermore, and as is the case in all types of contracts, since the conditions under which the services are rendered may be mutually agreed by both parties, lawyer and client, the corresponding liabilities may be restricted or extended. This, however, is not the usual practice.

The commencement of an action is time-barred five years from the date on which the cause of action accrued.

*Liability to non-clients*

Lawyers' liability to non-clients, can be differentiated in three different ways: liability before judges, before counterparties, and before third parties in general.

Regarding judges and counterparties, the liability is mostly of a disciplinary nature: lawyers are liable for their oral or written expressions that may be offensive to judges, for resorting to legal proceedings prohibited by the law, for alleging facts that have already been proved to be false, and for offending their counterparties or their attorneys. Non compliant lawyers may be admonished, fined or suspended for a period of one year.

Regarding third parties, lawyers are subject to the provisions applicable to general civil liability (tort), whereby they may be held responsible for their wrongful or negligent activities that cause harm to third parties.

*Recent developments with respect to liability*

There is a trend, evidenced by the doctrine and jurisprudence in Argentina, that is trying to reverse the burden of proof, regarding lawyers' liability. According to this trend, the client will not be under the obligation to prove that the lawyer did not comply with his duties. This position assumes the non-compliance, and therefore it is the lawyer who will need to prove that he acted in a diligent and competent manner, and thus, that he complied with his obligations.

This position has found no echoes in our country, and there are currently no new developments taking place. In fact, not so long ago the point was only dealt with in a theoretical manner, and there were no judicial cases thereon.

However, we would not be surprised if further developments arise in the near future, as has been the case regarding the responsibility of medical doctors, a subject that has experienced significant developments in the last few years.

## Insurance

*Professional indemnity insurance*
There is no professional indemnity insurance available for the legal profession in Uruguay.

# COUNTRY INDEX

## COUNTRY INDEX